Images of Modern America

BUSCH GARDENS
TAMPA BAY

Front Cover: Guests come face-to-face with a giraffe on the Serengeti Plain while the Montu roller coaster stands proudly in the background. (State Archives of Florida, Florida Memory.)

Upper Back Cover: The Hospitality House is at center, with the Anheuser-Busch brewery in the background. (State Archives of Florida, Florida Memory.)

Lower Back Cover (from left to right): A trainer shares a kiss with her feathery friend, the Python roller coaster barrels through its iconic corkscrew element (see page 43), and a camel teases a young girl. (All, State Archives of Florida, Florida Memory.)

Images of Modern America

BUSCH GARDENS
TAMPA BAY

Joshua McMorrow-Hernandez
Foreword by Jim Dean

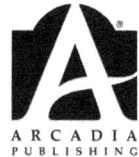

ARCADIA
PUBLISHING

Copyright © 2017 by Joshua McMorrow-
Hernandez ISBN 978-1-5402-1525-3

Published by Arcadia Publishing
Charleston, South Carolina

Printed in the United States of America

Library of Congress Control Number: 2016960058

For all general information, please contact Arcadia Publishing:
Telephone 843-853-2070
Fax 843-853-0044
E-mail sales@arcadiapublishing.com
For customer service and orders:
Toll-Free 1-888-313-2665

Visit us on the Internet at www.arcadiapublishing.com

For all Busch Gardens ambassadors past, present, and future; the millions of people who have made special memories at the park since 1959; and last, but certainly not least, my family and dear loved ones

Contents

Foreword		6
Acknowledgments		7
Introduction		8
1.	1957–1964: New Gardens Brew	11
2.	1965–1974: It's a Zoo!	23
3.	1975–1982: The Gardens Grow	37
4.	1983–1992: Extinction Is Forever	59
5.	1993–2008: Racing to the Top	75
6.	2009 and Beyond: The Future Blooms	89

Foreword

For me, Busch Gardens Tampa Bay is about family, from local families returning from childhood to those who travel from across the world. Since 1959, the park has hosted millions of guests, helping them to create lifetime memories. The experience that Busch Gardens provides has evolved from its humble beginnings as an Anheuser-Busch brewery tour and bird exhibit to what it is today, one of the most renowned theme parks in the world.

Whether it's the spine-tingling experience of sharing the front row of one of our many thrill rides, exploring the lush gardens throughout the park, the excitement of attending one of our award-winning shows, or having the opportunity to be part of a life-changing animal encounter, the combination of these exceptional attractions at one theme park can only be found here.

It was a very special family that started this park so many years ago, the Busch family. My wife, Trish, and our family feel so fortunate to be part of this history. For the past 32 years, my experience has provided me with a once-in-a-lifetime opportunity to work with many dedicated professionals with more passion for this park than I can express. It has been a privilege and an honor to be part of the team that makes Busch Gardens Tampa Bay the remarkable place that it is today. Many have come and gone over the years, leaving their imprint on the park, and we will forever be indebted for their commitment and dedication to Busch Gardens. The tradition continues as new team members join our park. They share the passion of our past and a commitment to shaping our future, keeping alive the unity of this extended family.

When Joshua McMorrow-Hernandez approached me with the idea for this book, I couldn't have been more excited. I knew that the history of Busch Gardens would certainly be a fascinating tale to be told and was honored to contribute. It is and always will be the family spirit that makes Busch Gardens Tampa Bay the incredible destination that it is today. What makes this narrative so interesting is that Joshua was once a part of the family here, and his father is still one of our ambassadors today. Joshua embodies the character that has made this park so successful for so many years. He has managed to capture the history of this incredible park in pictures and words that make the whole family proud.

—Jim Dean, 2016
President
Busch Gardens & Adventure Island, 2010–2017

ACKNOWLEDGMENTS

This book simply would not have been possible without a huge team of people who dedicated much effort and many hours assisting me throughout the course of more than a year. My deep gratitude goes out to everyone at SeaWorld Parks & Entertainment, including Jim Dean, Colleen Roop, Pierre Mathurin, Sally Imhoff, Jeffrey Schwartz, Bill Street, Robbi Parsons Lepre, Karen Varga-Sinka, Mark Rose, Gerard Hoeppner, Jeff Andrews, Bob Kroen, Joe Parr, Sonya Parham Shannon, Pete Geisler, Shellie Kalmore, Adam Lewis, Maritza Fernandez, Jonell Reed, Peggy Sue Christensen, Stacy Michele Spurlock, Jay Strong, Gloria Esther Casanova, and Tony Perry, among others.

There are also several former Busch Gardens team members who were gracious with their time, help, and support. They include Mark Peterson, Deborah Kern Bond, "Doctor" Dave Messick, Susan Foster, Andrew Hoyle, Ron Blalock, and Barbara St. Denis.

Lending me their invaluable support throughout the course of producing this book are "Little Jeannie" Baker, Kelly McMorrow-Hernandez, Michele Hernandez, James Libengood, and a group of beloved friends. My great appreciation goes to Jack Hanna, George Foreman, and Stefanie Powers, all of whom so kindly lent me permission to use their likenesses and quotes in this book. Also instrumentally helpful to me were Janos and Ilona Csikasz, Andrew Huse, Sarah King, Mark DeNote, and the staff at Arcadia Publishing, including my title manager, Jeff Ruetsche.

Finally, I must tip my hat to my dad, Frank "Rudy" Hernandez. He began working for SeaWorld Parks & Entertainment in 1979 and is the reason I have had the priceless experience of calling Busch Gardens Tampa Bay my "other home" throughout my life. My mom, Susan Melody McMorrow Hernandez, took me to Busch Gardens for the first time on November 2, 1981, the day I turned six months old. She made weekly family trips to Busch Gardens a tradition in my young life and for most of her remaining years, until she passed away in 2009. I remember my mom and those treasured family treks to the park every time I visit Busch Gardens today.

Many thanks to one and all!

Unless otherwise noted, images appear courtesy of SeaWorld Parks & Entertainment.

INTRODUCTION

The year was 1957. Dwight D. Eisenhower became the first US president to fly in a helicopter, Sputnik was launched as the first artificial Earth-orbiting satellite, a first-class US postage stamp cost 3¢, and "Jailhouse Rock" by Elvis Presley was the top song on the radio. Meanwhile, Anheuser-Busch, a world-famous beer manufacturer based in St. Louis, Missouri, purchased 160 acres of land in Tampa, Florida, to construct a new $20 million brewery. The brewery would rise in North Tampa Industrial Park, a new development in Tampa built on land that during World War II served as Hillsborough Army Air Field. The Army Air Forces training center was converted to a civilian airport after the war but closed by the late 1950s. Small sections of the airport's concrete runways remain today, including one segment adjacent to Busch Gardens near the northeast corner of Malcolm McKinley Boulevard and Bougainvillea Avenue.

In addition to building a brewery, Anheuser-Busch also planned to open a visitor center on the Tampa site including scenic gardens and aviaries. This was not to be the first time the brewer opened botanical gardens to the public. The first Busch Gardens attraction opened in Pasadena, California, in 1905 and served as a popular tourist destination for more than 30 years. The Pasadena Busch Gardens offered scenic waterfront vistas, a faithful replica of Banbury Cross Mill in England, and numerous species of beautiful trees and flowering plants.

Busch Gardens Tampa Bay was officially dedicated on March 31, 1959, and opened to the public on June 1 of that year. The park was an immediate success, drawing more than 350,000 guests during its first year of operation. Adult visitors enjoyed the park's free brewery tour and complimentary Anheuser-Busch products. Meanwhile, guests of all ages were captivated by the park's popular bird show, acres of lush foliage, and a colorful menagerie of parrots, flamingos, and other beautiful avian species.

Busch Gardens Tampa Bay grew quickly. In the 1960s, the park constructed a wire-frame geodesic dome that served as a space-age aviary. The park also unveiled a Swiss-themed restaurant that served up some of the top cuisine in Tampa for nearly 20 years. The decade also saw the opening of the Serengeti Plain, a man-made veldt for free-roaming animals that became the world's first zoological habitat of its type. Soon after, a state-of-the-art monorail ride opened, providing guests with stunning, up-close encounters with the large African animals of the Serengeti Plain.

As tourism in Florida ramped up during the 1970s, so too did construction activity at Busch Gardens Tampa Bay. In fact, it was during that decade that the park saw much of its growth. In the first half of the 1970s, Busch Gardens added its iconic Serengeti Express railroad, opened the Stanleyville Amphitheater, provided guests a new lay of the land with the Skyride, unveiled the Moroccan Village, and introduced the first major thrill ride at Busch Gardens Tampa Bay, the Stanley Falls log flume. The year of 1976 was particularly significant for the park, which was temporarily rebranded as "The Dark Continent"—a name that paid homage to the wonders and mystique of 19th-century Africa. It was also during 1976 that Python, the first roller coaster in the state of Florida to feature inversions (periods of being upside-down), opened in a section of Stanleyville that was soon renamed Congo.

By the end of the 1970s, two other Busch Gardens parks in the United States closed to accommodate brewery expansions, including a location near the Anheuser-Busch facility in Van Nuys, California, that entertained guests from 1964 through 1979 and an attraction adjacent to the company's Houston brewery that operated as a theme park from 1971 through 1973. Meanwhile, a European-themed Busch Gardens park in Williamsburg, Virginia, that opened in 1975 was attracting millions of guests on an annual basis by the end of the decade. Back at Busch Gardens Tampa Bay, one of the park's largest expansion projects was about to unfold.

In 1980, Busch Gardens Tampa Bay formally unveiled its Timbuktu section. The addition, since reimagined as Pantopia, provided several elements for guests, not to mention the completion of a walking loop around the entire park. Among the new attractions in Timbuktu were the Scorpion roller coaster and a German-themed restaurant that rolled out barrels full of "Oktoberfest" fun to guests on a daily basis. This was also the year that Busch Gardens opened its sister water park, Adventure Island. Located just one block east of Busch Gardens, Adventure Island became one of the first major water parks in Florida and boasts numerous waterslides, children's play elements, and other summer-fun attractions.

As the decade of the 1980s progressed, several new rides were added to the park's collection of attractions, including the Congo River Rapids and Phoenix. In 1986, *Kaleidoscope* became the nation's first Broadway-style theme park show when it debuted at the new Moroccan Palace Theater. Among the other additions during the decade were several innovative animal experiences, including a world-class elephant habitat and an expanded animal nursery. In 1987, Busch Gardens welcomed two special guests from China's Beijing Zoo: adorable giant pandas named Ling Ling and Yong Yong.

The Tanganyika Tidal Wave water ride made a splash during the park's 30th anniversary year in 1989, which was also when several properties were added to the Busch Gardens family of adventure parks, including SeaWorld. The 1990s was a thrilling decade for Busch Gardens Tampa Bay, a period when the exciting Questor motion-simulator ride opened, the record-setting Kumba roller coaster roared to life, and inverted roller coaster Montu rose up above the southern stretches of the Serengeti Plain.

The Anheuser-Busch brewery at Busch Gardens Tampa Bay closed in 1995 to make way for new park attractions, including a dueling wooden roller coaster known as Gwazi and an outdoor special events venue called Gwazi Park. Meanwhile, Myombe Reserve: The Great Ape Domain and the Edge of Africa opened, continuing the park's long legacy of providing innovative and immersive zoological experiences that enrich the lives of their animal residents and educate guests.

The first decades of the 21st century continue providing guests at Busch Gardens Tampa Bay with thrilling attractions, award-winning entertainment, unique up-close animal experiences, and diversified cuisine. These popular features include the addition of world-class thrill rides such as Cobra's Curse, SheiKra, Cheetah Hunt, and Falcon's Fury. Also built were one-of-a-kind animal education and interaction areas, including the state-of-the-art Animal Care Center, Cheetah Run, Jungala Tiger Trail, and marsupial-inhabited Walkabout Way. Meanwhile, Busch Gardens Tampa Bay added several popular annual events to its calendar, including Howl-O-Scream, Christmas Town, and the annual Food & Wine Festival. As the 21st century unfolds, Busch will continue offering new and exciting rides and entertainment for its guests while persevering in its mission to protect the world's animals and conserve our natural resources.

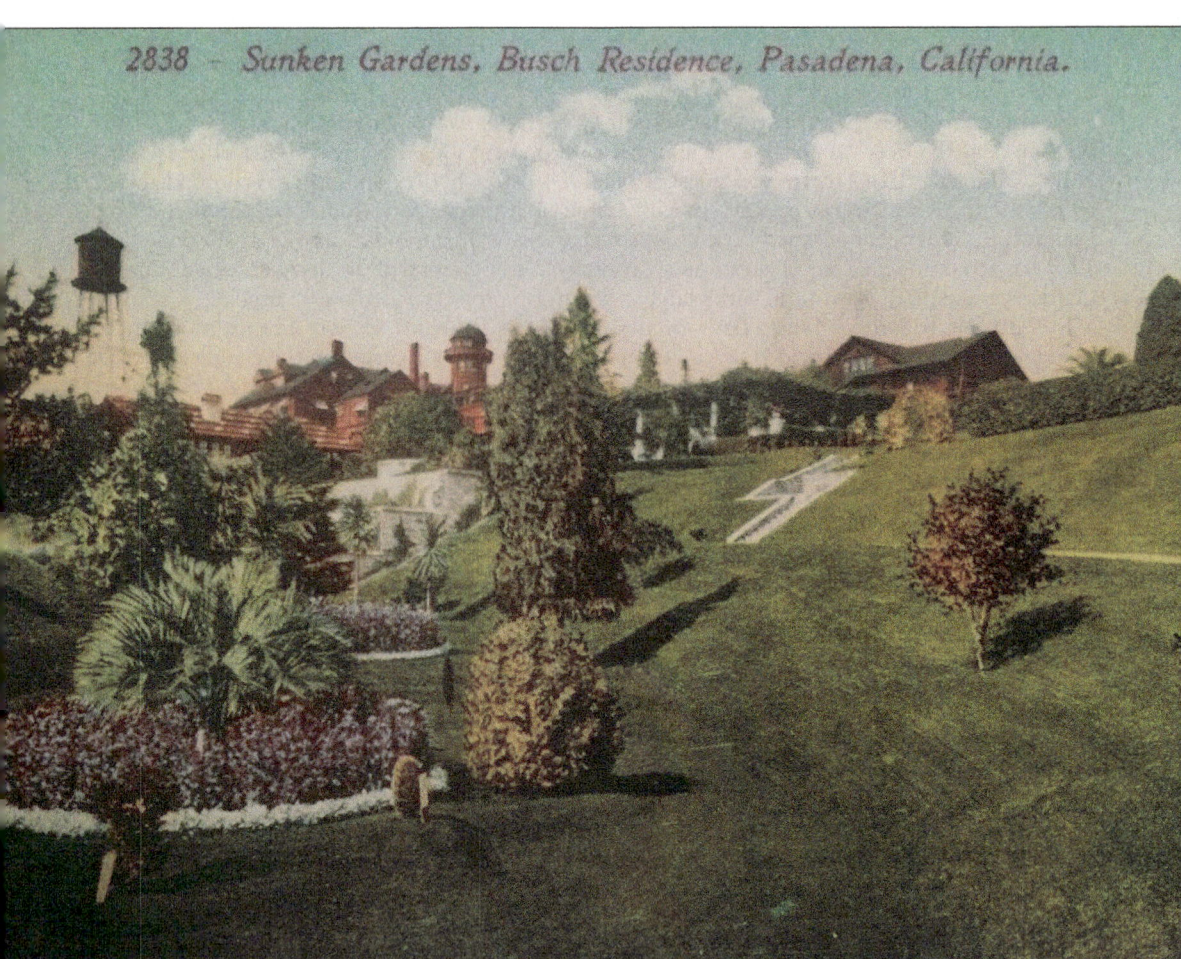

The first Busch Gardens park was located in Pasadena, California, in 1905. The landmark, which measured more than 30 acres in size, was immensely popular and was one of the biggest tourist attractions in Southern California. It also served as the backdrop for several films, including *Duck Soup* (1933), *The Adventures of Robin Hood* (1938), and *Gone with the Wind* (1939). The park, which was a forerunner to Busch Gardens Tampa Bay, closed to the public in 1937 and was later turned into a residential neighborhood.

One

1957–1964
New Gardens Brew

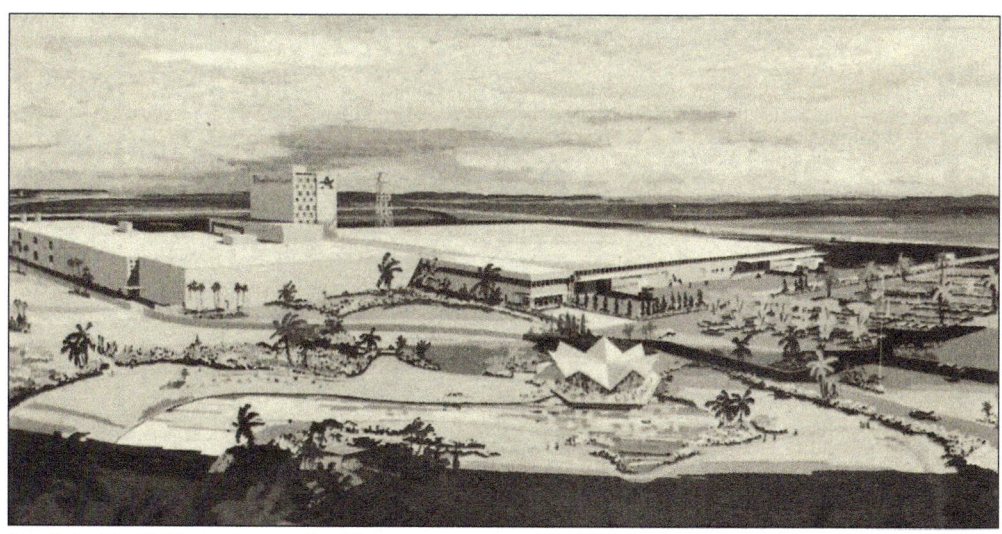

On July 25, 1957, Anheuser-Busch announced its purchase of 160 acres to open a $20 million brewery and tourist attraction in Tampa, Florida. The brewery was designed to produce 800,000 barrels of beer each year and manufacture other products essential to the brewing process, such as yeast. In addition to the brewery, Anheuser-Busch's plans for the new Tampa landmark included botanical gardens and a hospitality center where adults could sample free beer.

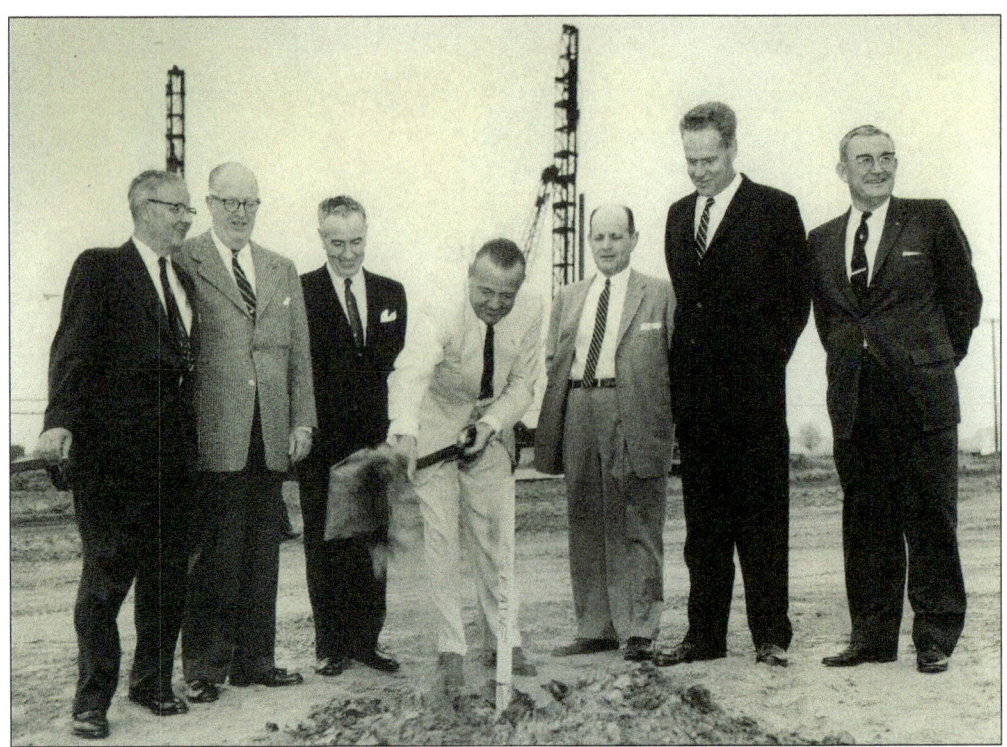

August Busch Jr. turns a shovel in March 1958 to officially break ground for his company's new brewery and tourist attraction in Tampa. Construction on the brewery and the original section of Busch Gardens, the Bird Gardens, would continue through 1958 and into the first months of 1959. (Tampa Bay History Center Collection.)

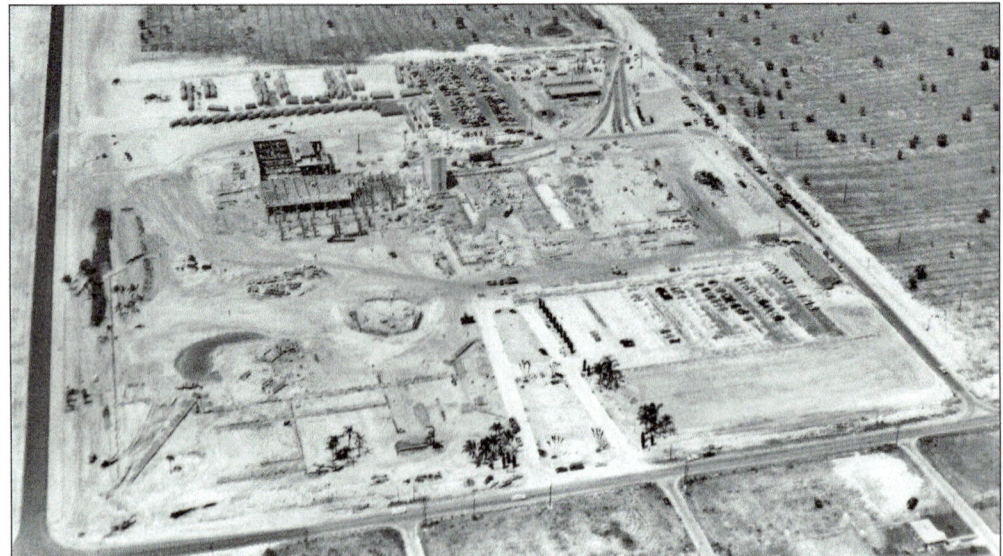

Construction is underway on Busch Gardens in this August 14, 1958, photograph. Looking north from Temple Terrace Highway (later renamed Busch Boulevard), one can see the brewery taking shape, impressions in the ground for lagoons, and the nucleus of the original parking lot. (Tampa-Hillsborough Public Library.)

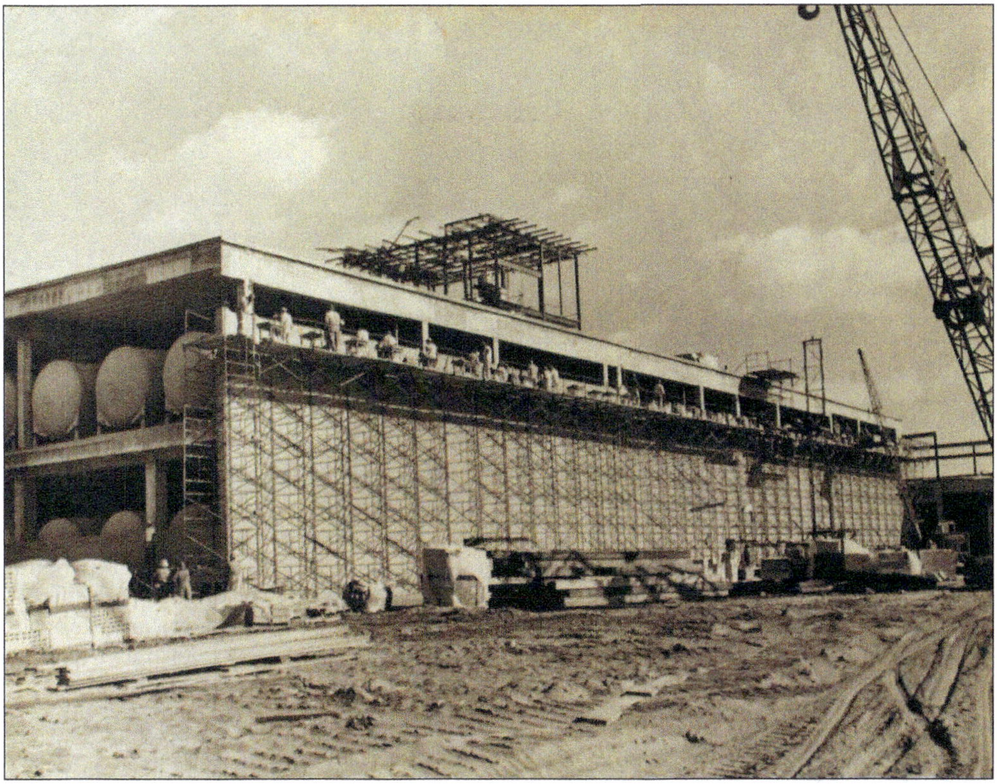

Crews work on constructing the Anheuser-Busch brewery in late 1958. The large tanks seen inside the building were used for holding thousands of gallons of beer. When the Anheuser-Busch brewery in Tampa first opened, it could manufacture up to 800,000 barrels of beer each year. A barrel is equivalent to 31 gallons, meaning nearly 25 million gallons of beer were flowing through the brewery annually.

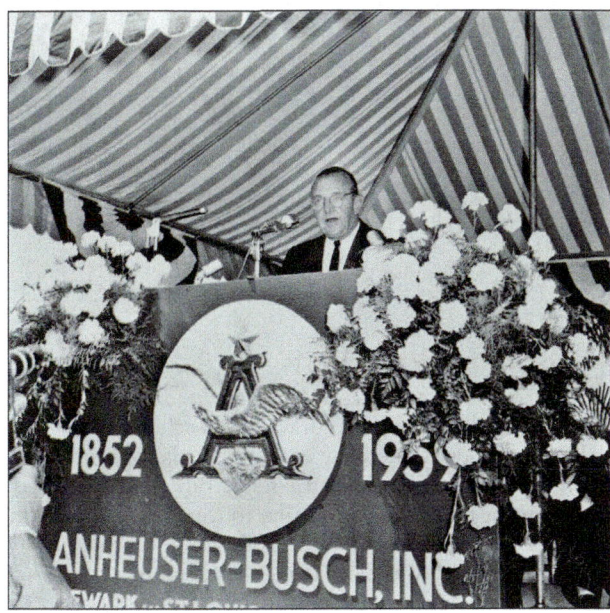

August Busch Jr. speaks at the dedication ceremony for Busch Gardens Tampa Bay on March 31, 1959. Founder Eberhard Anheuser was part owner of Bavarian Brewery, a St. Louis company established in 1852. Anheuser bought out the other investors by 1860 and renamed the brewery E. Anheuser & Company. Later, brewing supplier Adolphus Busch met Anheuser and married his daughter Lilly. Adolphus Busch worked for his father-in-law and purchased half-ownership of the brewery, which became Anheuser-Busch, Inc. In 2008, the company was renamed Anheuser-Busch InBev.

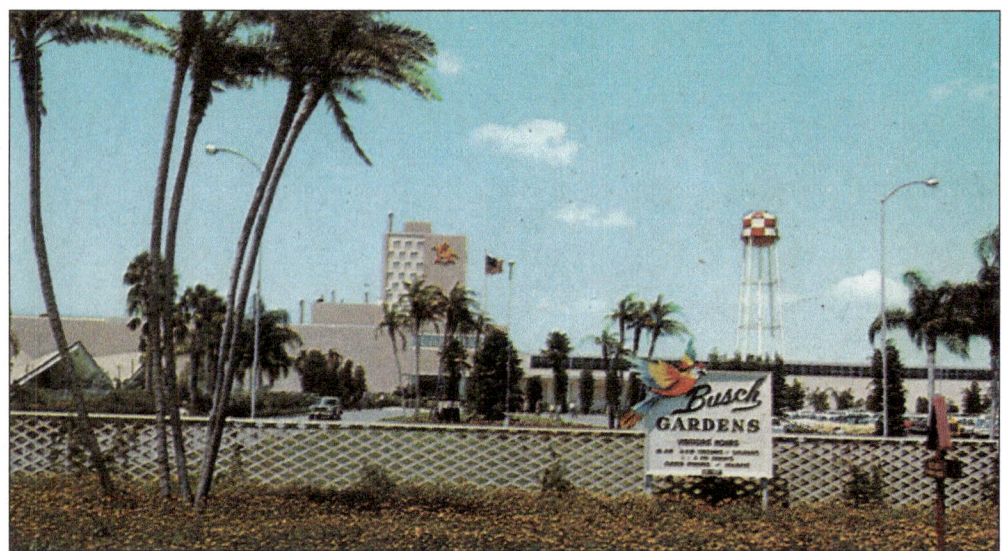

When Busch Gardens Tampa Bay opened to visitors on June 1, 1959, they entered the park from Busch Boulevard, which was then named Temple Terrace Highway. The original park entrance was located across from Thirty-Third Street and brought guests onto the grounds through a driveway adjacent to the east side of the Bird Gardens Gift Shop (now known as Xcursions), which became the park's first standalone gift shop when it opened in October 1964.

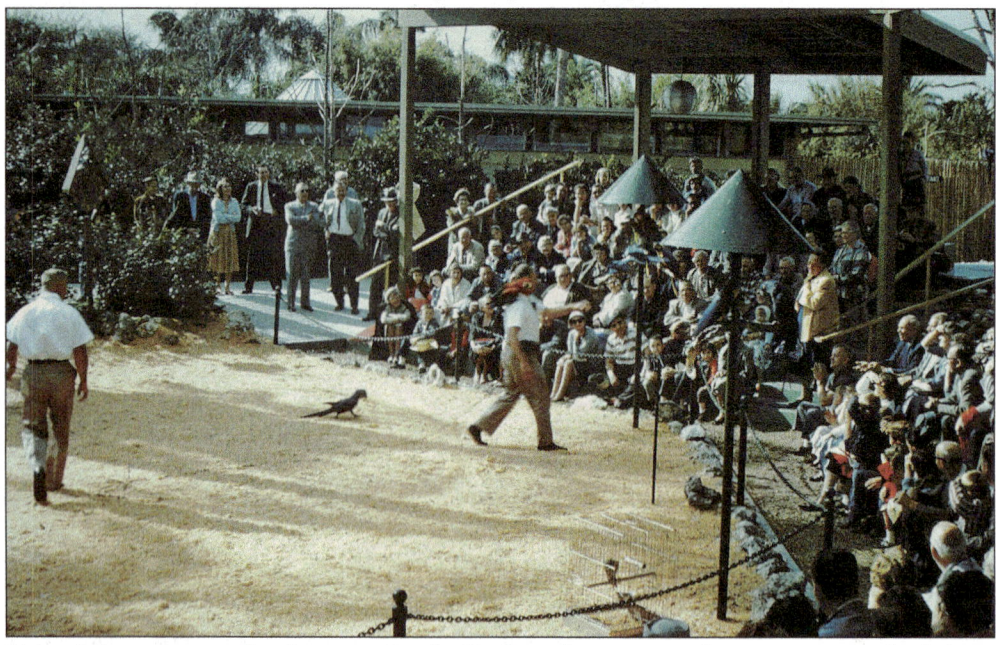

One of the most popular draws at Busch Gardens during its early years was the bird show. The show allowed an array of exotic birds to demonstrate an array of natural behaviors before adoring crowds. The Busch Gardens Bird Show debuted with the opening of the park in 1959 and continued in a format similar to the original program until 2007. *Critter Castaways*, another show featuring domestic and exotic animals, played at the Bird Gardens Theater until 2014, when the theater was closed and later demolished; the *Critter Castaways* crew began performing at Pantopia Theater later in 2014. (Author's collection.)

Guests who came to tour the Anheuser-Busch brewery at Busch Gardens entered the large factory via the Stairway to the Stars escalator, which took visitors to an entryway at the top of the building. When it first opened, Stairway to the Stars was said to be the world's longest escalator, measuring more than 80 feet high. (Author's collection.)

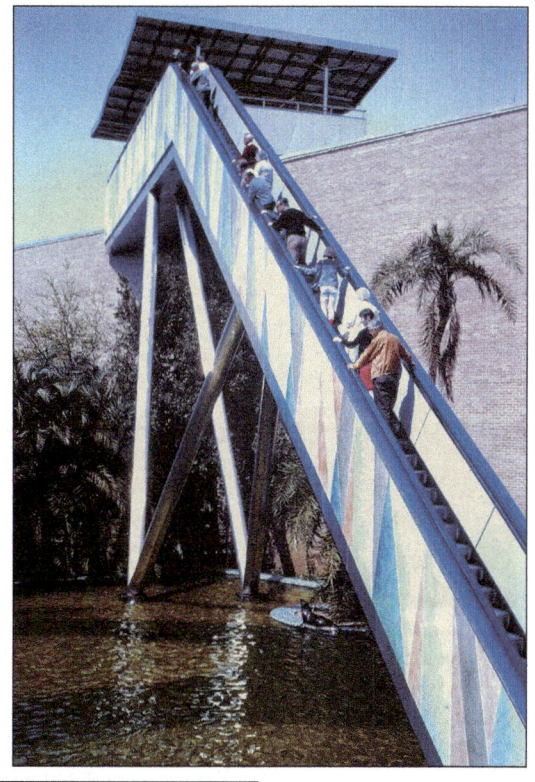

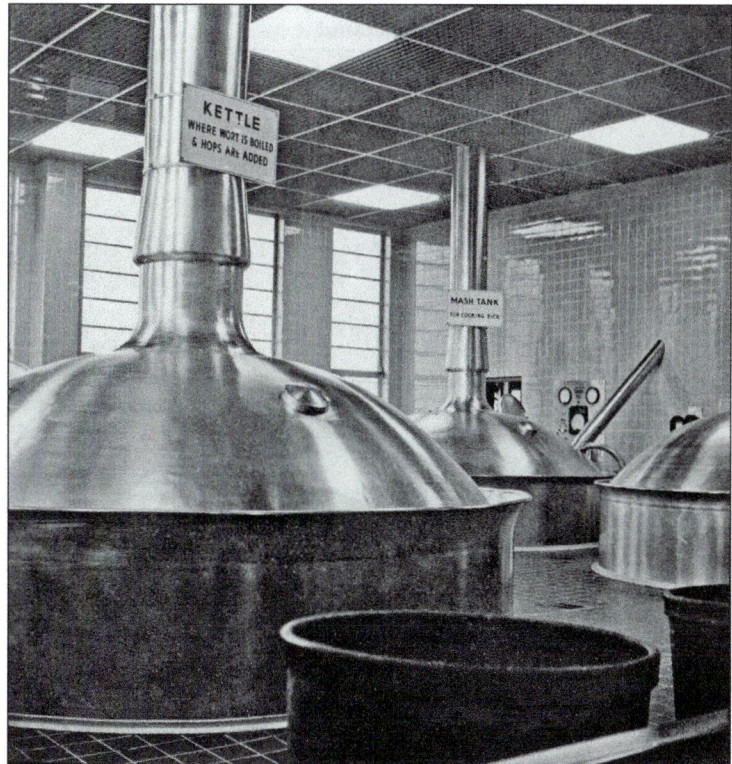

Guests touring the Anheuser-Busch brewery could watch beer be manufactured through every step of the process. In this room, visitors see the kettle (front vat) where wort is boiled and hops are added. Wort contains sugars that are fermented by brewing yeast, and hops are a type of plant that stabilize beer and add flavor. In the rear is the mash tank, which uses hot water to steep barley and start the fermentation process. (State Archives of Florida, Florida Memory.)

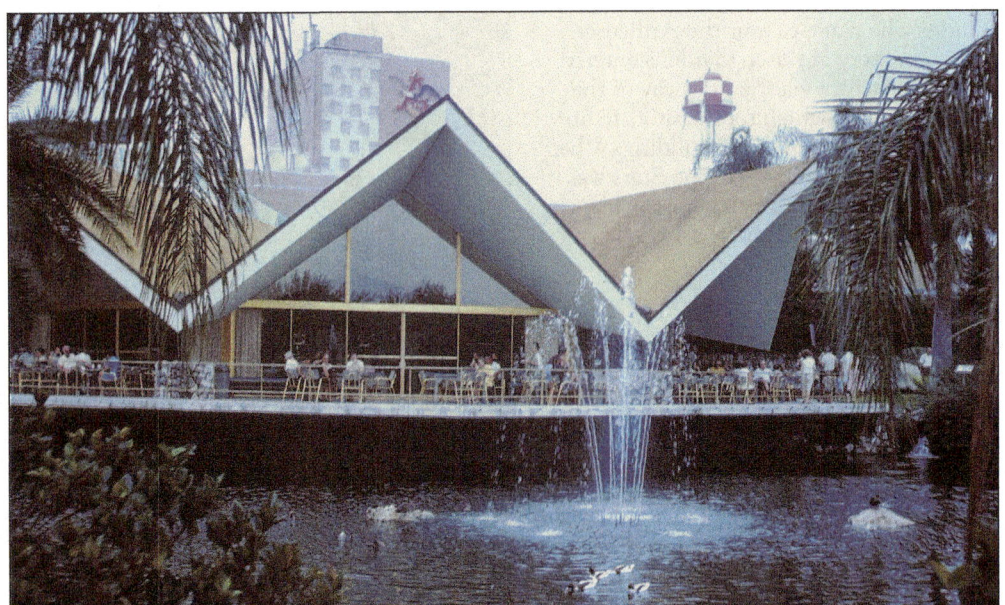

Adults could sample Anheuser-Busch beer products at the Busch Gardens Hospitality House. However, free beer was not the only attraction here. Guests also could enjoy soft drinks and snacks while taking in views of the adjacent lagoon where waterfowl delighted in the beautiful, exotic surroundings. The Busch Gardens Hospitality House's unique, seven-sided floating roof was the brainchild of William B. Harvard. The St. Petersburg, Florida, architect designed many local landmarks, including the St. Petersburg Pier's inverted pyramid, which stood over the waters of Tampa Bay from 1973 until 2015. (Author's collection.)

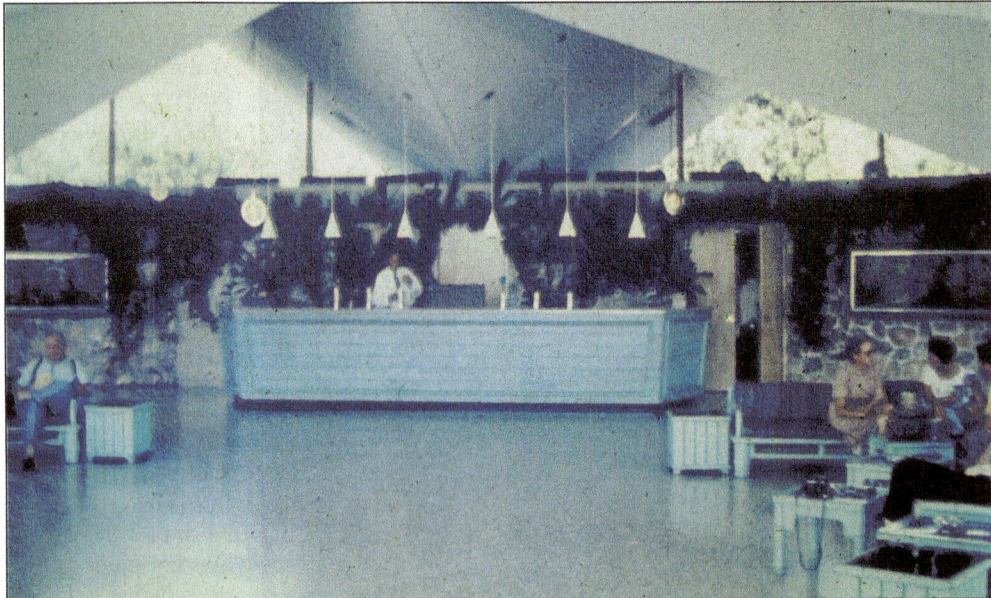

Visitors enjoy free beer and other refreshments inside the Busch Gardens Hospitality House in this 1962 photograph. The Busch Gardens Hospitality House continued offering free beer until 2009, when the restaurant was re-themed as the Garden Gate Café. The family-friendly dining venue serves craft beer, pizza, pasta, salad, desserts, and more. (Author's collection.)

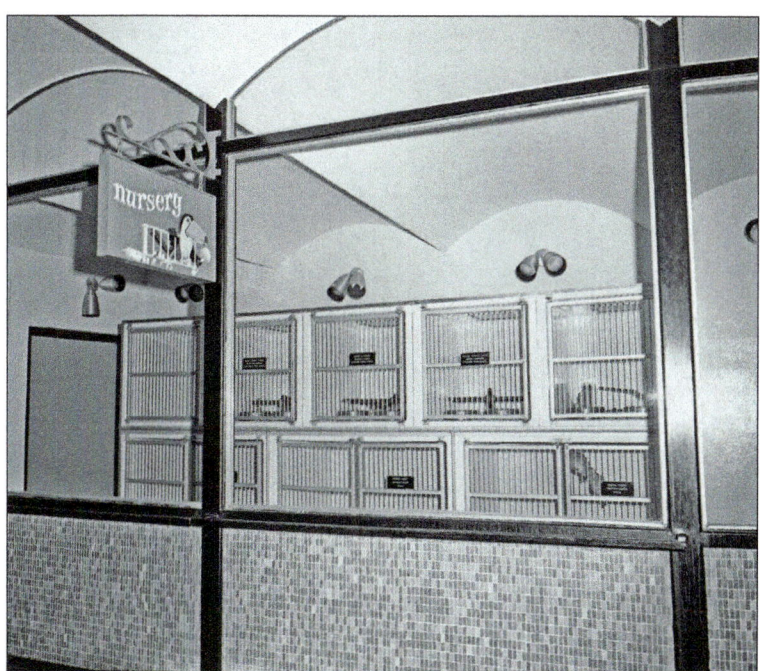

The Bird Gardens Nursery was one of the park's earliest animal care centers and allowed guests to watch on as zoological staff handled everything from incubation to dietary preparations. The Bird Gardens animal care center was housed in a distinctive scallop-roofed building once located just steps north of where Walkabout Way is today. (State Archives of Florida, Florida Memory.)

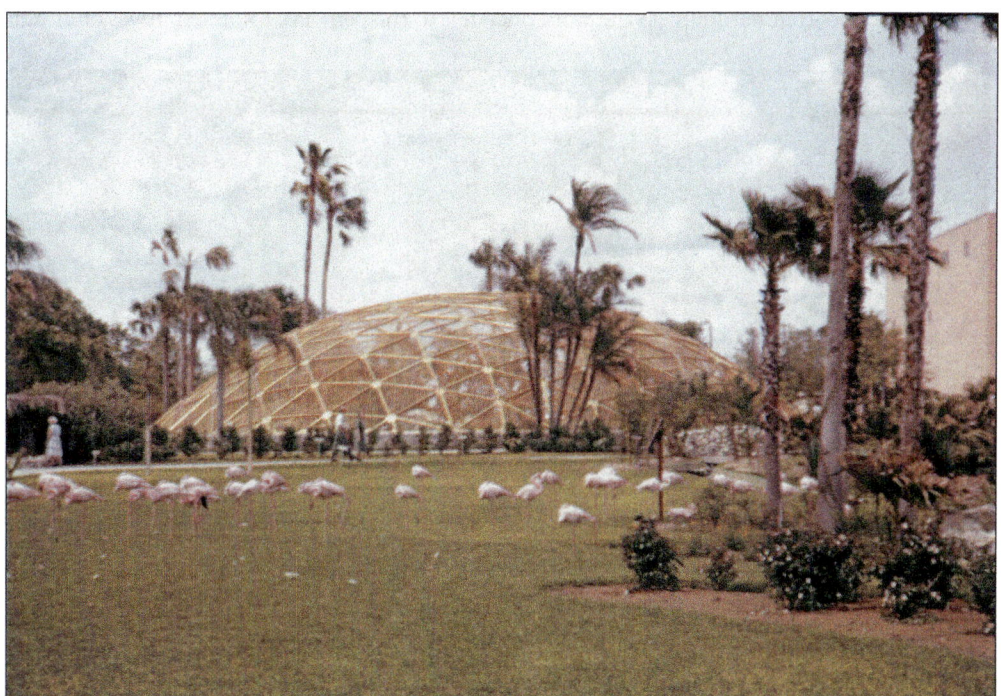

The Adolphus Busch Space Frame was a gold-anodized aluminum geodesic dome that served as an aviary. Named for an Anheuser-Busch founder, it was dedicated on March 22, 1960, and housed an array of exotic birds and other species in various ponds and gardens encompassed within an enclosed area measuring 99 feet in diameter. The Adolphus Busch Space Frame was removed in 1988 to accommodate a brewery expansion. (State Archives of Florida, Florida Memory.)

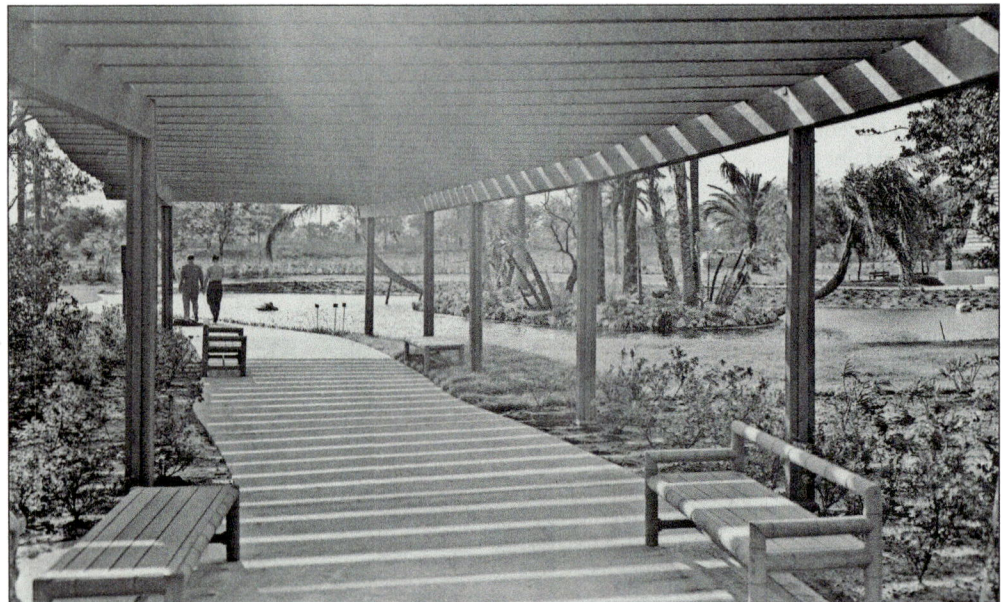

Several beautiful pergolas covered stretches of walkway throughout the original Bird Gardens during the park's early days. The pergolas afforded guests areas of shade when the park's trees and other vegetation were still young and small. Today, Busch Gardens Tampa Bay boasts many large shade trees that naturally do the work once left to the pergolas. (State Archives of Florida, Florida Memory.)

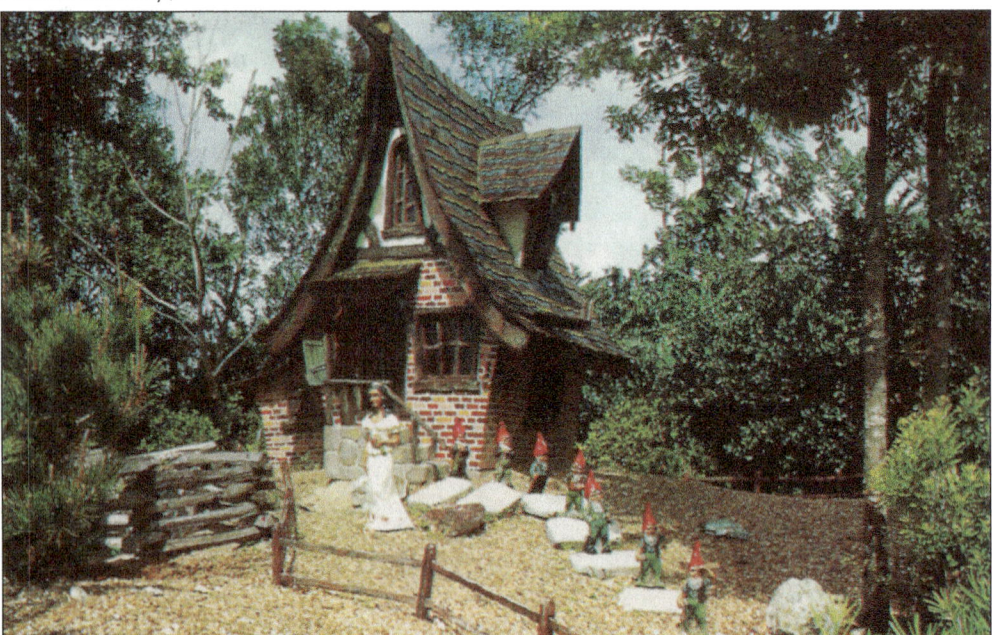

Dwarf Village was an area of the Bird Gardens featuring handmade gnomes imported from Germany. Set amid a forested backdrop, Dwarf Village showcased several whimsical scenes from popular children's fairy tales, including "Snow White and the Seven Dwarfs," seen here. The Dwarf Village area was later re-themed into a children's play area and eventually became Sesame Street Safari of Fun.

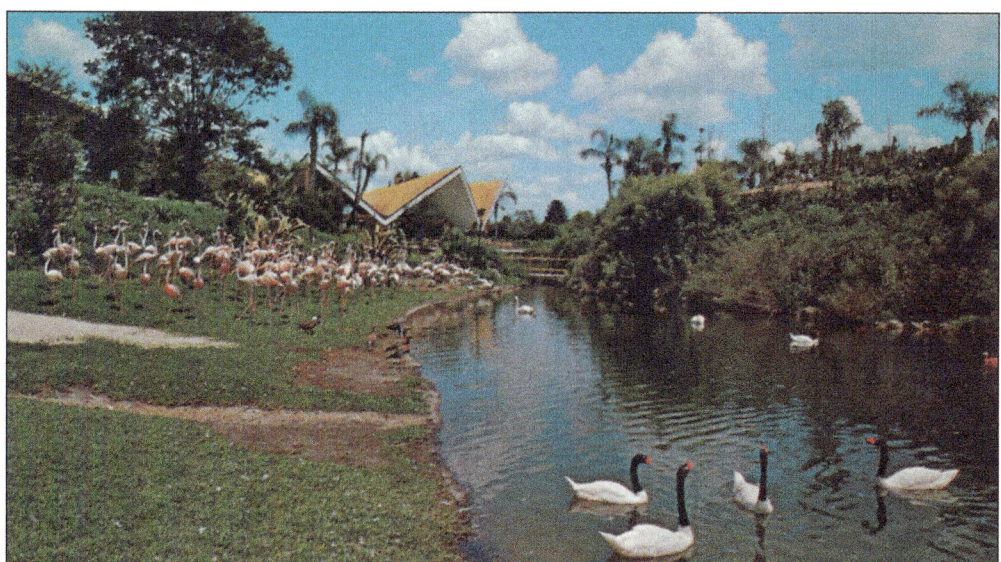

Flamingos have made their home in the Bird Gardens since 1959. They take residence around a picturesque lagoon just west of the Busch Gardens Hospitality House building, where they have been since the park opened. Flamingos stand approximately 3.5 feet tall and weigh between three and nine pounds. Chicks are born white or gray and turn pink after one to two years. The distinct pink color of their feathers is a direct reflection of beta-carotene in the flamingo's diet, which typically includes food such as shrimp and plankton.

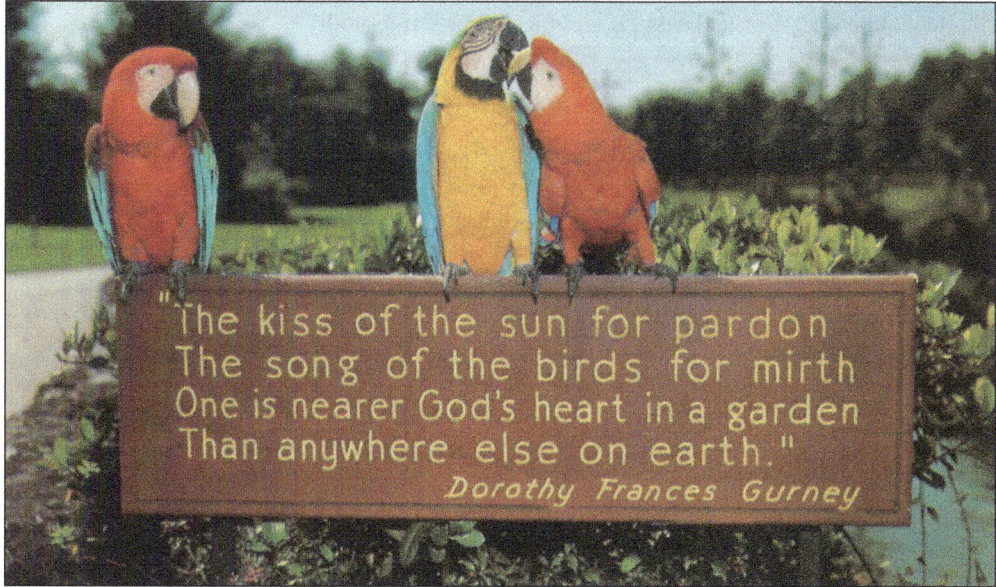

These famous words by English poet and hymn writer Dorothy Frances Gurney (1858–1932) were displayed on this plaque in the Bird Gardens for many years after the park's opening. The quote is from the second-to-last verse of her 1913 poem "God's Garden." Her passage is still often seen on signs and markers in gardens throughout the world. Parrots, such as those atop this plaque, represent diverse species of bird and are found in warm climates such as Australasia, South America, and Central America. Parrots are intelligent, charismatic creatures, and many can imitate human speech.

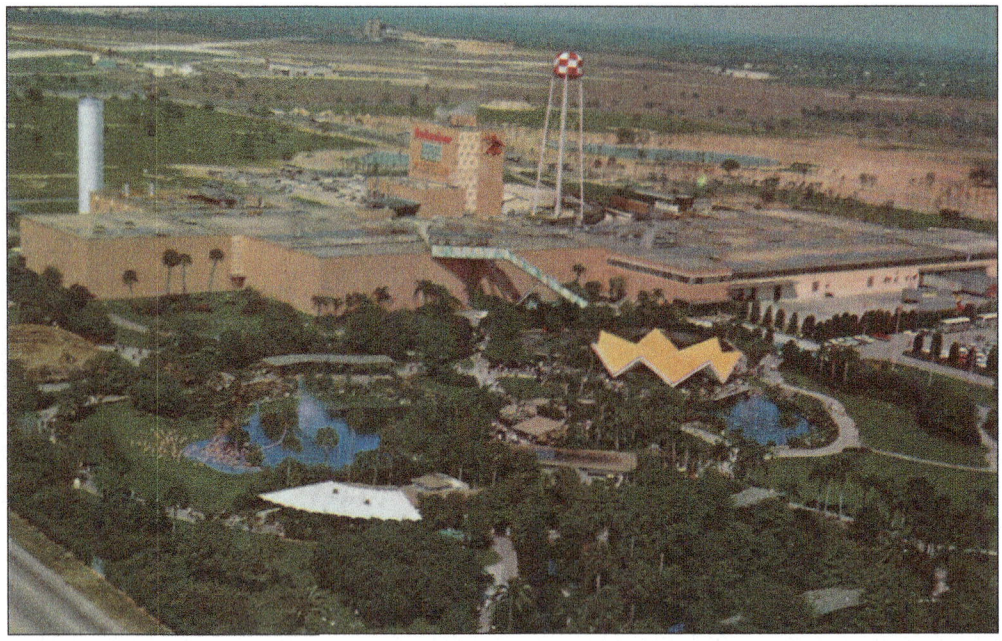

When Busch Gardens opened in 1959, the park featured several lagoons, some 300 trees, and more than 36,000 flowering plants. Today, Busch Gardens has thousands of species and millions of native and exotic plants from every corner of the globe, including more than 50 species of palm. Interestingly, palms are not actually trees, but rather are related to grass. That means Florida's state tree, the sabal palm, is technically not a tree at all!

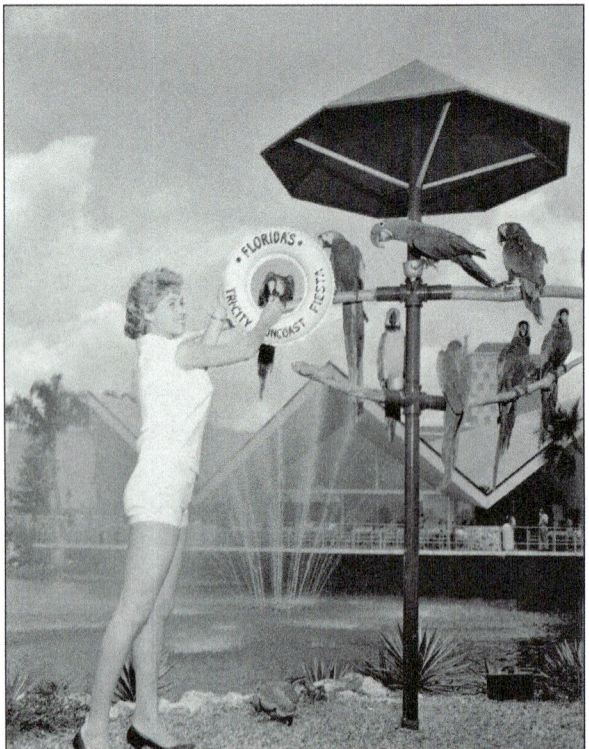

Norma Lado is seen feeding a parrot at Busch Gardens in May 1960 while posing for a photograph promoting the Florida Tri-City Suncoast Fiesta. The Tri-City Suncoast Fiesta was an annual event lasting from June through August in the cities of Tampa, St. Petersburg, and Clearwater. Parades, cookouts, and other events were staged by local organizations to promote the Tampa Bay Area as a tourist destination. (State Archives of Florida, Florida Memory.)

Busch Gardens has a long legacy of world-class animal caretakers and handlers, including Al Mello, who began working at the park during its early days and trained the resident avian species seen in the bird show for many years. Here he is working with Billy, a sulphur-crested cockatoo. The cockatoo is a family of 21 species of birds belonging to parrots, and they generally hail from Australasia. Cockatoos have colorful crests and curved bills and are larger than other parrots.

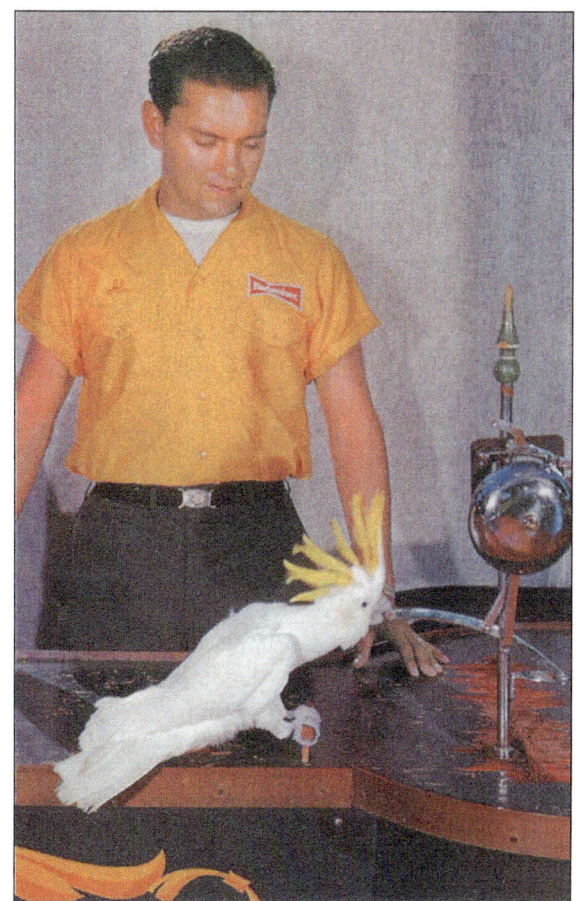

Beginning on October 1, 1964, guests had a new way to get around the park in what became the precursor of the parking lot tram system. The Busch Gardens Special was a trackless, diesel-powered train that took visitors between the Bird Gardens and the Old Swiss House restaurant, which opened on the east side of the park in October 1964. The Old Swiss House, now known as the Serengeti Overlook Restaurant, is seen in this photograph before its distinctive clock tower was built in 1965.

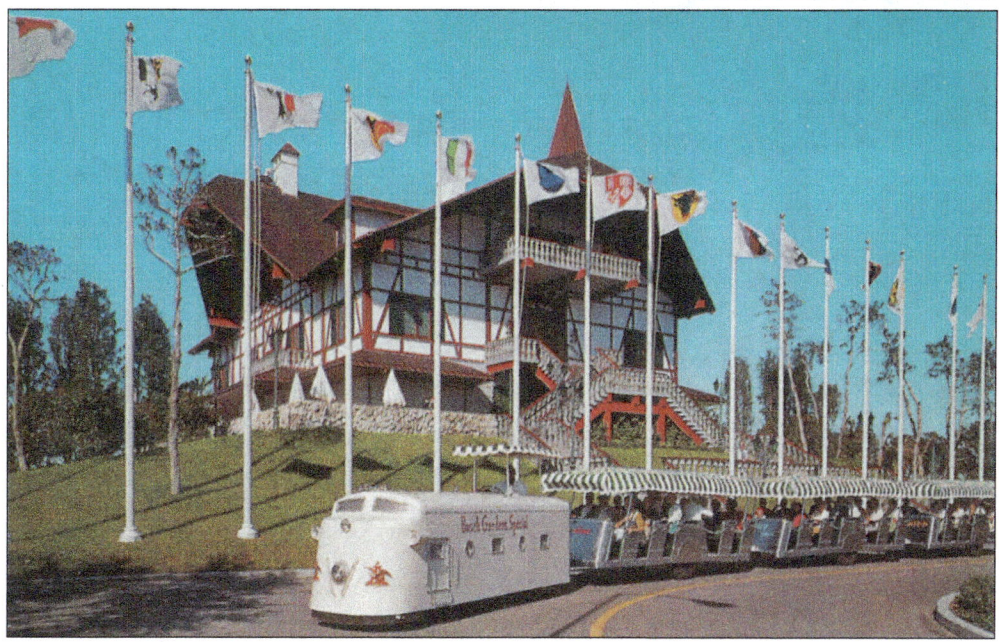

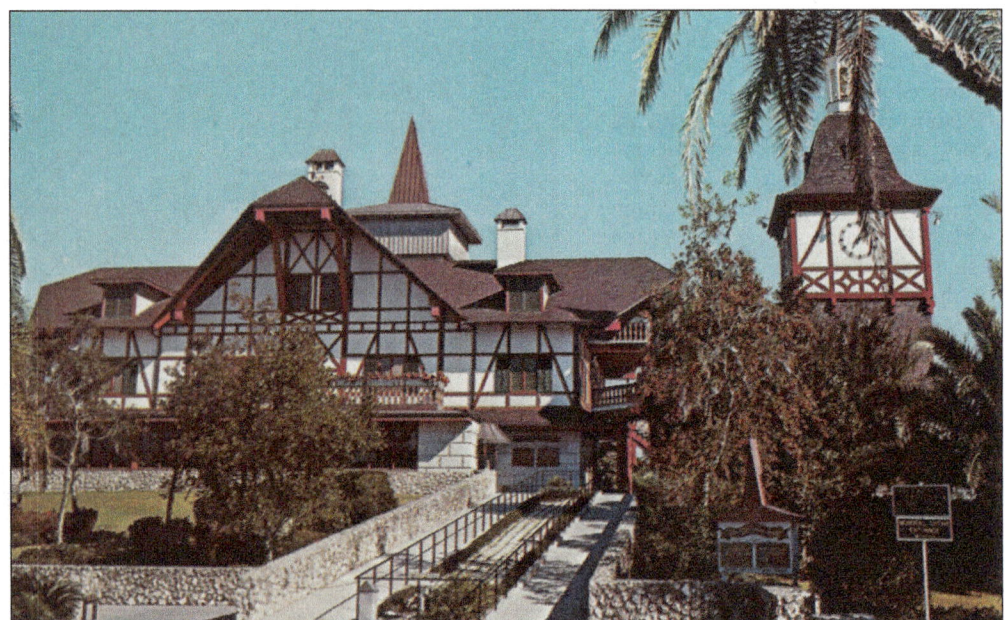

The Old Swiss House opened in October 1964 and was built by August Busch Jr. as a gift for his wife, Trudy; her family owned a similar restaurant operating under the same name in Lucerne, Switzerland. The Old Swiss House at Busch Gardens served up high-class fare, including Bavarian sauerbraten, braised sirloin tips, and roast beef. The Old Swiss House closed in 1982 and reopened in 1990 as the re-themed Crown Colony House restaurant, offering full-service dining upstairs and a café downstairs. In 2016, the restaurant received a makeover and was renamed the Serengeti Overlook Restaurant. (Below, State Archives of Florida, Florida Memory.)

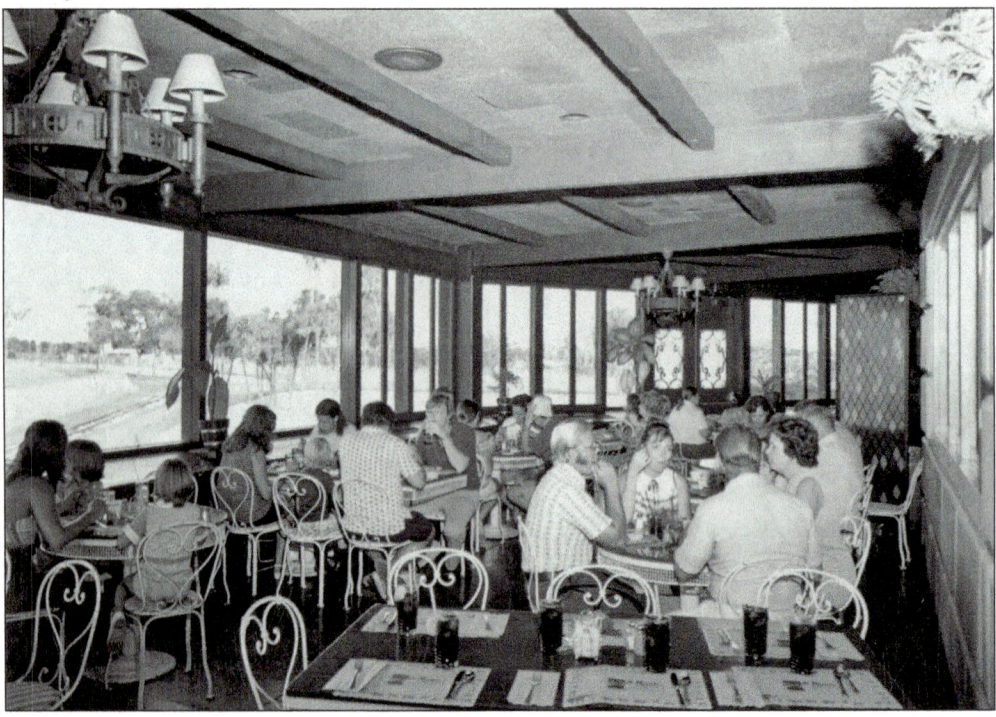

Two
1965–1974
It's a Zoo!

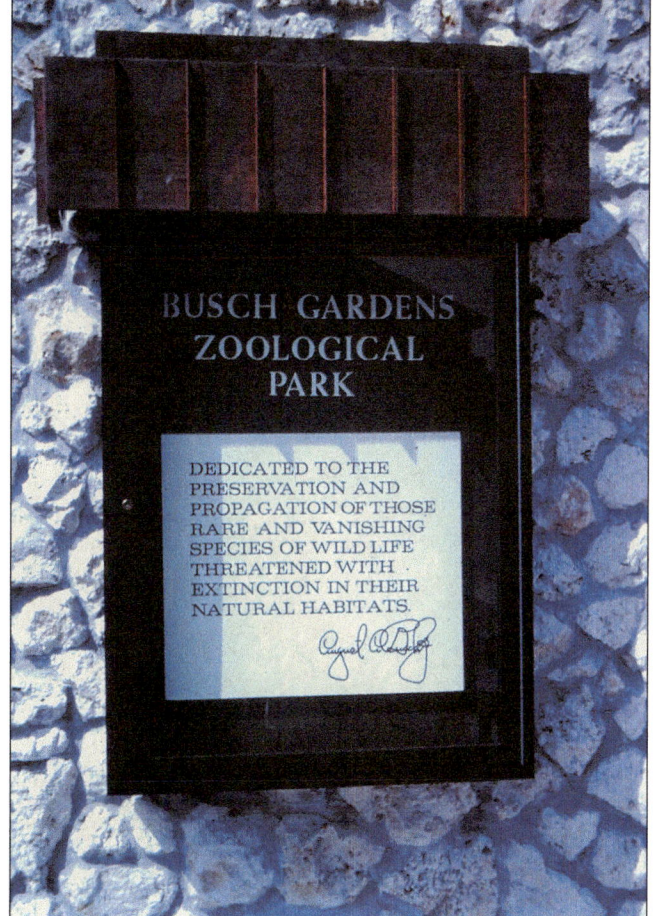

During its early years, Busch Gardens Tampa Bay transitioned into a full-fledged zoological sanctuary for endangered species great and small. Even in the mid-1960s, Busch Gardens was a leader in ecological conservation, as exhibited on this plaque once located near the Serengeti Plain. It reads: "Busch Gardens Zoological Park, dedicated to the preservation and propagation of those rare and vanishing species of wild life threatened with extinction in their natural habitats—August A. Busch." (Author's collection.)

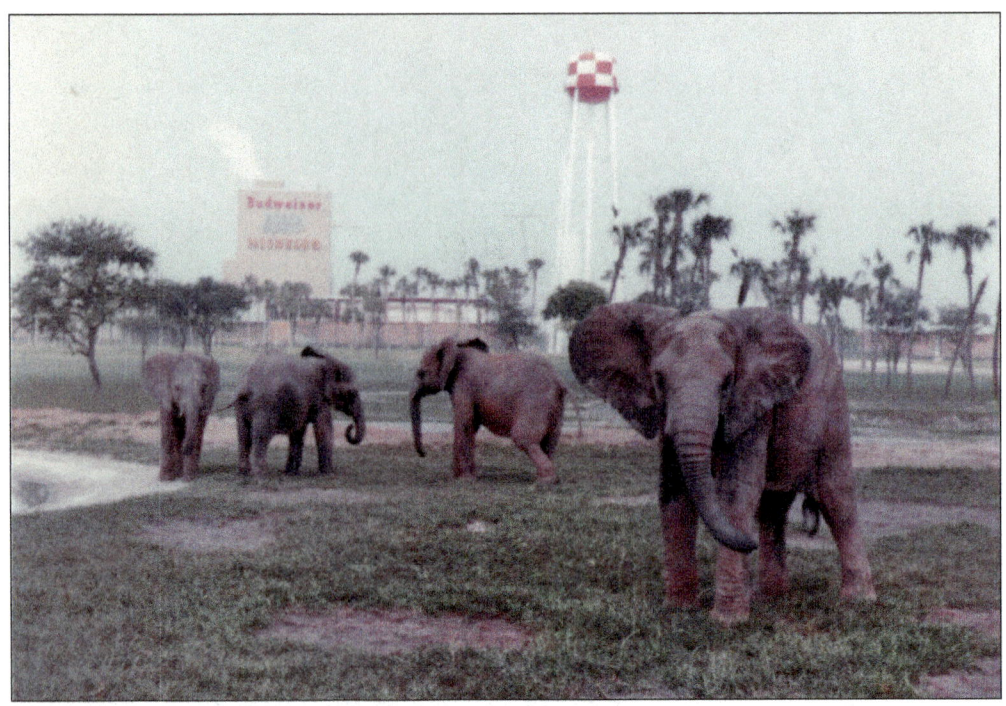

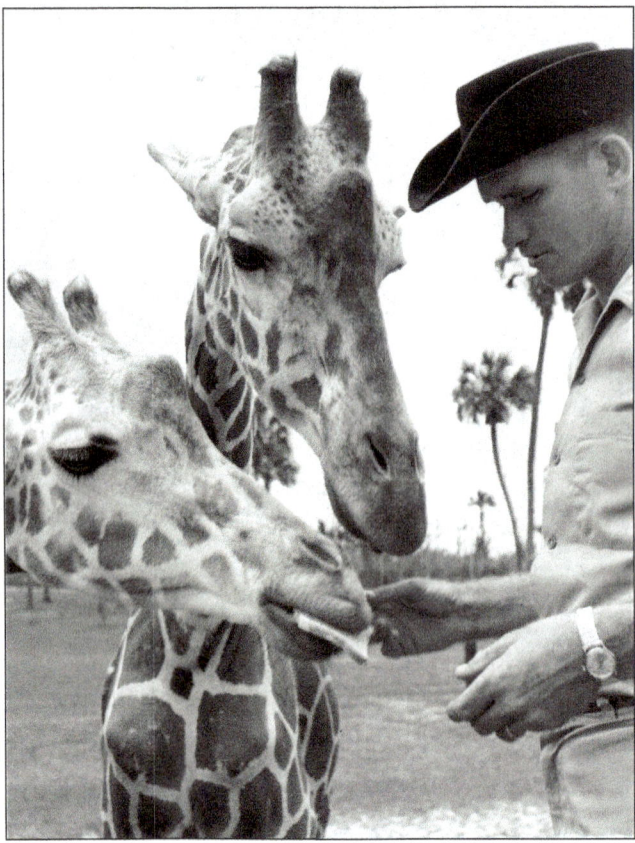

In 1965, Busch Gardens unveiled its Serengeti Plain, which was the first zoological habitat of its kind in the world. Elephants (above) and giraffes (left) were just two of the many exotic, endangered species to call this unique sanctuary home during its early years. The Serengeti Plain, which quickly grew from 29 acres to 70 acres in the 1960s, is widely known as "the Veldt," a word with Afrikaans origins that translates to "field" in English.

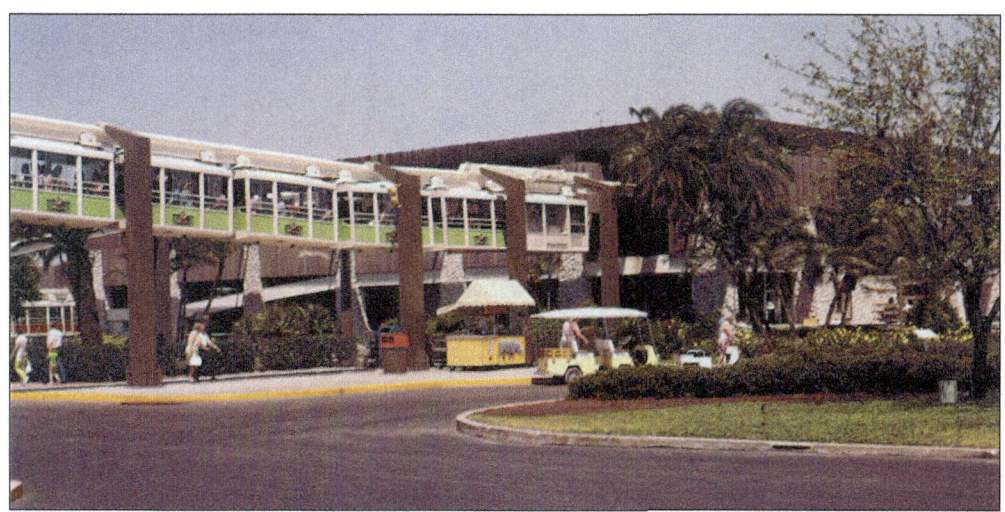

The monorail was dedicated on September 13, 1966. Originally called the Skyrail, the monorail was designed by Arrow Development, a California-based firm that was well known for building theme park rides, including some that rose at Busch Gardens in the 1970s. The 1.3-mile-long monorail took guests on an adventure through the Serengeti Plain years before the Trans-Veldt Railway, Skyride, or Serengeti Safari would offer guests other opportunities to encounter the animals that live in the sprawling naturalistic habitat.

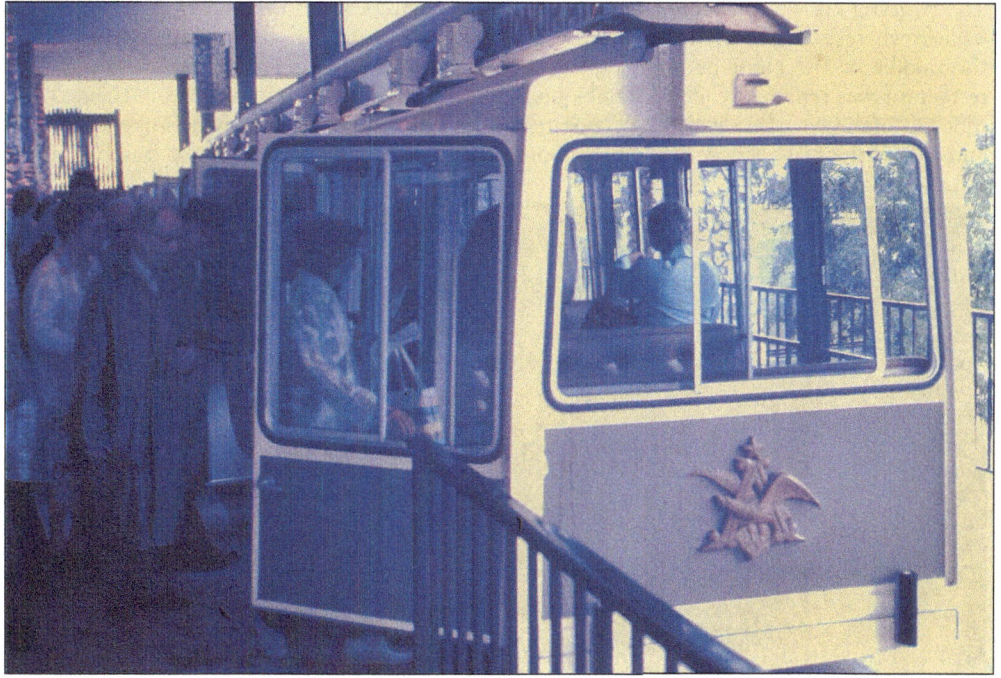

These guests are seen entering the monorail in 1975. Originally, a ride on the monorail cost $1 for adults and 40¢ for children 18 and under, but the separate monorail admission fees were rolled into a single park ticket price during the early 1970s. Aside from the addition of new vehicles in 1988, the monorail changed little during the course of its 33-year life. After the monorail closed in 1999, the station was converted into the queue house for the Cheetah Hunt roller coaster, which opened in 2011. (Author's collection.)

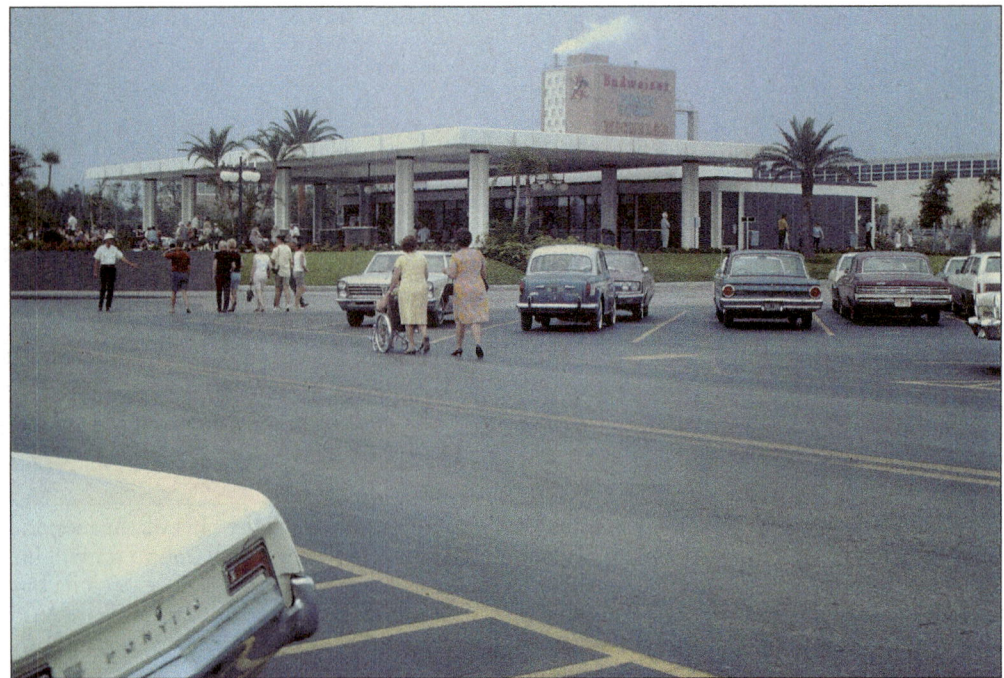

The building known as Zagora Café has not always been located in the heart of the Moroccan Village where it stands today. When the dining venue opened in 1967, it was a snack bar in the middle of the guest parking lot, between the Bird Gardens and monorail station. The restaurant was renamed Café Mozambique in the early 1970s. Its exterior was re-themed with Moorish archways when it was incorporated within the Morocco area, which opened in 1975 and is now the first section of the park most guests encounter during a day at Busch Gardens. (Author's collection.)

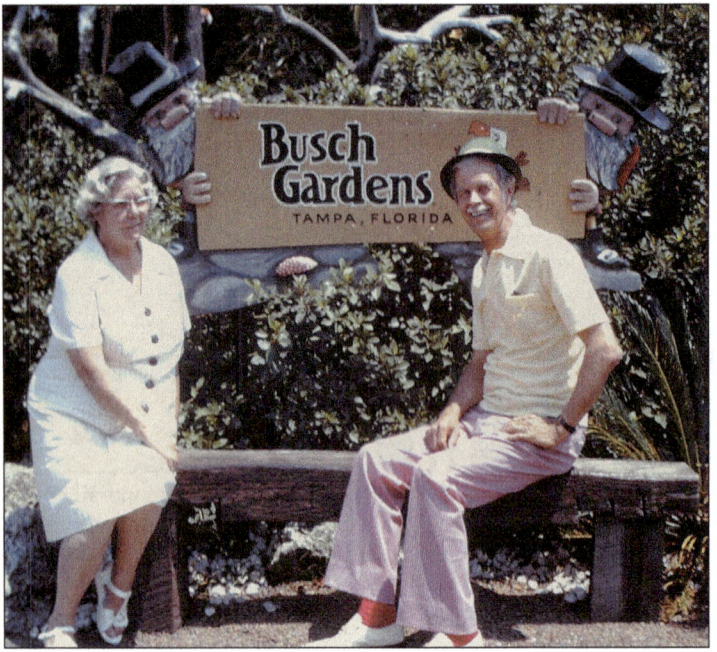

This couple smiles for the camera at a posing area around 1970. Since its earliest days, Busch Gardens Tampa Bay has been a photographer's paradise, providing endless opportunities to snap pictures of exotic animals, lush landscaping, or even beloved friends and family members. (Author's collection.)

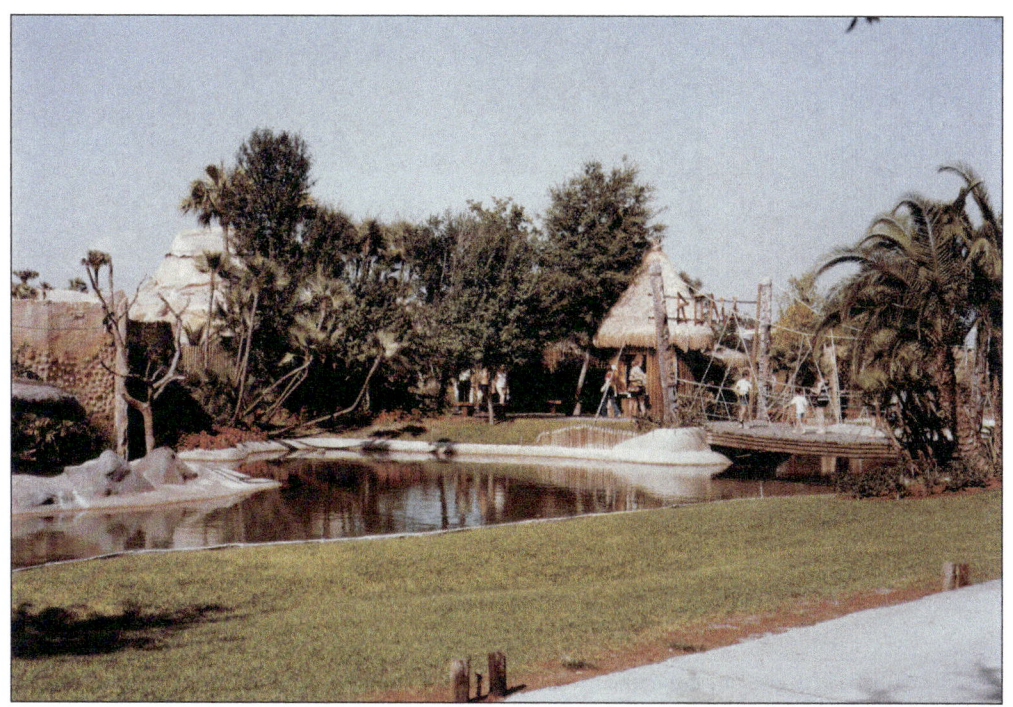

Boma premiered on July 30, 1970, and became the park's first themed area. Boma, a Swahili word for "animal enclosure," was a section of the park where guests could encounter an array of animals, including gibbons, ostriches, sloths, kangaroos, gorillas, orangutans, and chimpanzees. Boma, which eventually formed the nucleus of the Nairobi area, was converted into the Myombe Reserve: The Great Ape Domain habitat in the early 1990s.

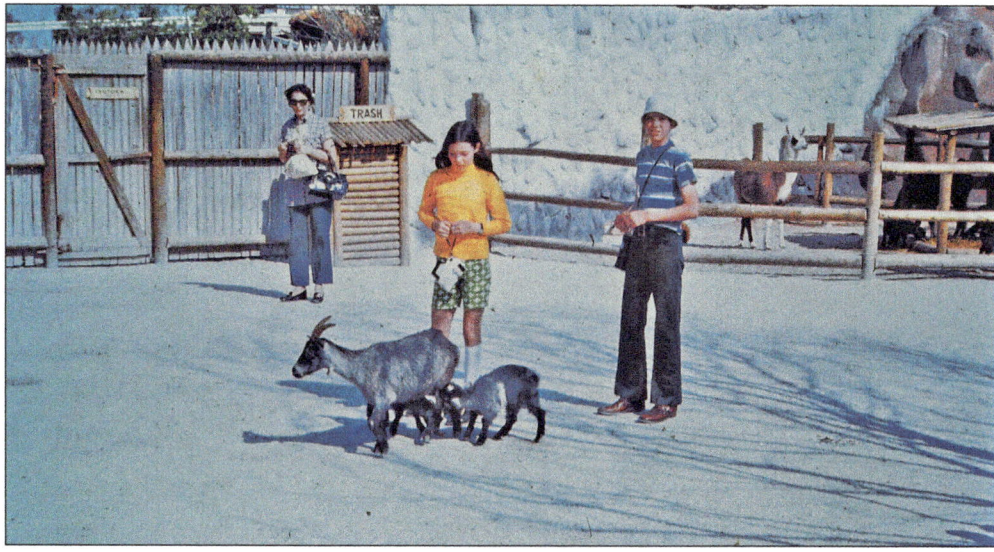

These guests interact with African pygmy goats in 1972 at the Boma petting zoo. In addition to the petting zoo, Boma offered a subterranean aquarium where guests could view exotic fish through glass portals at the bottom of a pond and the unique Nocturnal Mountain, an indoor animal habitat where creatures of the night played during the day. Nocturnal Mountain was re-themed when the area was reopened as Myombe Reserve in 1992. (Author's collection.)

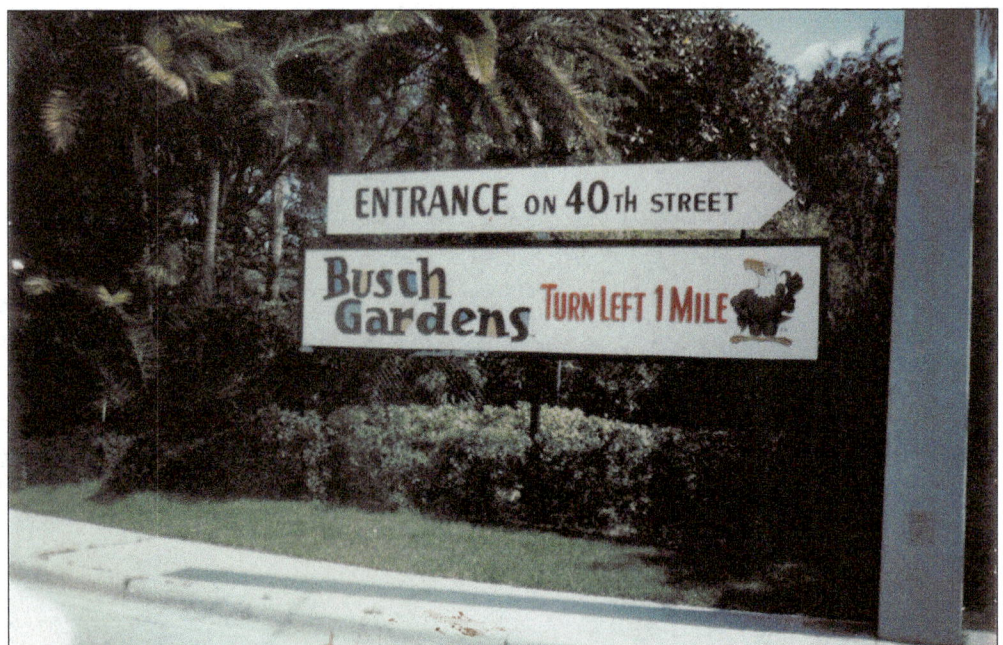

By December 1970, guests were entering Busch Gardens via Fortieth Street/Malcolm McKinley Boulevard, which is where the park's main entrance is today. The park's main guest entrance has evolved remarkably over the past decades. Various park logos necessitated the revising of entryway signage, and Montu rose in 1996, vastly changing the appearance of the entrance. A dual tunnel was installed under Malcolm McKinley Boulevard in 2005, creating a new pedestrian crosswalk and motor vehicle pathway between the park itself and eastern guest parking areas.

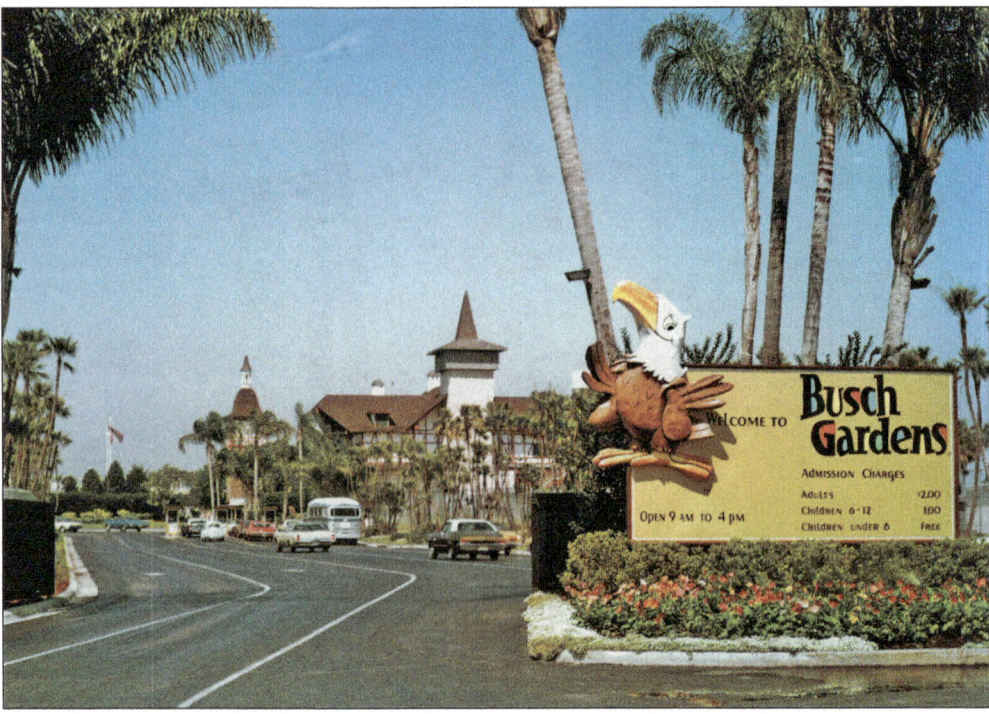

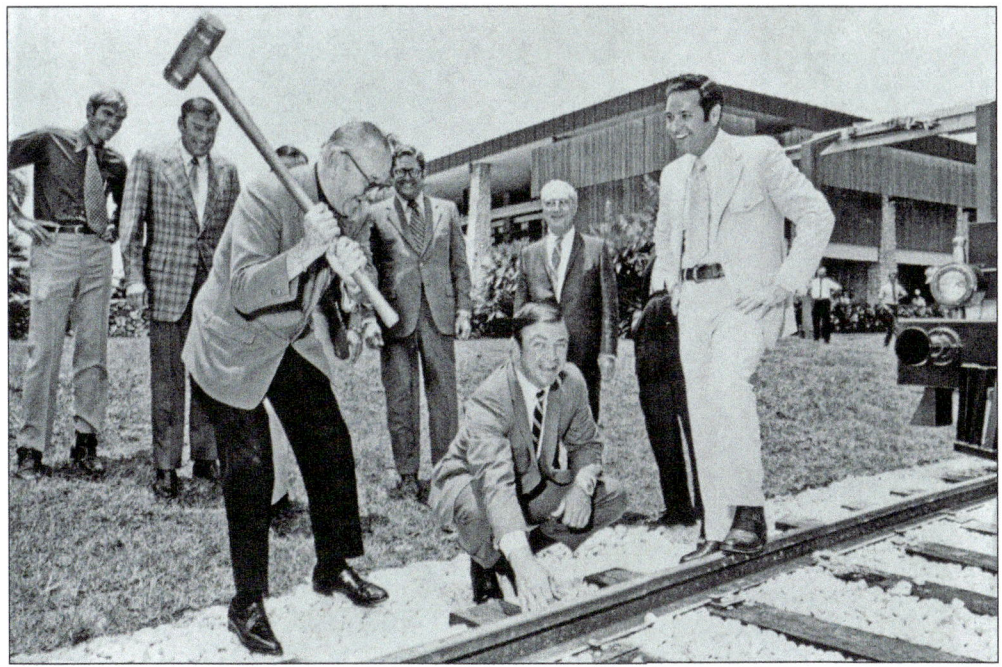

August Busch Jr. wields a mallet that will pound the final spike, held by his son August Busch III, officially completing the Trans-Veldt Railway. The narrow-gauge railroad opened on July 3, 1971, and takes guests on a two-mile trek around Busch Gardens, serving not only as a people mover but also a pleasant joyride. For many years, the Trans-Veldt Railway—now known as the Serengeti Express—was possibly the only narrow-gauge rail system in the United States to cross an operating standard-gauge rail line, the latter serving the Anheuser-Busch brewery in the park.

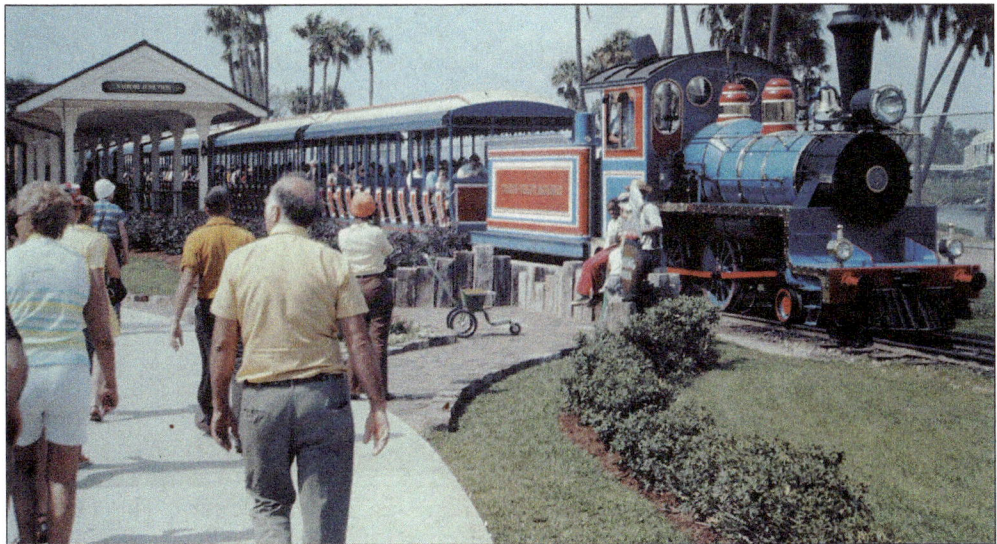

Guests board the train at the Nairobi Junction train station in 1972. Four steam locomotives serve the Serengeti Express. Two engines are modeled after the kind typically seen in the days of the American Old West, while the other two are patterned after 1890s African locomotives, such as the faithful replica seen in this image. (Author's collection.)

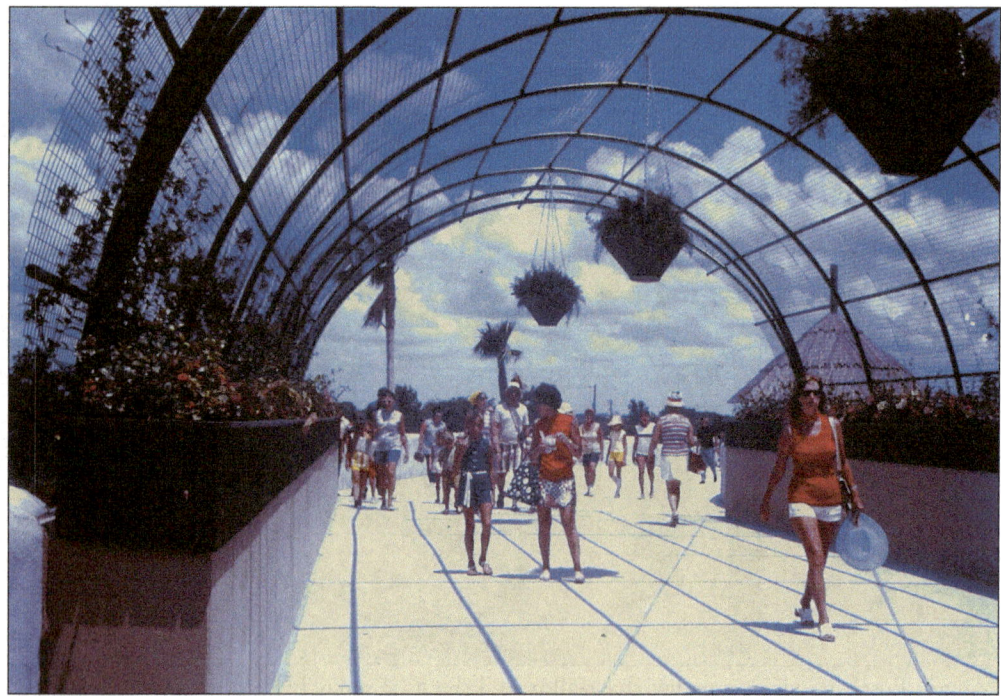

The Stanleyville area opened on June 19, 1972, as an African village. This image, taken in early 1973, shows the pedestrian footbridge that brings guests from the Bird Gardens into Stanleyville. Today, guests who walk northward along this bridge into Stanleyville see the SheiKra roller coaster rise 200 feet into the sky just to their right. (Author's collection.)

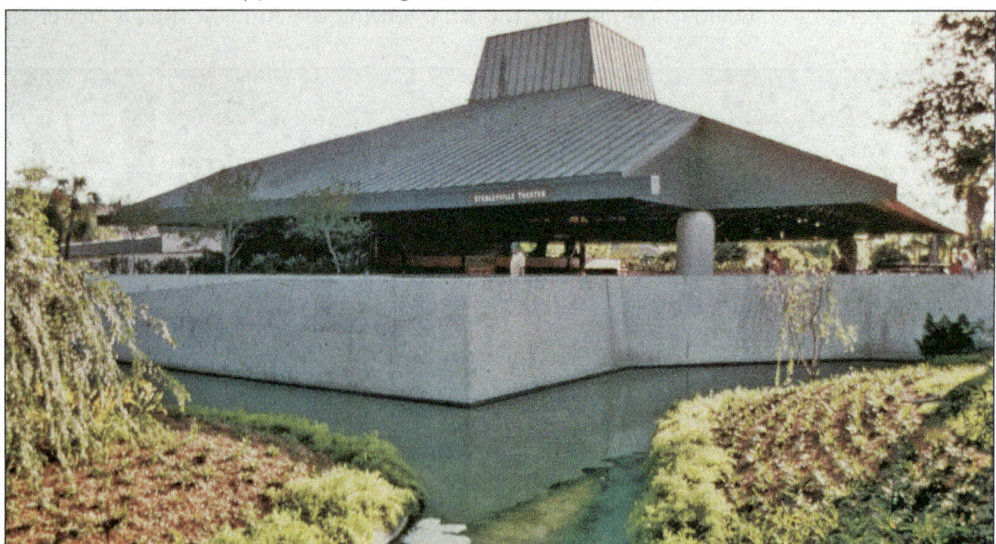

The Stanleyville Theater opened on June 19, 1972, as the Tanzania Theater. This 1,000-seat amphitheater has seen a wide array of performances over its years, including concerts, events, and animal presentations. It was also the location of the *Stanleyville Theater Variety Show* from 1980 through 1994 and later hosted a popular Russian circus performance known as *The Akishin Show*. The semi-outdoor theater venue was enclosed in 2013 to allow for enhanced lighting and visual effects. (State Archives of Florida, Florida Memory.)

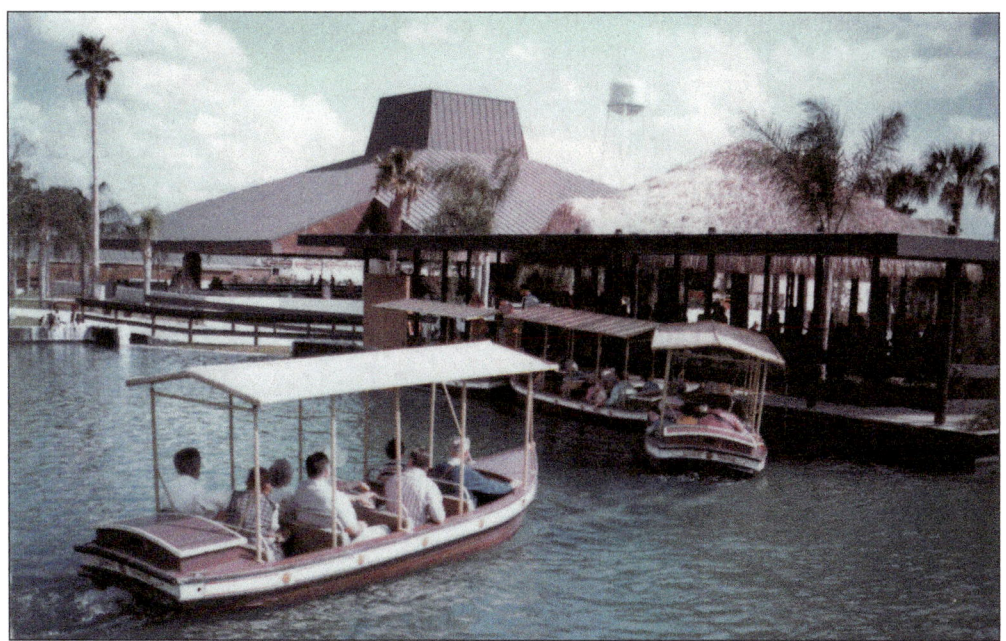

Livingstone's Landing opened in the summer of 1972 as a jungle cruise adventure. The Stanleyville-area boat ride operated under this format for a few years before it was completely overhauled in time for the 1977 season, when it reopened as the longer, more thrilling African Queen Boat Ride.

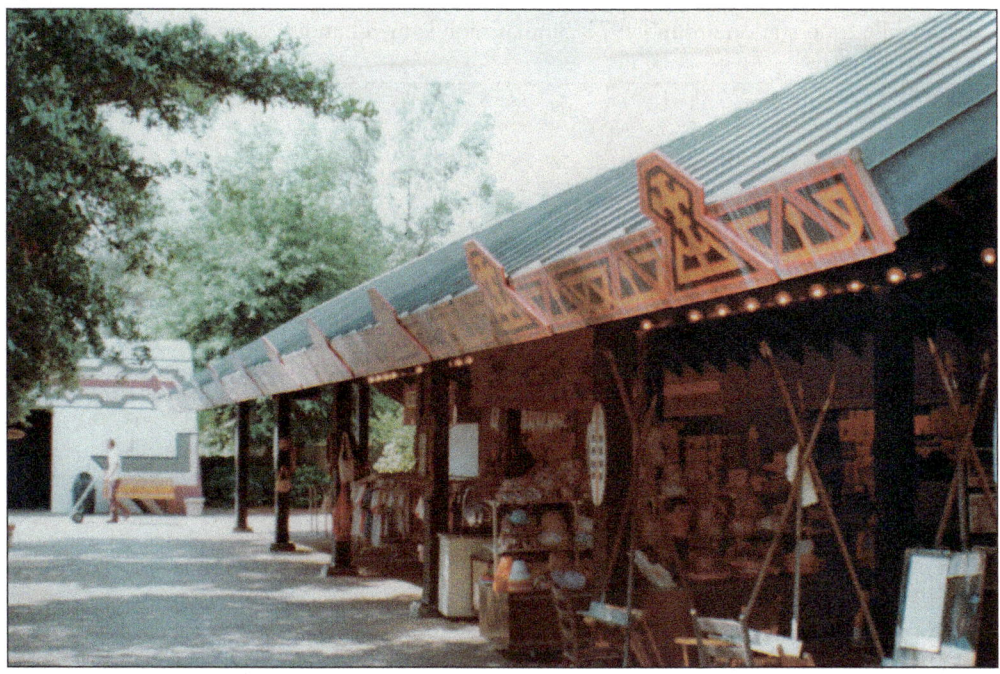

Stanleyville Bazaar was a collection of shops and refreshment bars located roughly between Stanleyville Theater and the Stanley Falls log flume. Much of the Stanleyville Bazaar was razed to make way for guest enhancements that opened in 2005, including new snack bars, game kiosks, and the 200-foot dive coaster, SheiKra.

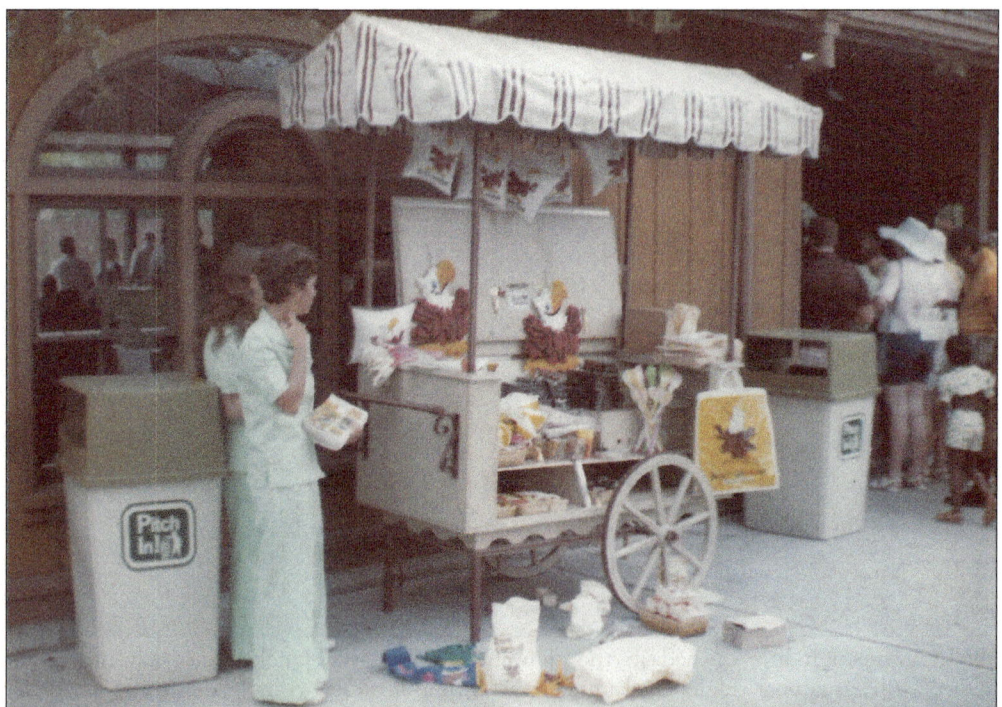

The Friendly Eagle, who officially served as the Busch Gardens Tampa Bay mascot from the late 1960s into the mid-1970s, is seen adorning much of the merchandise on this gift cart near the Stanleyville train station around 1973. Similar mobile merchandise carts are still in use today at Busch Gardens.

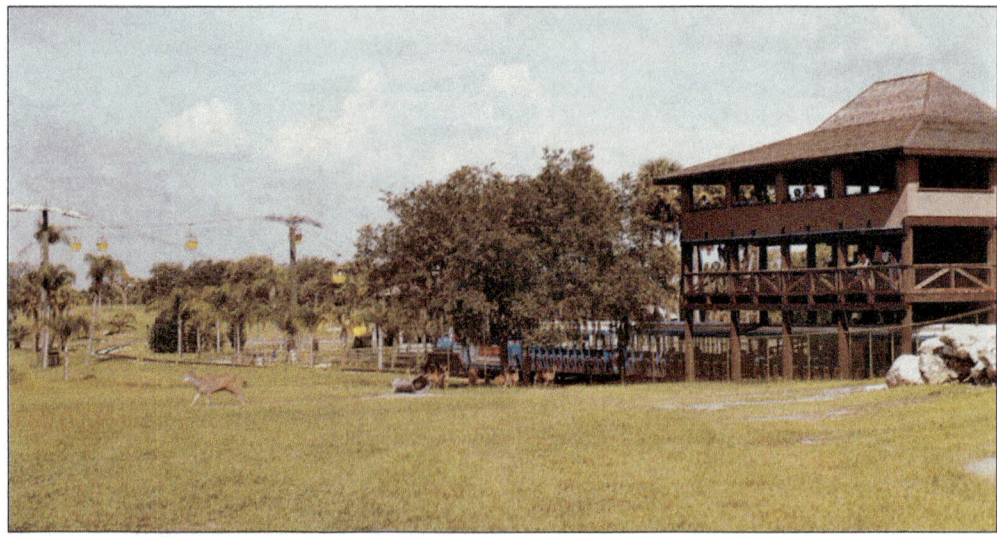

Treetops was a three-level wooden structure situated on the north end of the Serengeti Plain near the Skyride midway station. Treetops opened in 1972 and was only accessible by the train until the Skyride opened in 1974. The attraction's main draws were the incredible views of the Serengeti Plain, a variety of refreshments, and live entertainment. Treetops closed by the early 1980s, when the nearby Congo train station provided new disembarking opportunities for guests who wanted to enjoy the exciting attractions in Timbuktu, the area now known as Pantopia.

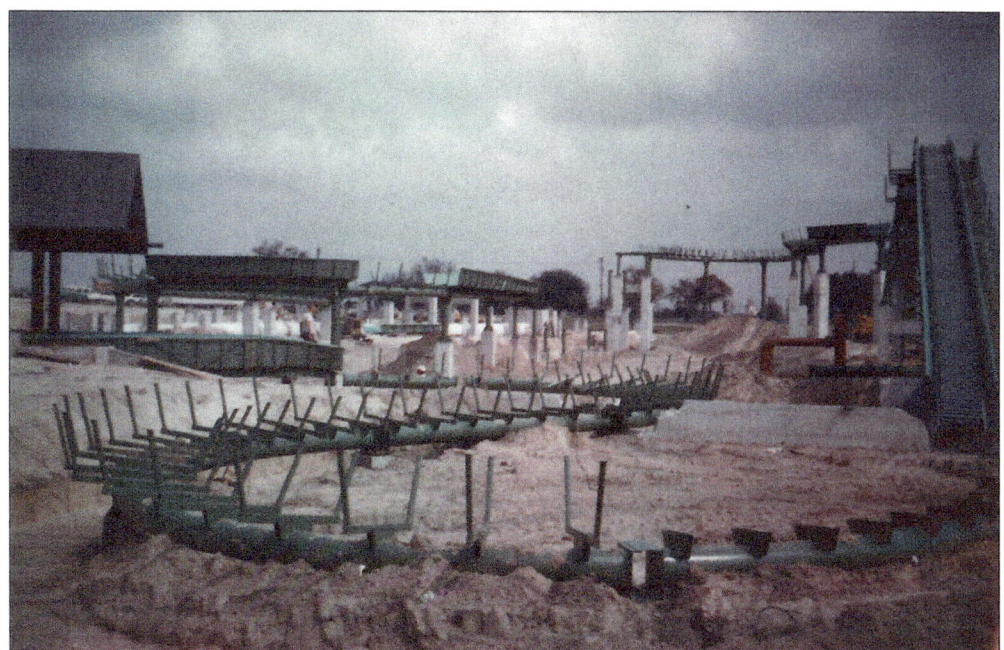

This March 16, 1973, photograph shows the construction of Stanley Falls. The log flume, which became the first major thrill ride at Busch Gardens, was built by Arrow Development of Mountain View, California, the same company that constructed the monorail.

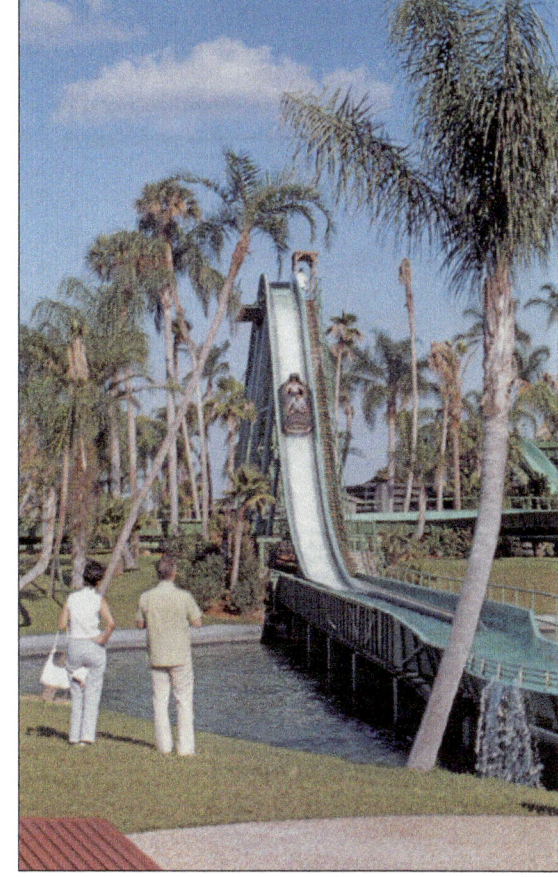

Stanley Falls, which opened on June 1, 1973, features two thrilling drops, including a 43-foot plummet that provides a breathtaking and drenching finale. Stanley Falls has changed little over the course of its history. At nearly a quarter-mile long, this popular attraction serves as one of the largest flume rides in the Southeast. (State Archives of Florida, Florida Memory.)

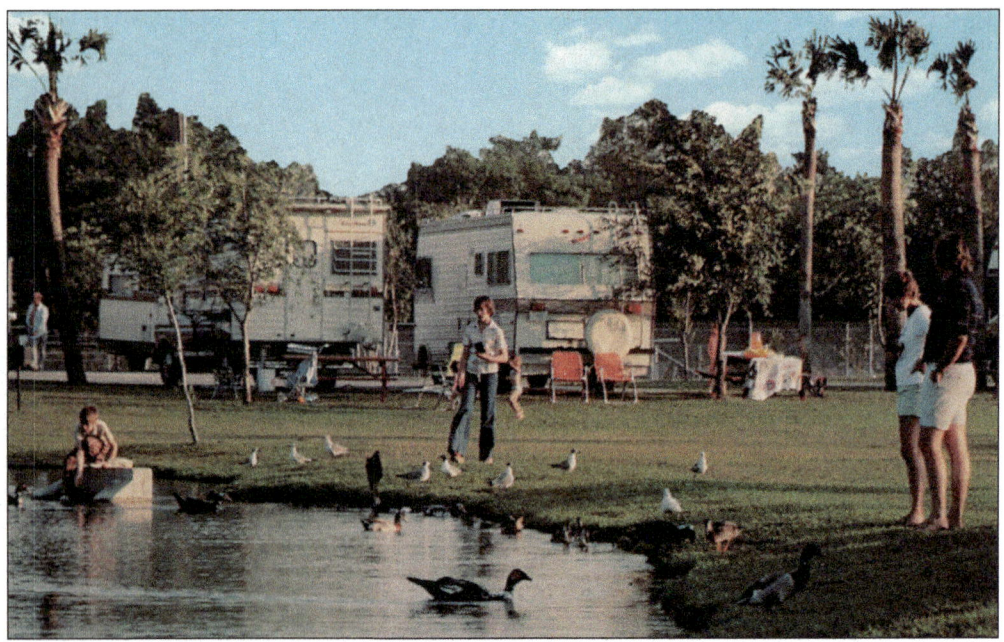

The Busch Gardens Travel Park opened in May 1973 and provided accommodations for nearly 200 vans or camper trailers. The travel park, situated near the northeast corner of North Malcolm McKinley Drive and East Linebaugh Avenue, offered its guests badminton, a playground, and a 56-foot heated swimming pool. While the travel facility was convenient for guests who enjoyed Busch Gardens just across the street, it closed by the early 1990s to provide room for expansions at the adjacent Busch Gardens sister water park Adventure Island.

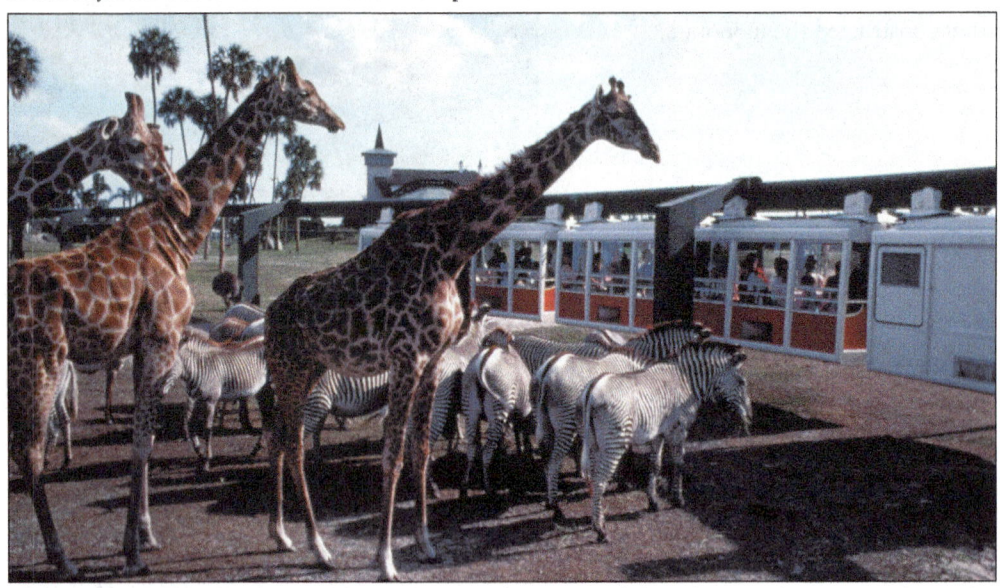

Giraffes, zebras, and other Veldt residents greet guests gliding by on the monorail. In the early 1970s, taking the monorail tour of the Serengeti Plain, in addition to riding the Trans-Veldt Railway, was one of the best ways to view the beautiful animals of the Veldt up close before the Serengeti Safari became a popular option for guests in the 1990s. (State Archives of Florida, Florida Memory.)

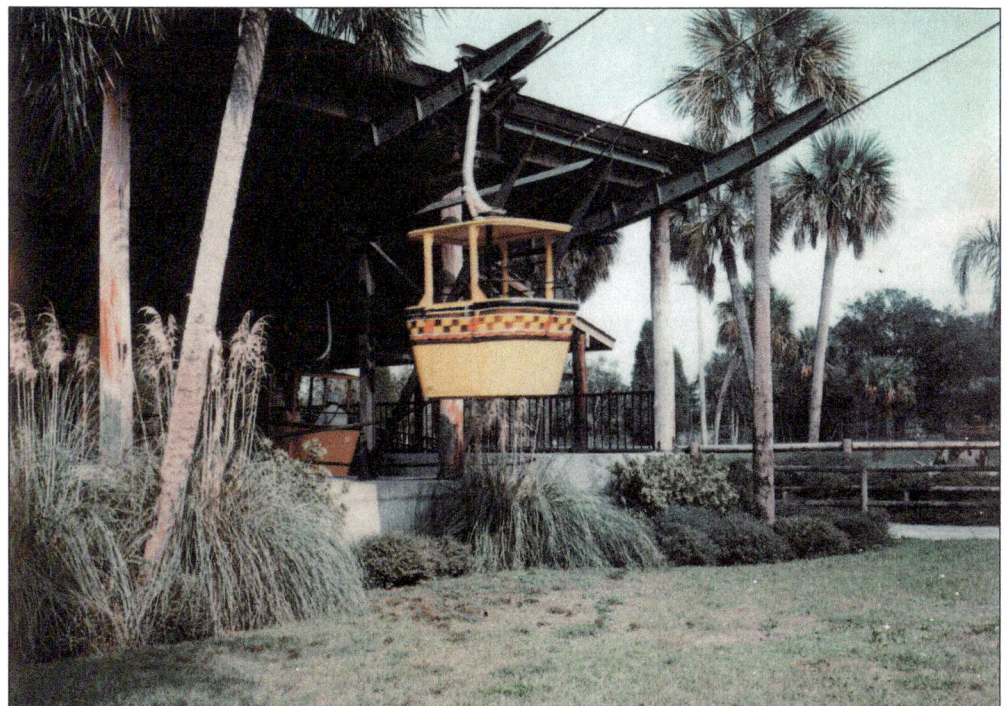

The Skyride opened in May 1974, taking guests up to 50 feet into the air along a cable path that travels from the former monorail station (now the Cheetah Hunt roller coaster queue station) to the Congo area near Stanley Falls. The Skyride at Busch Gardens Tampa Bay is a Von Roll 101 model similar to the Skyride attractions at two of Busch Gardens' sister parks, Busch Gardens in Williamsburg, Virginia, and SeaWorld in San Diego, California.

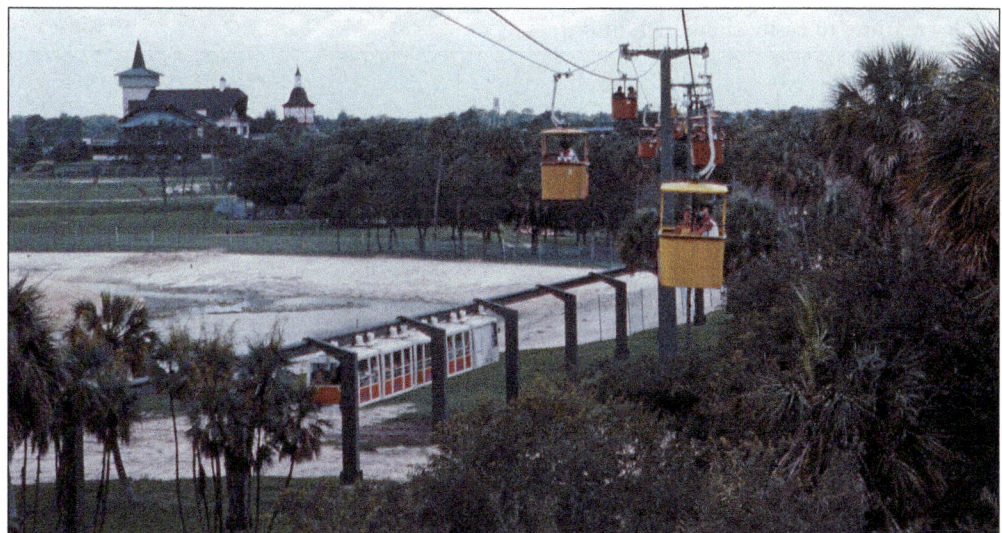

The Skyride provides unparalleled views of the Serengeti Plain and provides a lay of the land for guests. The Skyride gondolas have changed in appearance somewhat over the years, originally sporting yellow, tan, and brown colors. Today, those aboard the Skyride see the green, box-shaped track of the Cheetah Hunt launch coaster fly over the cables near this section of the ride. (State Archives of Florida, Florida Memory.)

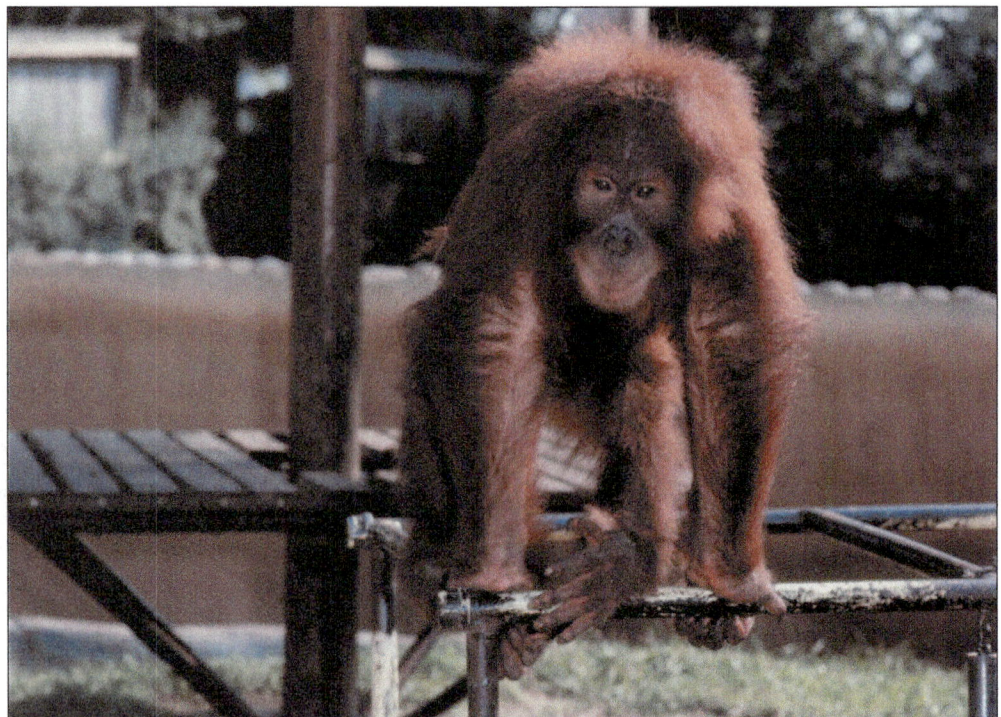

This young orangutan explores his interactive habitat in Stanleyville. The word *orangutan* is Malay in origin, with *orang* translating to "person" in English and *utan* deriving from *hutan*, which means "forest." The arms of the hairy "person of the forest" can stretch out longer than its body—up to eight feet from fingertip to fingertip on a very large male. Orangutans, like humans, have opposable thumbs, and they also enjoy the use of opposable big toes, which allow these agile creatures to easily climb high into trees.

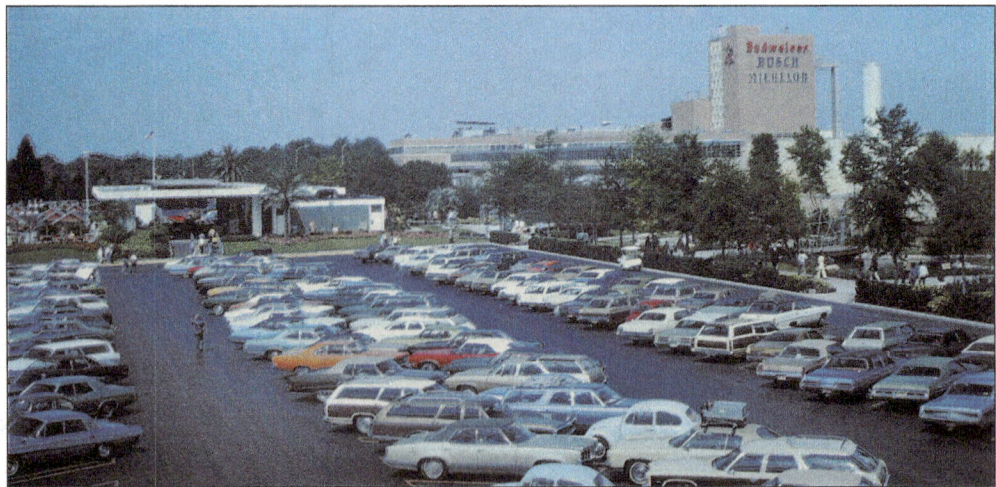

The Busch Gardens parking lot is packed on this day in 1972. Café Mozambique (now known as Zagora Café) is seen on the left, and the entrance to Boma sits off to the right. This scene would soon change, as the construction of the Moroccan Village beginning in 1973 consumed most of the parking area visible in this photograph and helped to usher in a new era for Busch Gardens. (Author's collection.)

Three

1975–1982
THE GARDENS GROW

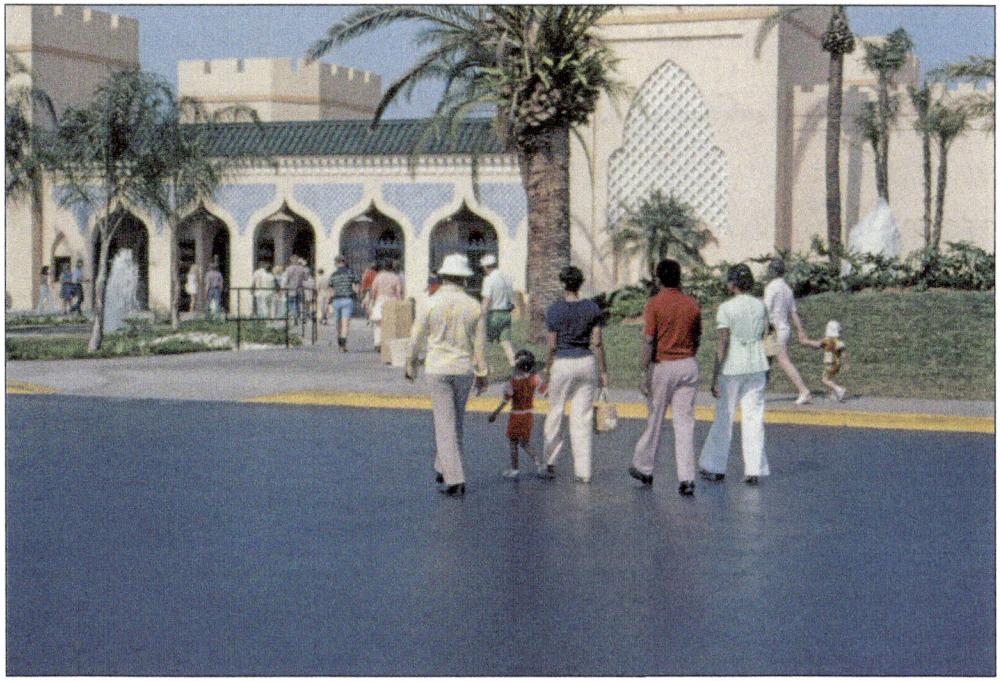

Guests start their day at Busch Gardens Tampa Bay walking up to the Moorish turnstile building at the front of the Moroccan Village. This park entrance, which still greets guests upon their arrival at Busch Gardens, opened on April 16, 1975, and introduced a new era for the Tampa tourist attraction. With the opening of the Morocco area and several other major additions over the course of the 1970s, Busch Gardens became, and has remained, one of Florida's most popular theme parks. (State Archives of Florida, Florida Memory.)

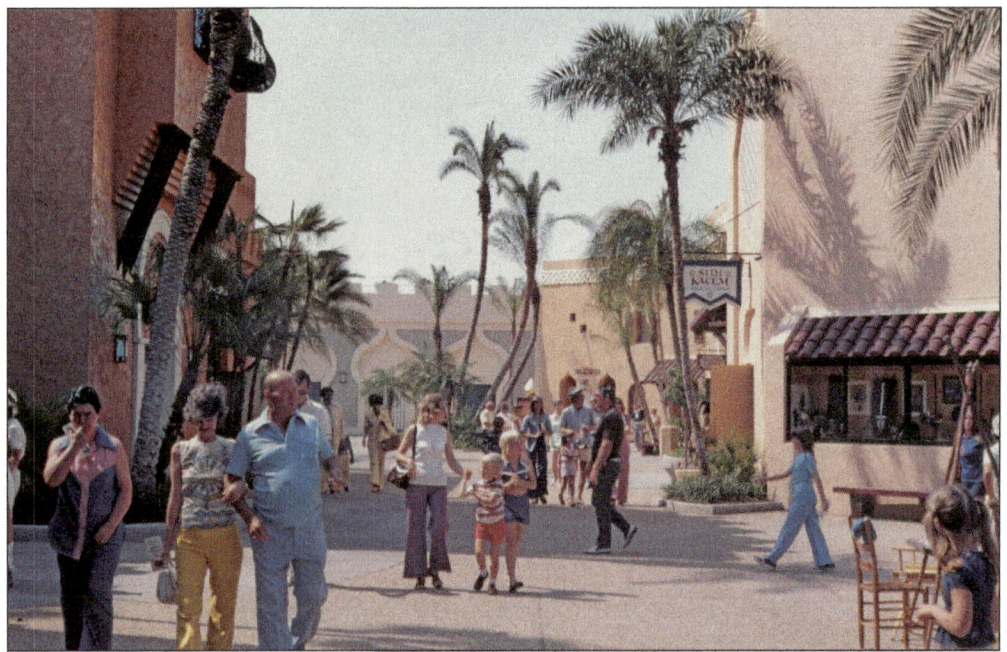

Guests enjoy a stroll through the newly opened Moroccan Village in 1975. The Morocco area offers several tantalizing treats for park guests, including handmade crafts, delicious meals, tasty ice cream and baked goods, and a variety of enchanting performers. (State Archives of Florida, Florida Memory.)

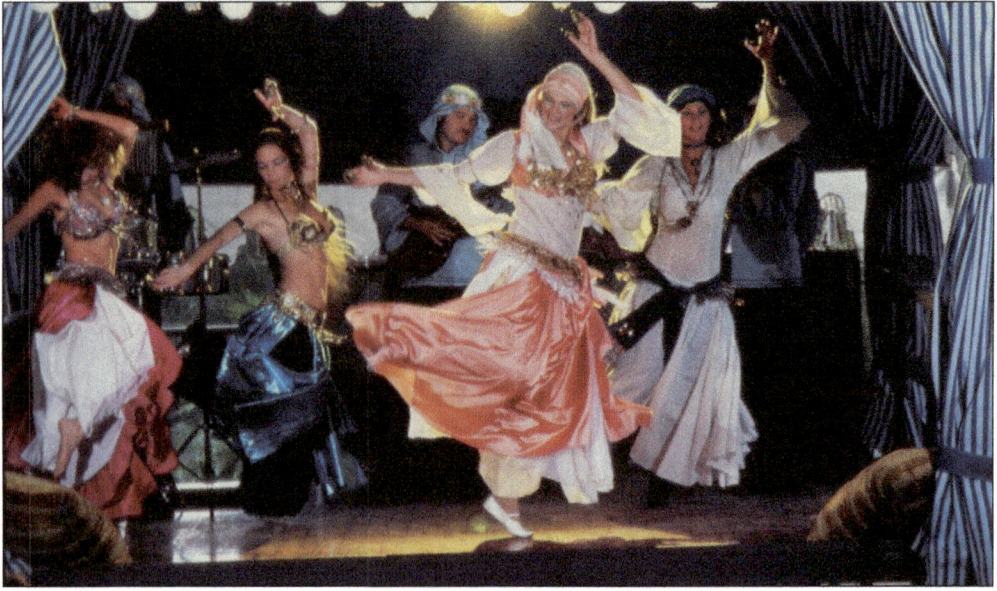

Belly dancers have been performing at Busch Gardens since the earliest days of the Moroccan Village. Some cultural experts believe that belly dancing is the oldest form of dance, theorizing that it first arose in India some 5,000 years ago before spreading to North Africa, the Middle East, and the Mediterranean. While traditional belly dancing music reflects its diverse cultural origins, this mesmerizing form of dance is often performed today to an array of modern beats. (State Archives of Florida, Florida Memory.)

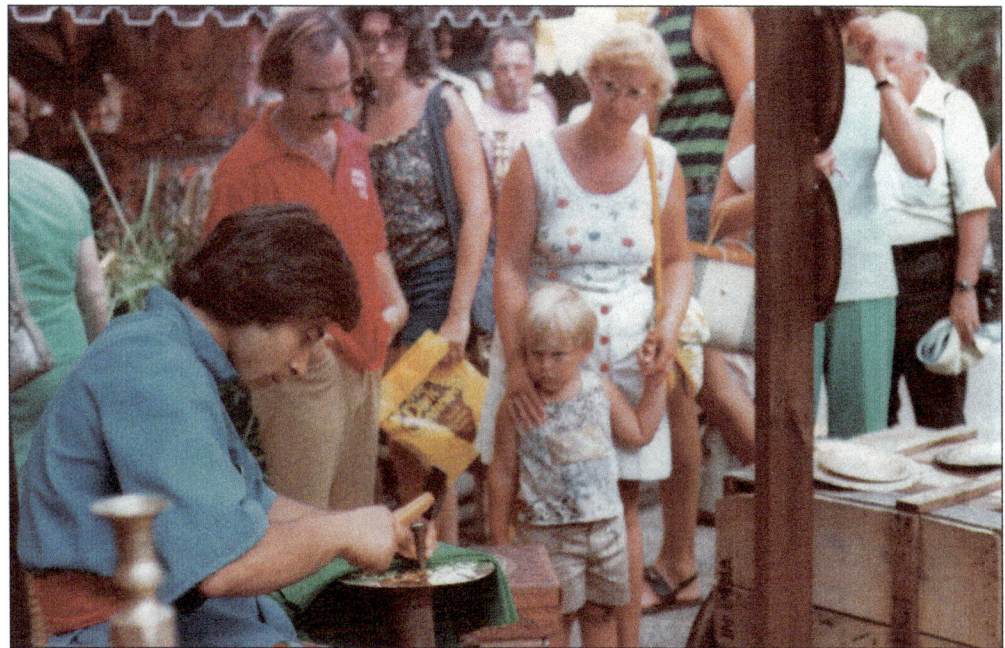

This brass crafter creates a unique piece of art before curious onlookers. Many crafters who work in the Moroccan Village hail from exotic places and use their amazing crafting skills to make one-of-a-kind keepsakes for Busch Gardens Tampa Bay guests. Today, shoppers can still find unique gifts both made on-site by talented artists and imported from native craftspeople in Africa, India, and other faraway places.

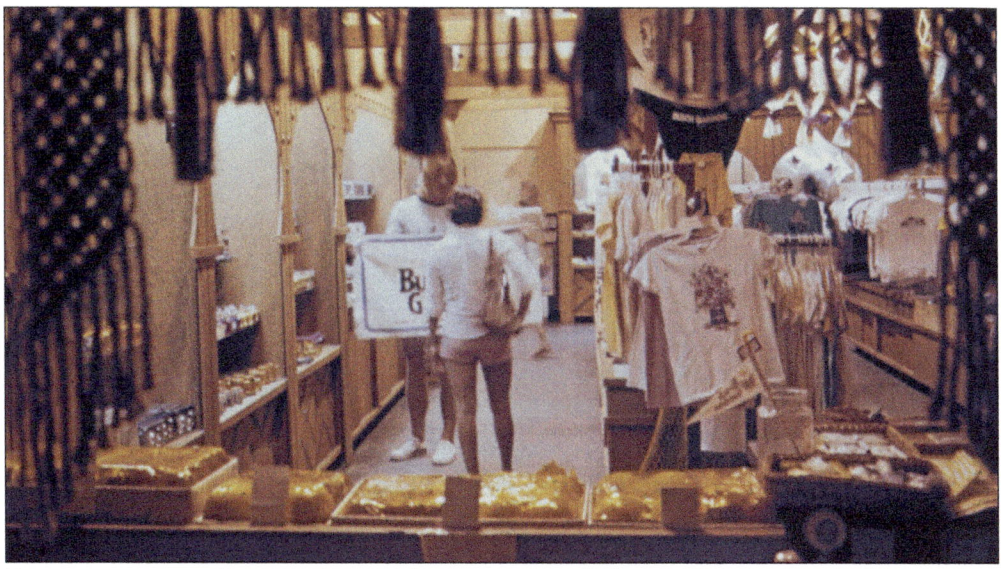

Two guests contemplate a purchase at the Emporium gift shop in the Moroccan Village in 1975. Since its opening, the Emporium has served as one of the park's main gift shops, carrying a wide array of Busch Gardens Tampa Bay logo–emblazoned items, including T-shirts, mugs and steins, hats, towels, toys, and more. The Emporium has been remodeled and expanded several times over the years as the park has grown and merchandise selection evolved. (State Archives of Florida, Florida Memory.)

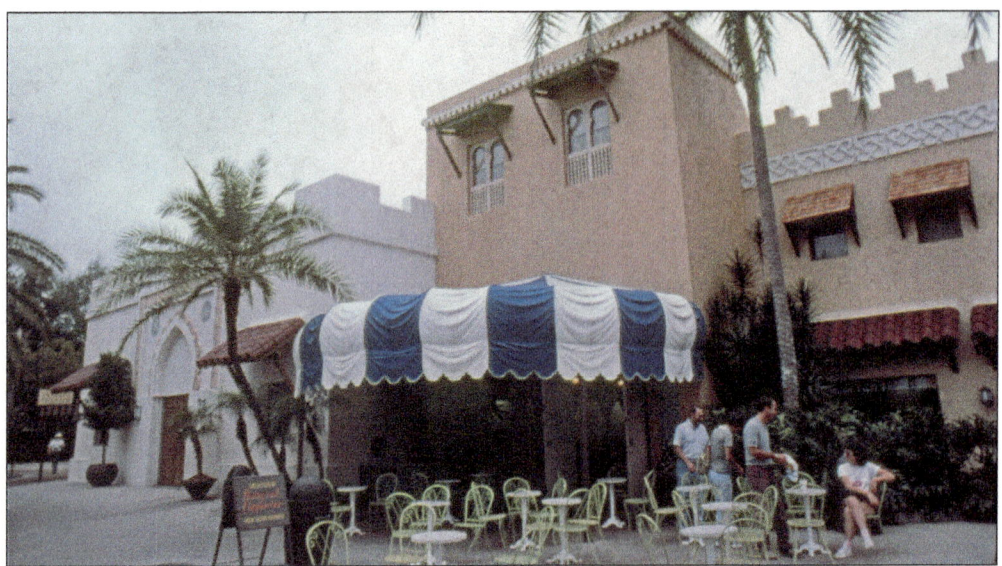

This 1975 image shows the Tangiers Theater on the left and Boujad Bakery in the middle with the blue-and-white awning. The Tangiers Theater showed a variety of educational and informational films from 1975 until the early 1990s, while Boujad Bakery served up fresh fudge, tasty tortes, and an array of other mouthwatering munchies for more than 20 years. The individual spaces occupied by the Tangiers Theater and Boujad Bakery became one by 1999, when the expansive Sultan's Sweets store began offering indulgent fare there. (State Archives of Florida, Florida Memory.)

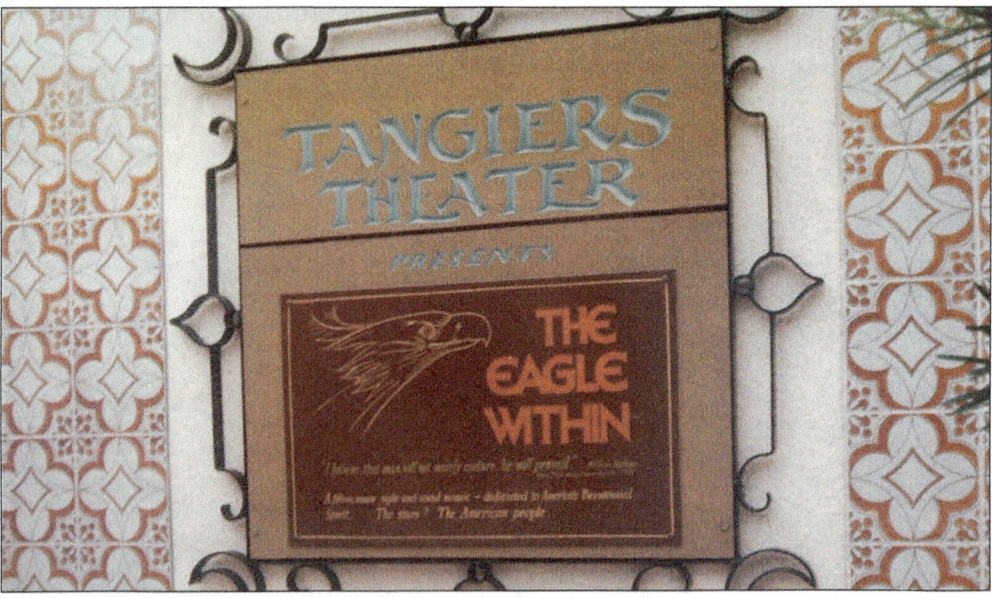

The Eagle Within was a patriotic-themed inspirational film that played at Tangiers Theater in 1976. The 15-minute film was billed as a "sight and sound mosaic dedicated to America's Bicentennial Spirit. The stars? The American People." A quote on the marquee by acclaimed American author William Faulkner reads, "I believe that man will not merely endure, he will prevail." The Tangiers Theater continued as an entertainment venue into the 1990s, when Tampa Bay Area personality Jack Harris hosted his live afternoon television show there before studio audiences consisting of park guests.

One of the improvements included with the opening of the Moroccan Village in 1975 was the renovation of the former Café Mozambique. The building, which opened as a parking lot snack bar in 1967, was retrofitted with Moorish archways and other thematic upgrades to integrate the semi-enclosed restaurant into its new Moroccan Village surroundings.

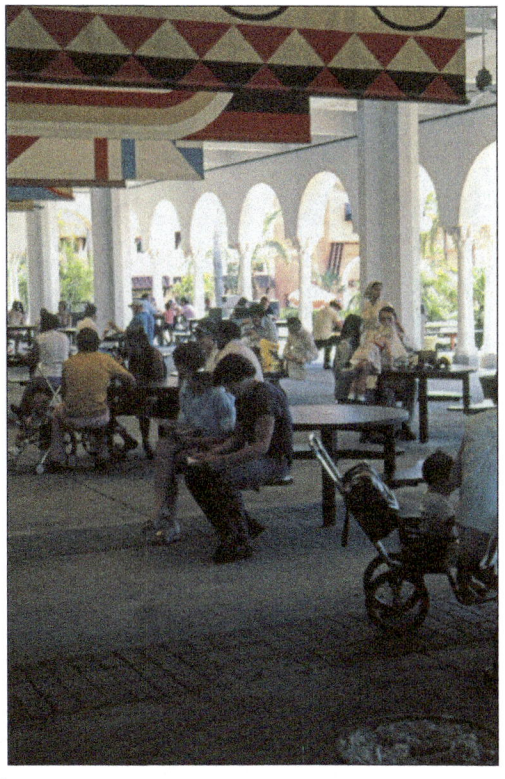

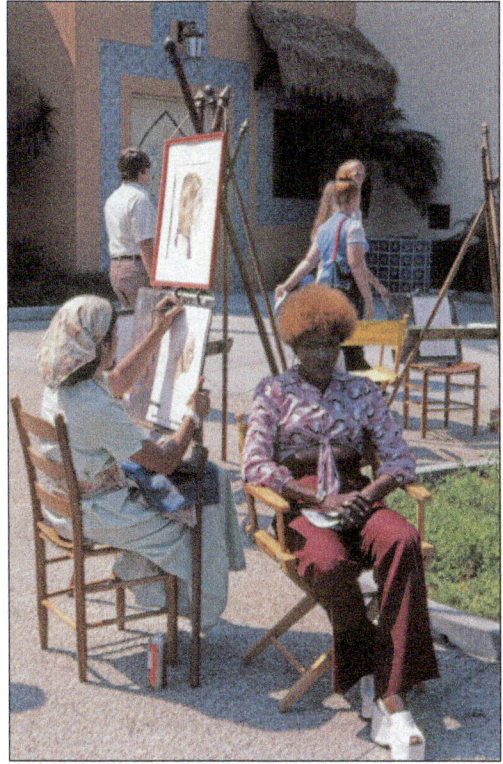

Skilled artists have been sketching up fun for guests at Busch Gardens for decades, as seen in this 1975 photograph of a portraitist creating a masterful piece of work for a guest in the Moroccan Village. Guests can still sit for portraits at Busch Gardens Tampa Bay today, and they can have their likenesses memorialized in goofy caricatures, detailed paintings, and an array of other artistic styles. Guests may even choose unique artwork that goes on their bodies, including henna, face paintings, hair wraps, and more. (State Archives of Florida, Florida Memory.)

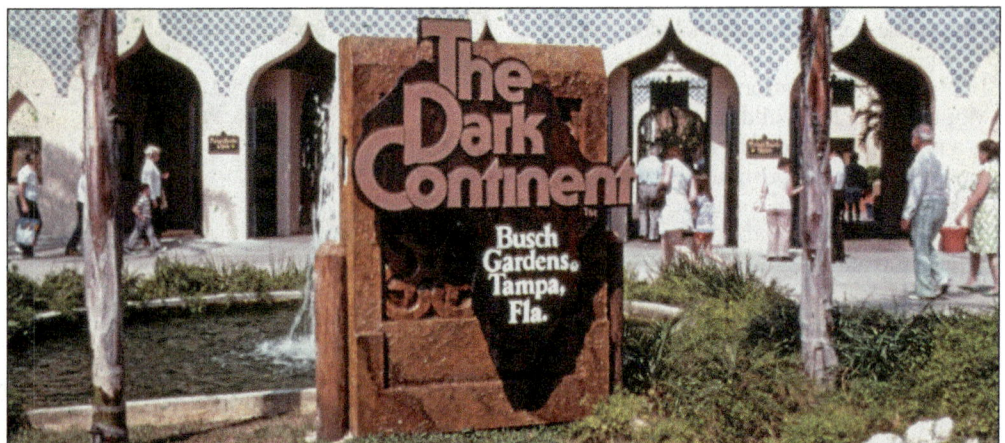

Busch Gardens Tampa Bay was temporarily rebranded as the Dark Continent beginning in 1976. The name change reflected the park's theme at the time, which was late-19th-century Africa, and referenced the hidden wonders and mystiques of the beautiful African continent. However, most locals and many tourists still referred to the Tampa Bay landmark simply as "Busch Gardens." Consequently, "The Dark Continent" was de-emphasized starting in late 1983 and dropped altogether by the end of the 1980s. (State Archives of Florida, Florida Memory.)

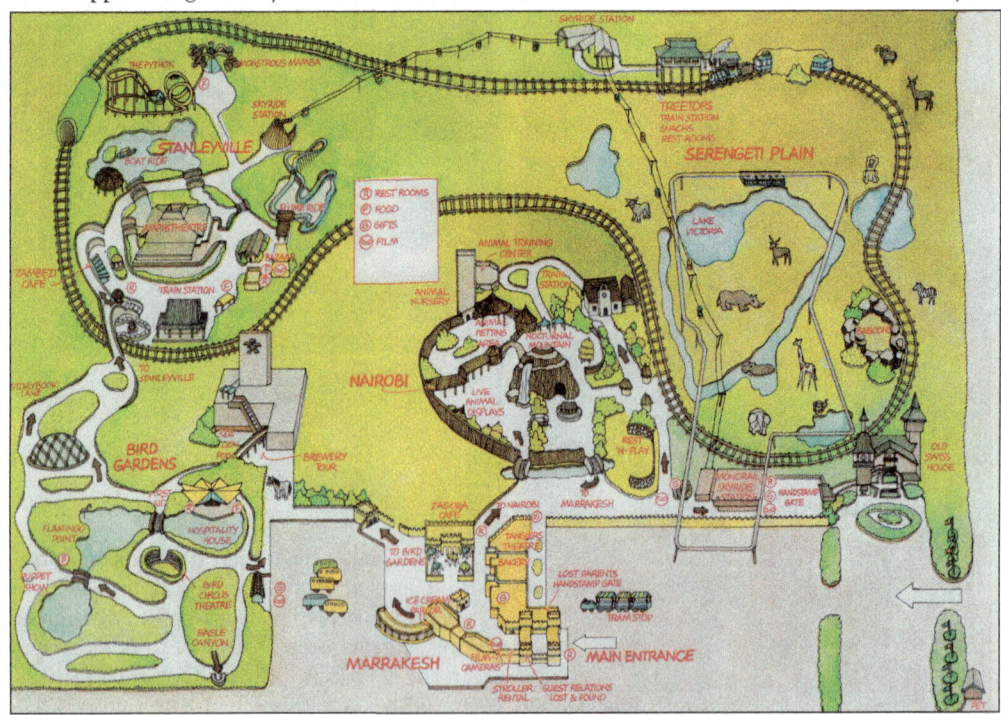

This 1976 Busch Gardens map reflects most of the expansions that occurred in the park during the 1970s, including the addition of Nairobi (originally called Boma) in 1970, the 1972-vintage Stanleyville section, and the Moroccan Village, referred to as Marrakesh on this map, in 1975. The Python roller coaster and Monstrous Mamba flat ride, which opened in 1976 as Stanleyville additions, would be reassigned to the newly created Congo area in 1977. By the end of the 1970s, the large gap in the top-center area of the map between Stanleyville and the Serengeti Plain was filled in with the addition of Timbuktu, which was later reimagined as Pantopia.

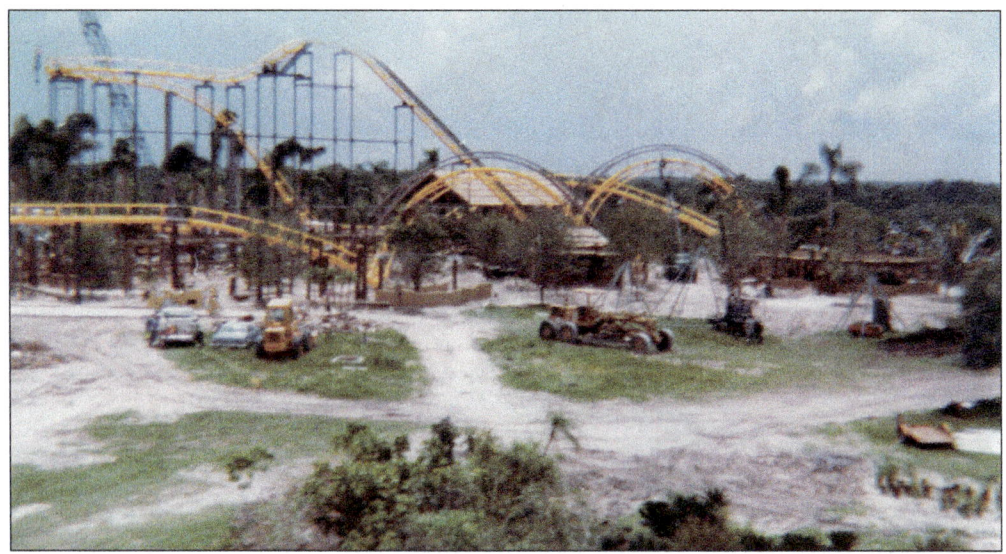

This spring 1976 photograph shows the construction of Python, the first roller coaster to rise at Busch Gardens Tampa Bay. Python was constructed by Arrow Development, which was the same firm that also built Stanley Falls and the monorail. Arrow Development built the first roller coasters since the early 1900s to turn their riders upside down. Meanwhile, Python was one of the earliest steel roller coasters in the United States to hurtle its riders through inversions and the first in Florida to do so.

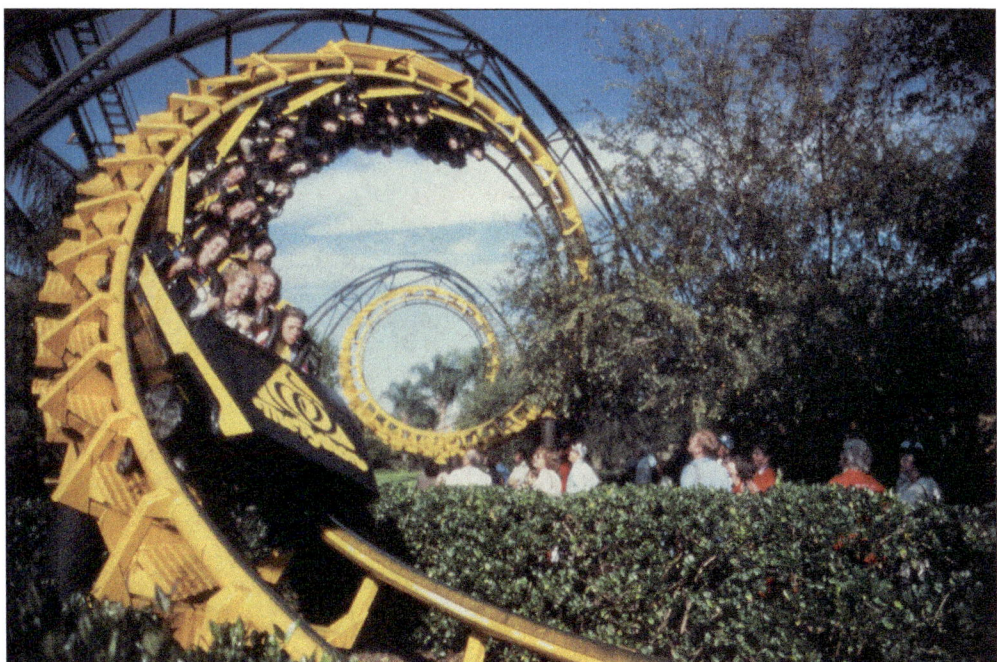

Python, seen here soon after its July 1, 1976, opening, was 1,250 feet long, featured a 55-foot vertical drop, and spun its brave riders through two corkscrew barrel rolls at speeds of up to 50 miles per hour. Python gave its last ride on October 31, 2006, and was demolished soon after. Most of its metal went into the construction of the Jungala attractions that took the place of the popular roller coaster. (State Archives of Florida, Florida Memory.)

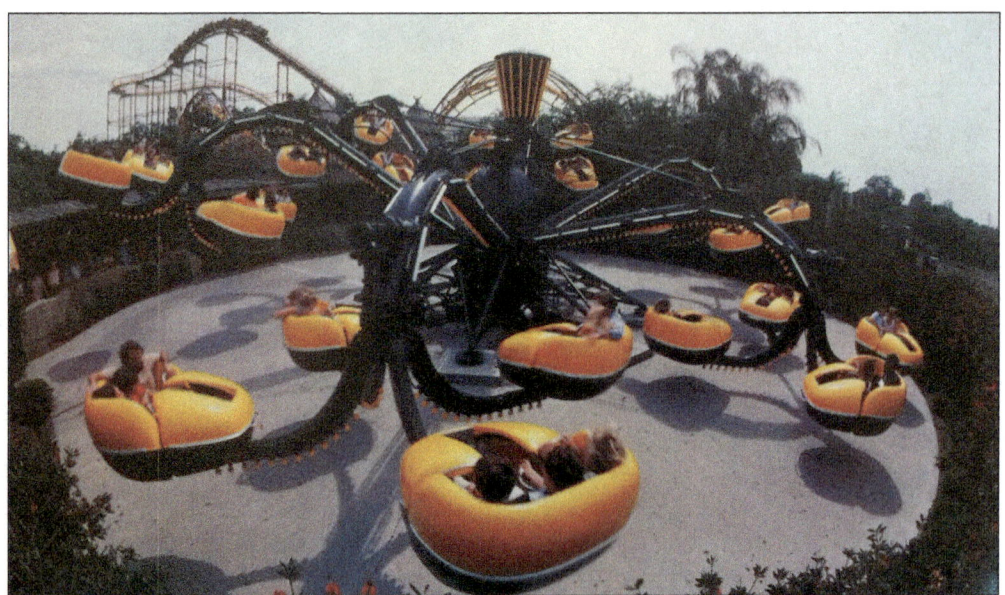

Monstrous Mamba was a Monster flat ride built by Eyerly Aircraft Company in 1976. Monstrous Mamba could seat some 50 guests at a time in 24 independently spinning capsules that moved up and down and provided thrilling, unexpected twists and turns as well as the sensation of weightlessness. The ride closed in the fall of 1995, and the space was used as outdoor seating for the adjacent Vivi Storehouse restaurant. Ultimately, the space once occupied by Monstrous Mamba was incorporated into the Jungala area, which opened on April 5, 2008.

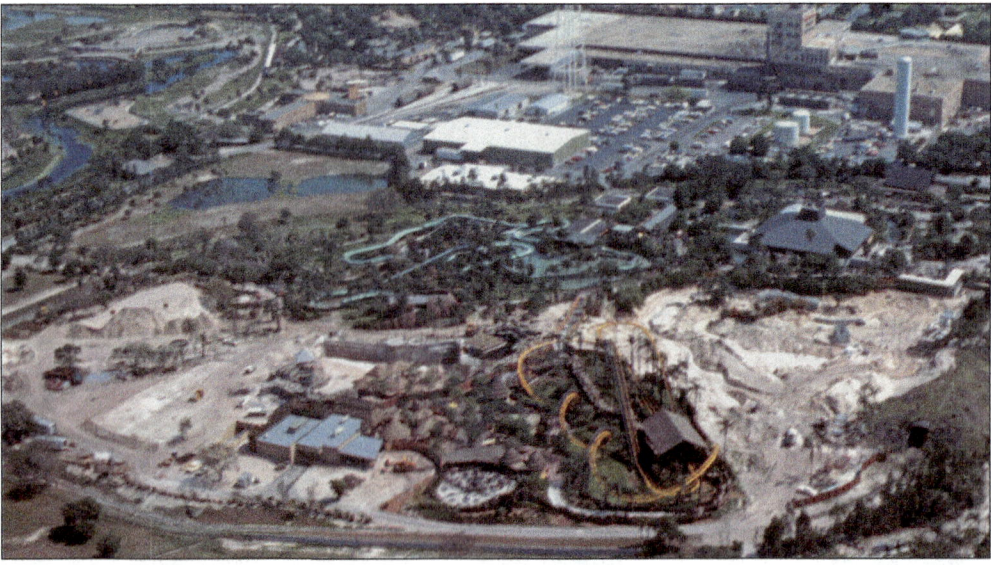

Busch Gardens was under constant expansion for the duration of the 1970s. This aerial photograph, taken in 1977, shows the yellow Python roller coaster and its neighboring Monstrous Mamba and Vivi Storehouse sandwiched by new development nearly all around. On the right, a revamped Livingstone's Landing soon became the African Queen Boat Ride, while construction on the left half of the photograph brought new Congo-area attractions, including Ubanga-Banga bumper cars and the innovative Claw Island Bengal tiger habitat. (State Archives of Florida, Florida Memory.)

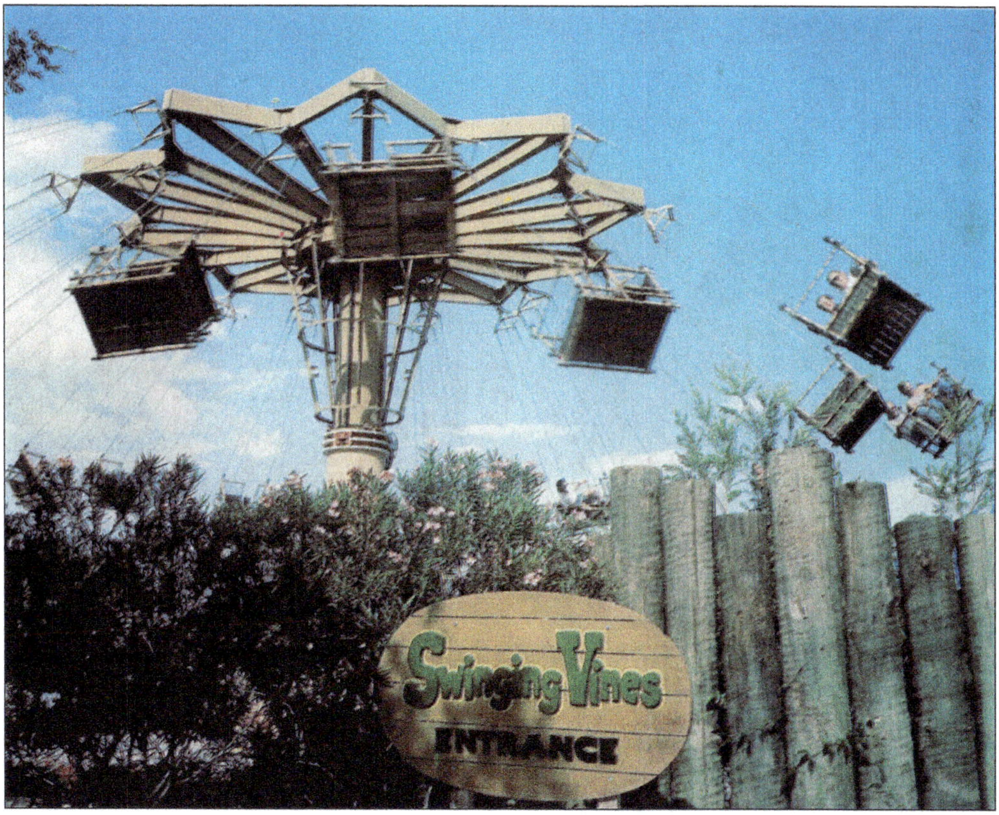

One of the new attractions under construction in the previous photograph was Swinging Vines. This major swing ride opened in July 1977 and was manufactured by Intamin, a Swiss firm that built several other thrilling attractions at Busch Gardens Tampa Bay, including the Congo River Rapids, the Phoenix, and Cheetah Hunt. Swinging Vines, which was situated just west of the Ubanga-Banga bumper cars, was removed around 1991.

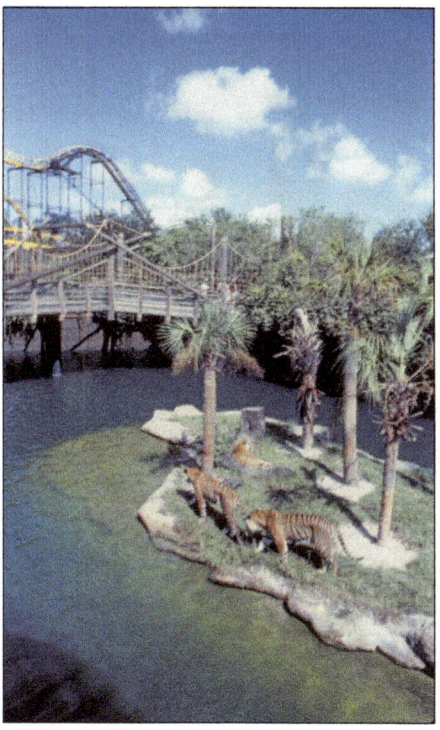

Claw Island opened in July 1977 to provide a sprawling, natural setting for the park's Bengal tigers. Claw Island was unique in that it allowed guests to enjoy close encounters with tigers while keeping both the animal residents and their human observers safe. Claw Island closed in 2006 and received a complete makeover when much of the Congo area was reimagined as Jungala. Tiger Trail, which opened with Jungala in 2008, took many design cues from Claw Island while also implementing many innovative habitat upgrades. (State Archives of Florida, Florida Memory.)

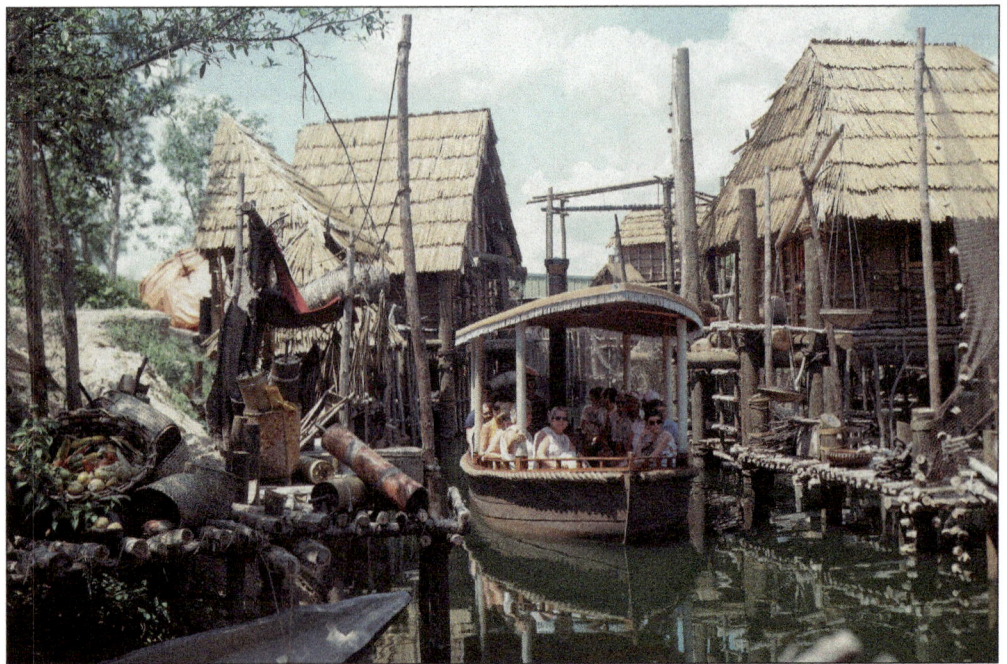

The African Queen Boat Ride, which was developed from Livingstone's Landing, opened in July 1977. The jungle cruise took its courageous riders through an African village, much to the chagrin of at least one "native" who was known to jump out from his hut and surprise unsuspecting guests. The African Queen Boat Ride was reopened in 1989 as the Tanganyika Tidal Wave, which retained some elements of the African Queen Boat Ride, including the village seen here, with the addition of a thrilling 55-foot drop and drenching finale.

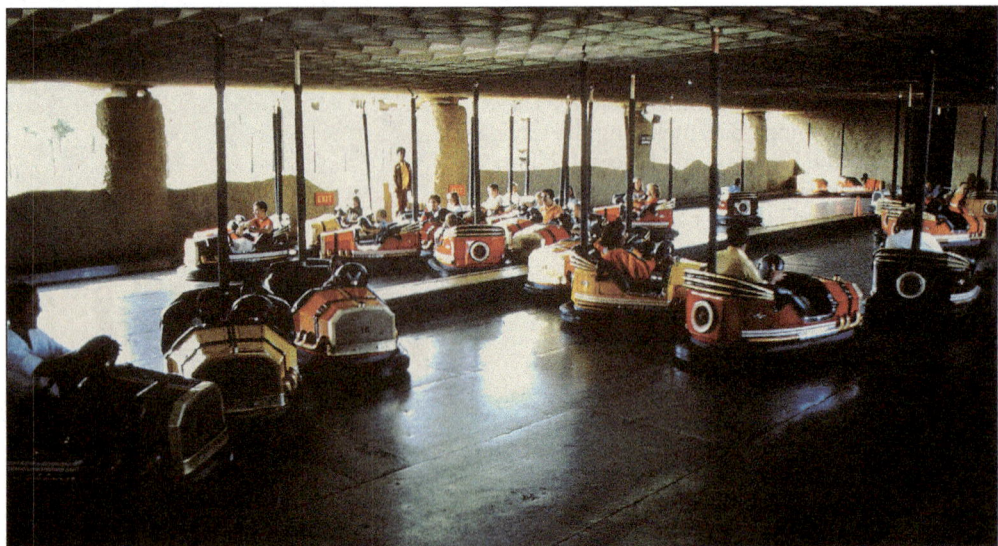

Ubanga-Banga bumper cars is seen here shortly after its opening in 1977. For many children, Ubanga-Banga offers a first (and jarring) experience behind the wheel of a vehicle. Perhaps for some parents, Ubanga-Banga has been the perfect place to teach their young drivers how not to get around on the road. For all, this timeless attraction has been a fun and safe place to tease family and friends, rib fellow park guests, and cause a giddier style of gridlock. (Author's collection.)

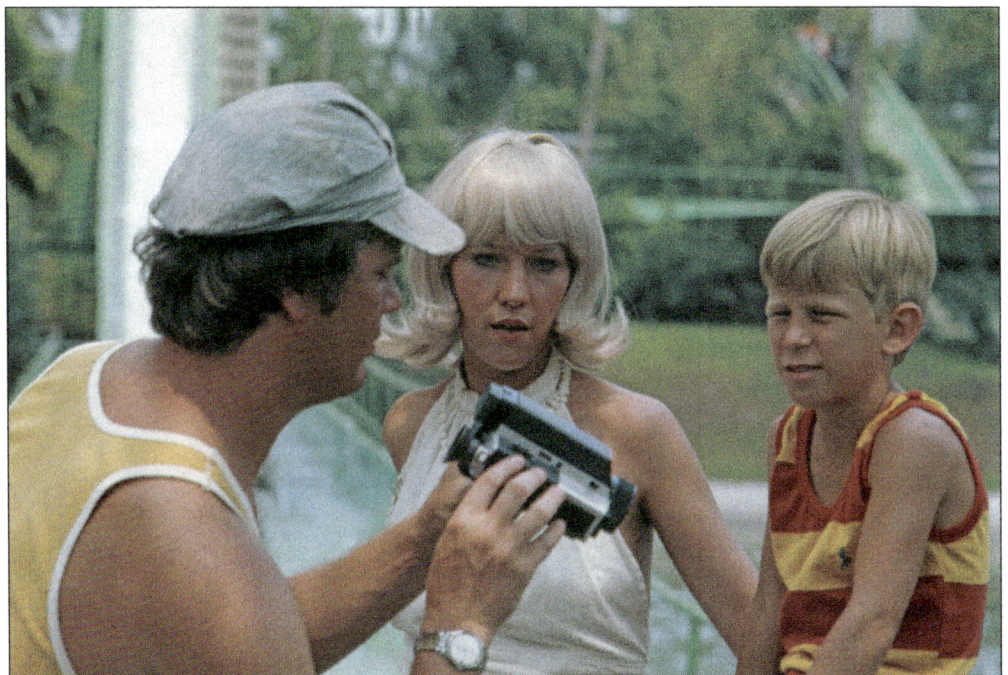

This young family is recording their day at Busch Gardens Tampa Bay on 8-millimeter film near Stanley Falls in 1975. Technology may have changed over the years, but guests still enjoy taking video, pictures, and snaps of their visits to Busch Gardens. Today, guests have the added technological capability of instantaneously uploading their videos and photographs to social media so they can share their memories of Busch Gardens with the rest of the world. (State Archives of Florida, Florida Memory.)

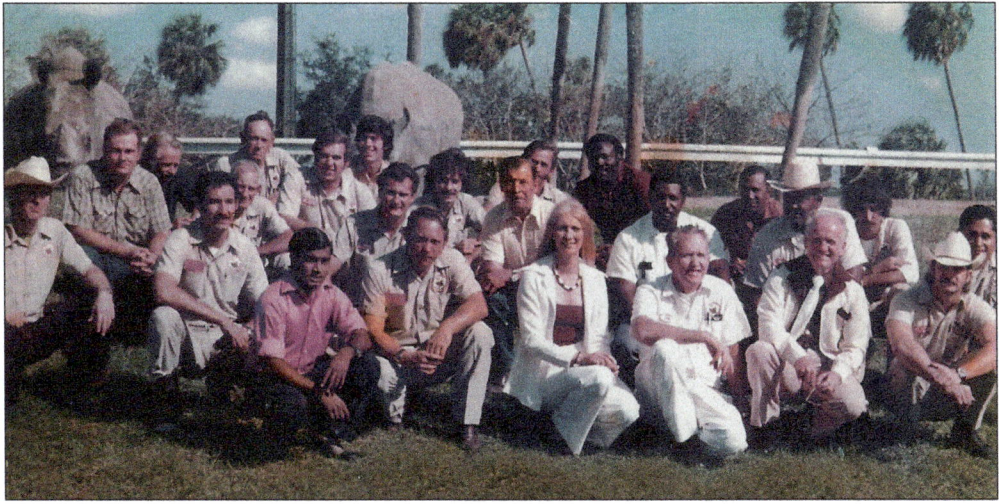

Two dozen zoo associates are seen posing on the Serengeti Plain in the mid-1970s. They include, from left to right, Buddy Farrar, Mike Massey, Karlis Fiser, Arnold Stillman, George Hindmarsh, Bill Webb, Shazam Ali, Wally Schlenke, Chris Palmer, Lynn Ash, Bobby Scrape, Tony Losito, Bill Cox, Ken Thompson, Peggy Downum, Willie Jackson, Eddie Vicks, John Jernigan, Sam Cleggett, Thornell Floyd, Raymond Dorsett, John Oliver, Mark Peterson, and Serapio Villarreal. (Mark Peterson.)

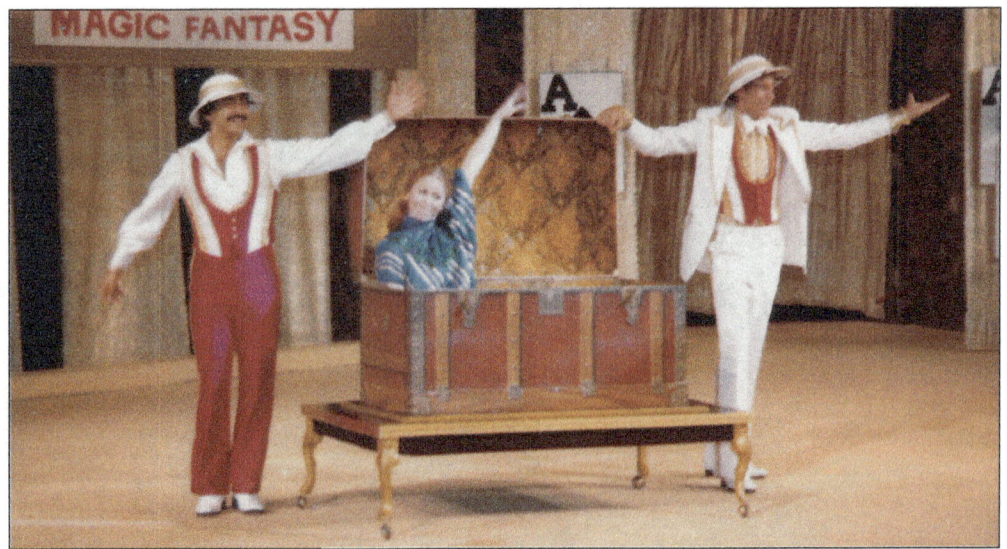

Mark Wilson's Magic Fantasy was one of several shows at the Stanleyville Theater in the 1970s. Seen here from left to right in 1979 are performers Frank "Rudy" Hernandez, Lesley Utley, and Gary Kebschull. Magicians have appeared at the Stanleyville Theater and other venues at Busch Gardens many times over the decades. In the summer of 2003, singing magician Darren Romeo performed his first Busch Gardens engagements at the Stanleyville Theater. His mentors, world-renowned magicians Siegfried Fischbacher and Roy Horn, made a cameo appearance onstage during one of Romeo's Stanleyville Theater performances. (Author's collection.)

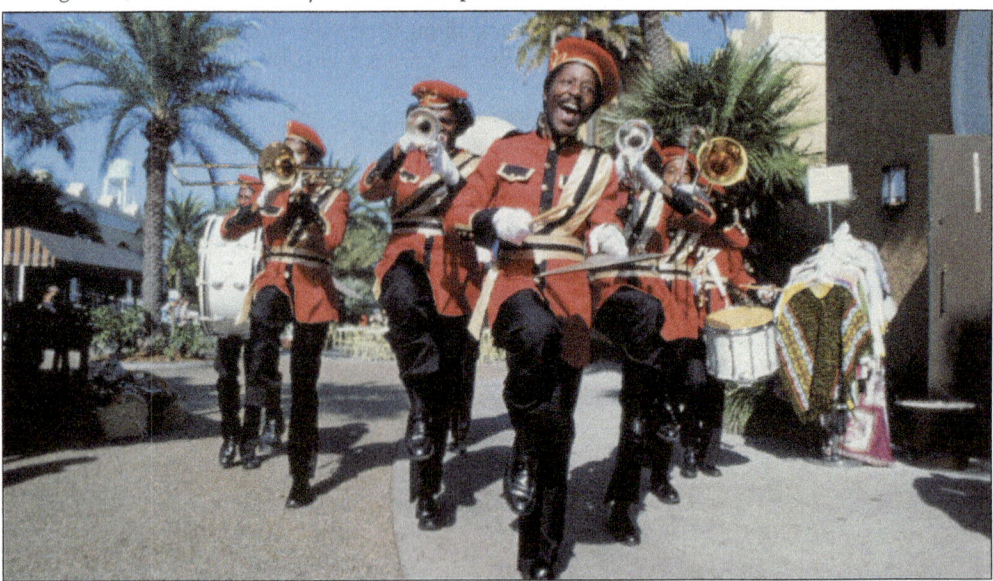

The Mystic Sheiks of Morocco were a marching brass ensemble entertaining guests at Busch Gardens from 1976 through 2010. The talented band members were as snazzy on the valves as they were quick on their feet, dancing along to most of their numbers and engaging with audiences young and old. The Mystic Sheiks of Morocco usually played throughout the park, though they occasionally performed at Stanleyville Theater and other park venues. They were also traveling ambassadors, representing Busch Gardens throughout Tampa Bay, across the United States, and around the world. (State Archives of Florida, Florida Memory.)

The ostrich, seen here in the Serengeti Plain in 1977, is the world's largest bird. Though flightless, ostriches can sprint up to 45 miles per hour, enabling them to outrun predatory animals such as leopards. Ostrich eggs are 24 times heavier than chicken eggs, measure six inches long, and can weigh three pounds. Those may be big eggs, but they are certainly fitting of a bird that can stand as tall as nine feet. (State Archives of Florida, Florida Memory.)

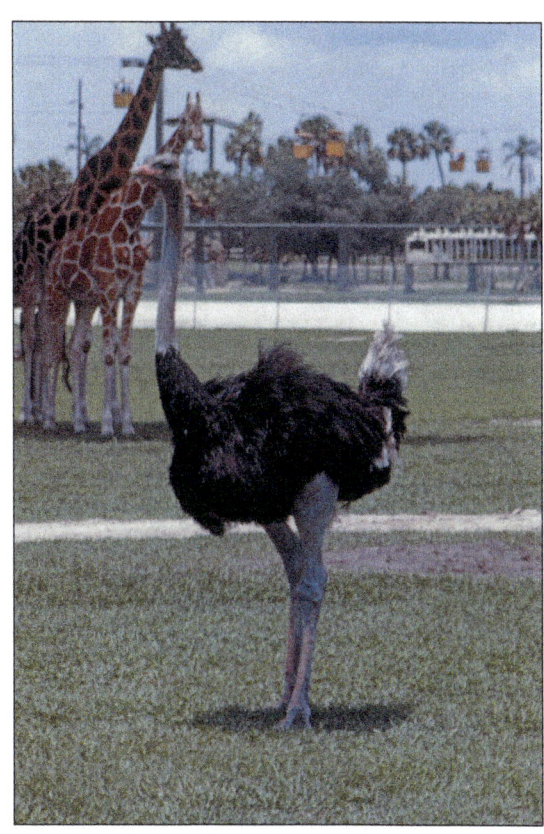

The Old Swiss House was as much of an attraction in-park as it was a draw for diners in Tampa Bay who wanted to enjoy a good meal and unparalleled views. Diners could enjoy meals at the Old Swiss House without having to pay park admission. This August 1979 photograph shows a billboard that stood just south of the park along Busch Boulevard near Thirty-Fourth Street, inviting passersby to stop in for a pleasant Veldt-side meal they would not soon forget.

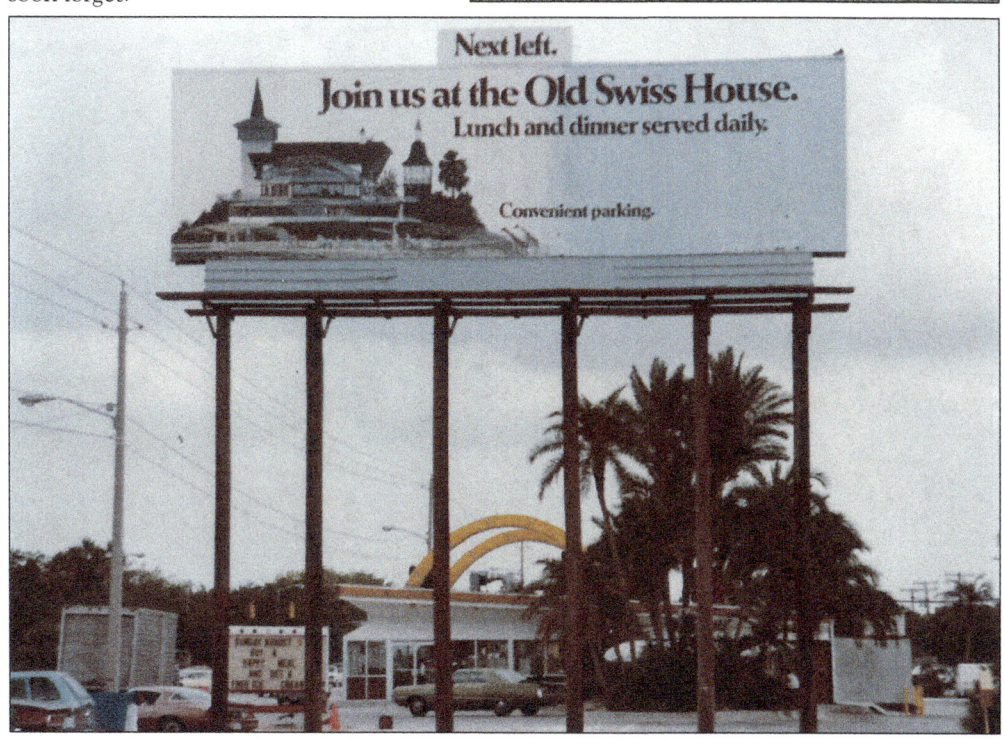

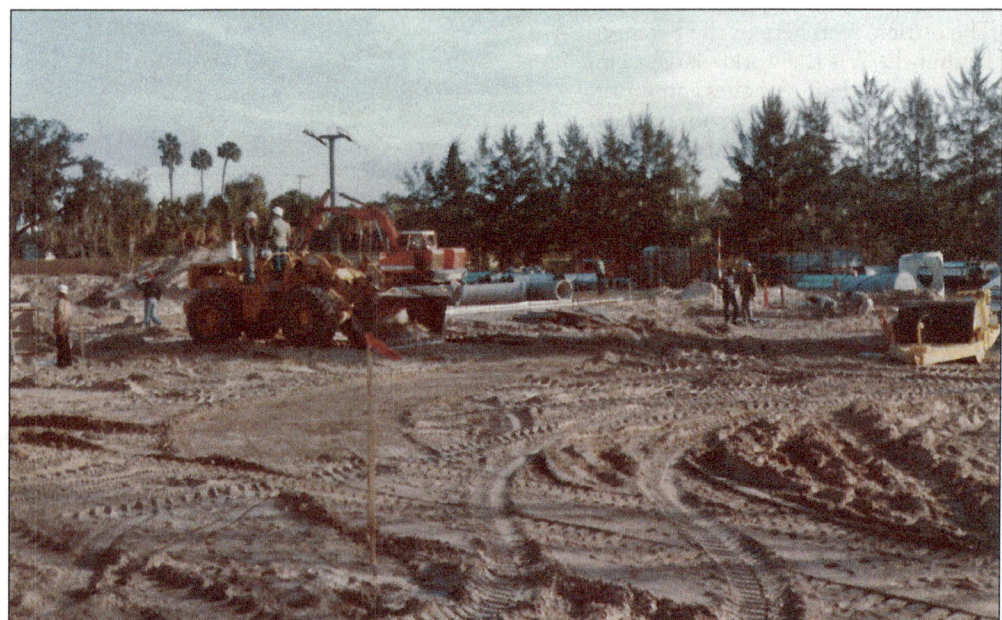

Construction crews were busy at Busch Gardens throughout 1979 as they built what was the park's largest expansion: Timbuktu, the area now known as Pantopia. Timbuktu was an ambitious project that marked the park's 20th anniversary and added several new attractions, including rides, shows, a games area, and restaurants. The work crew in this photograph is preparing the foundation of the Dolphin Theater, which was later renamed Pantopia Theater.

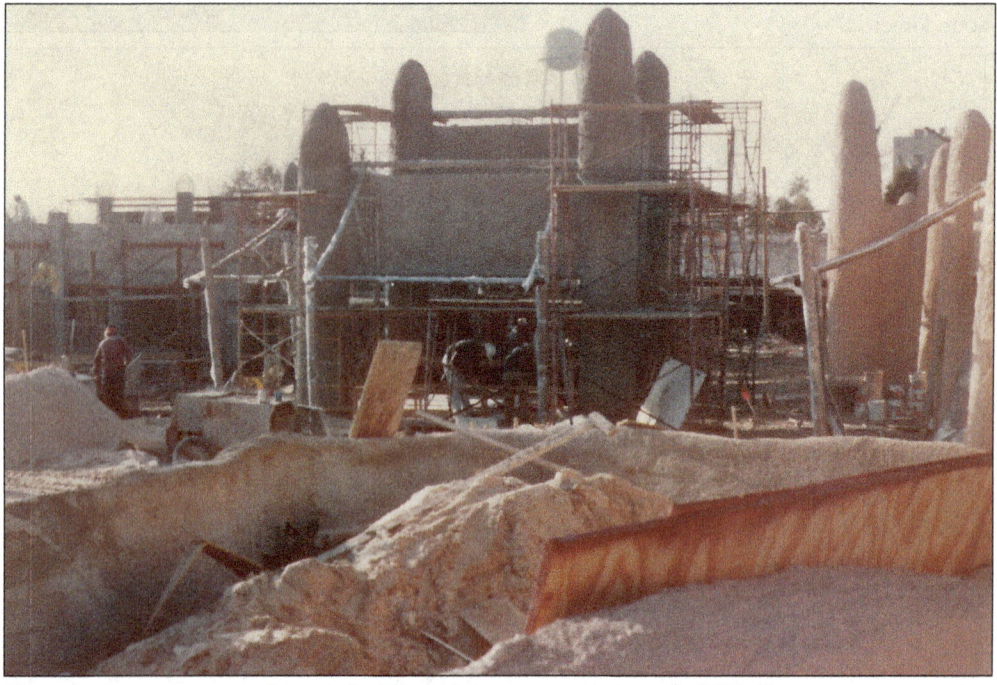

Construction comes together on the Timbuktu games area in early 1979. Guests continue trying their hand and pushing their luck at various games of skill and chance today in the reimagined land of Pantopia, which utilizes most of the buildings seen in this image.

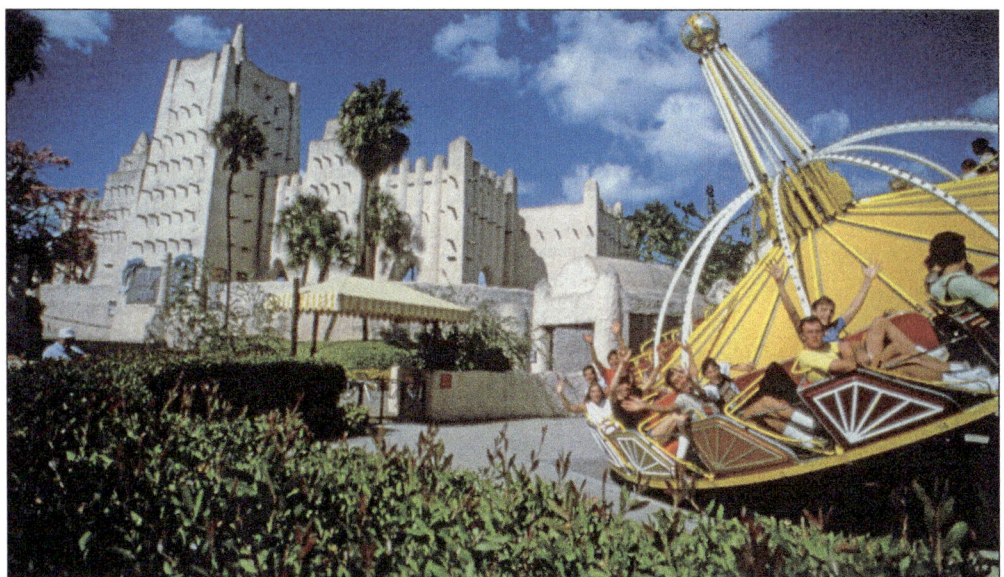

The Crazy Camel thrilled many guests from 1979 through 2003 in the Timbuktu area adjacent to the Dolphin Theater, seen in the background. This Chance Rides Trabant was replaced by Cheetah Chase, a Wild Mouse–style roller coaster that opened in 2004 and was renamed Sand Serpent in 2011. (State Archives of Florida, Florida Memory.)

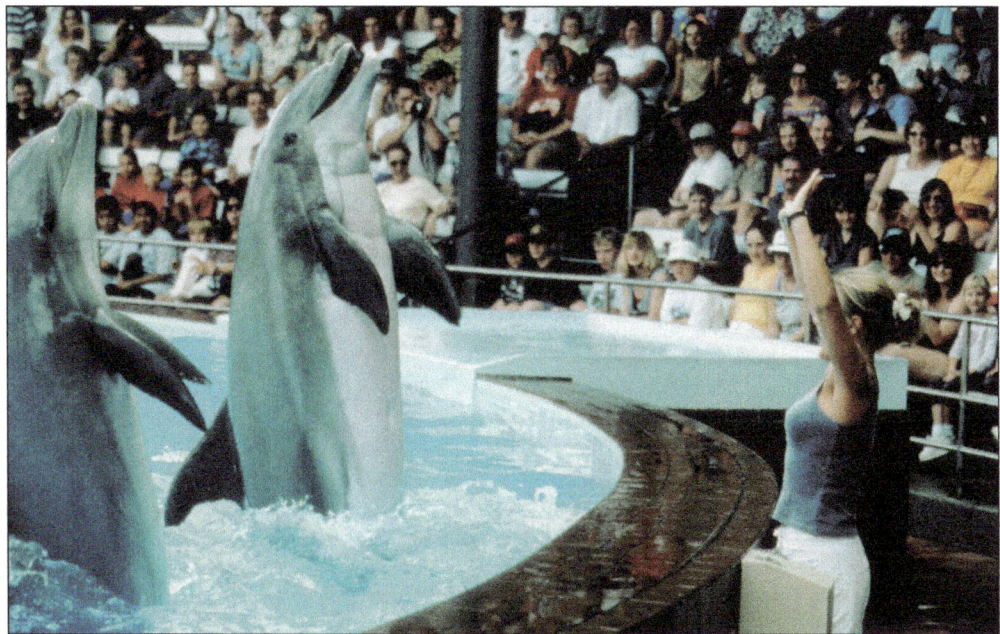

Dolphins of the Deep was a wildly popular show that starred Mich and Bud, two bottle-nosed dolphins with bubbly personalities. The cetacean stars showcased an array of natural behaviors in an engaging, family-friendly presentation that educated park-goers from October 1979 through September 2002. The Dolphin Theater was converted into an enclosed entertainment venue known as Timbuktu Theater, which opened in 2004 with the premiere of *R.L. Stine's Haunted Lighthouse 4-D Movie*. A decade later, Timbuktu Theater was refurbished and became Pantopia Theater with the debut of *Opening Night Critters* in 2014.

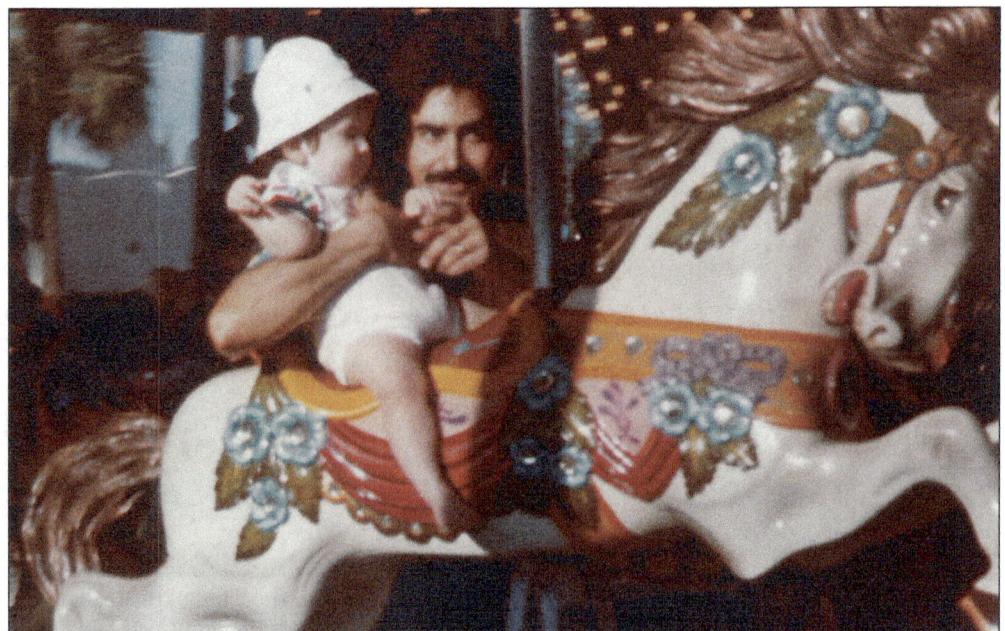

The Carousel Caravan opened in 1979 just south of the Dolphin Theater. This classic Chance Rides attraction was later renamed Grand Caravan Carousel and features horses, camels, and chariots. Riders who enjoy galloping can buck on the horses, while those who prefer less motion on the carousel may prefer riding on the camels or chariots, which are stationary. (Author's collection.)

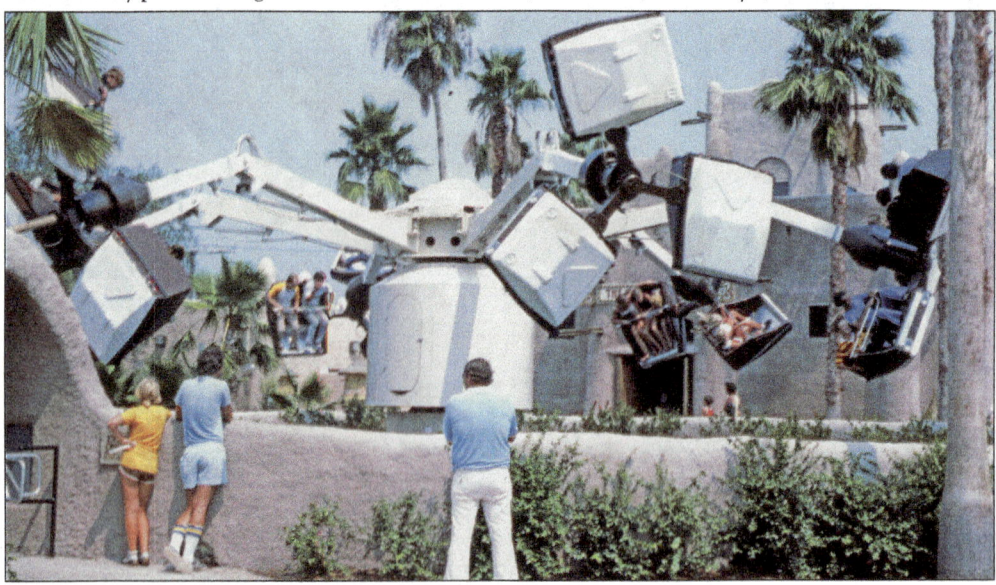

The Sandstorm was a Tivoli Orbiter ride that thrilled guests in the area now occupied by the Falcon's Fury drop tower. The spinning flat ride came to life in 1979 and provided high g-forces in cars that mechanically orbited on two axes: one on the end of each ride arm and the other based around the center of the ride. The Sandstorm was removed in 2013 to make way for Falcon's Fury. The Sandstorm was moved to sister park Sesame Place® in Langhorne, Pennsylvania, where it was refurbished, painted with bright colors, and became the Honker Dinger Derby. (State Archives of Florida, Florida Memory.)

Crowds are seen streaming through Timbuktu during the early 1980s. Timbuktu became one of the most popular areas of the park not just for its many rides but also for its entertainment and cuisine. A delicious German-style meal and wunderbar German dance and song show could be enjoyed simultaneously at Das Festhaus, seen in the background of this image. Das Festhaus was renamed Desert Grill in 2004 and became Dragon Fire Grill in 2015 when the area was re-themed as Pantopia. (State Archives of Florida, Florida Memory.)

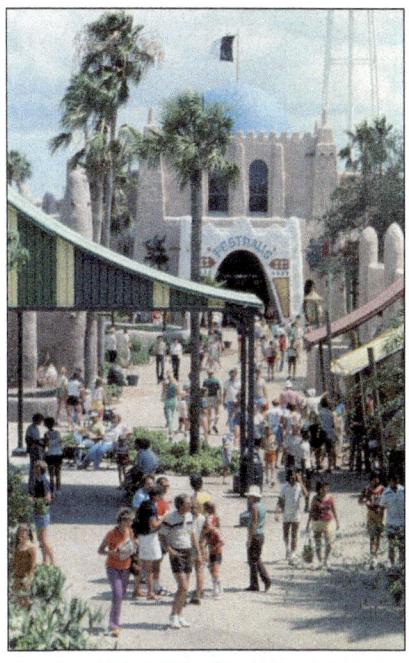

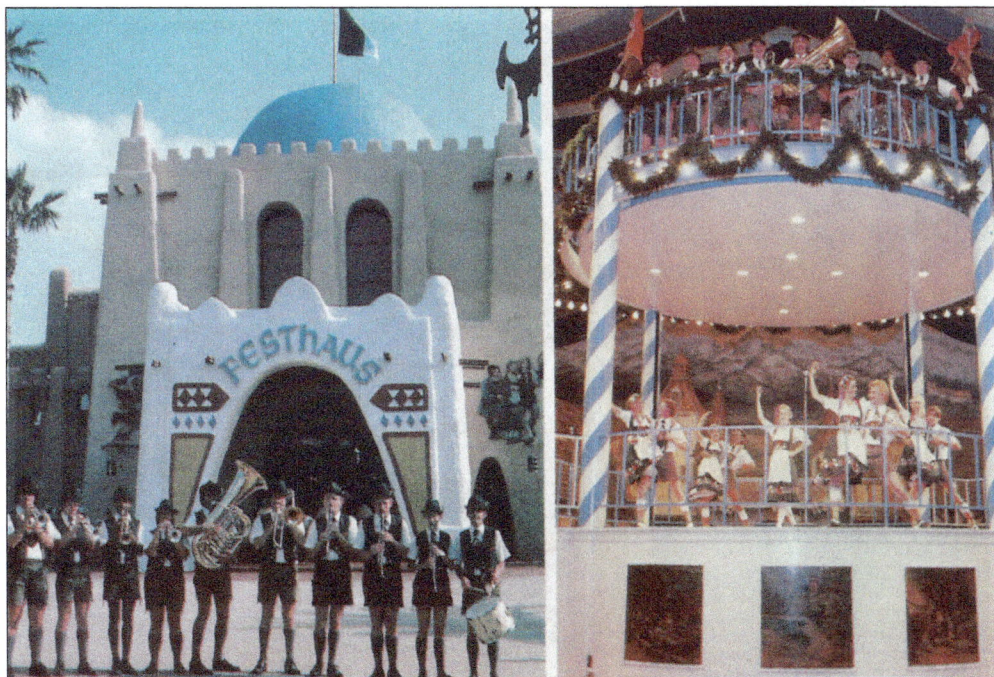

The Bavarian Colony Dancers and Band entertained diners enjoying German sausages, scrumptious sauerkraut, authentic German potato salad, and other delicious Deutsch delights at Das Festhaus. The reason a German beer hall anchored the African-themed Timbuktu area was straightforward: 19th-century German explorer and scholar Heinrich Barth, known in part for his marvelous muttonchops, traveled through the actual North African Timbuktu during the 1850s. Barth made friends with native rulers and locals, perhaps raising a prost or two with many of them during his African adventures.

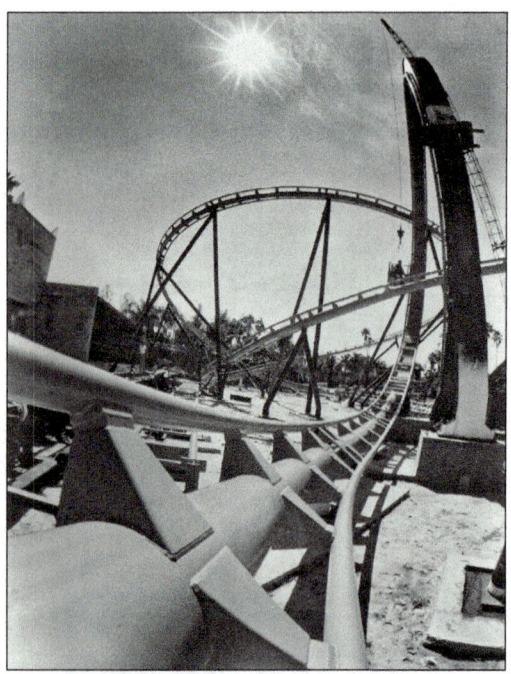

The last of the original Timbuktu attractions was the Scorpion roller coaster, seen here during its construction in April 1980. The Scorpion was built by Anton Schwarzkopf and is now one of the last remaining Silver Arrow–model roller coasters in the world. The Scorpion's trademark vertical loop, seen here, provides thrilling g-forces and is the first major element in the ride, which features a series of seemingly unrelenting helixes.

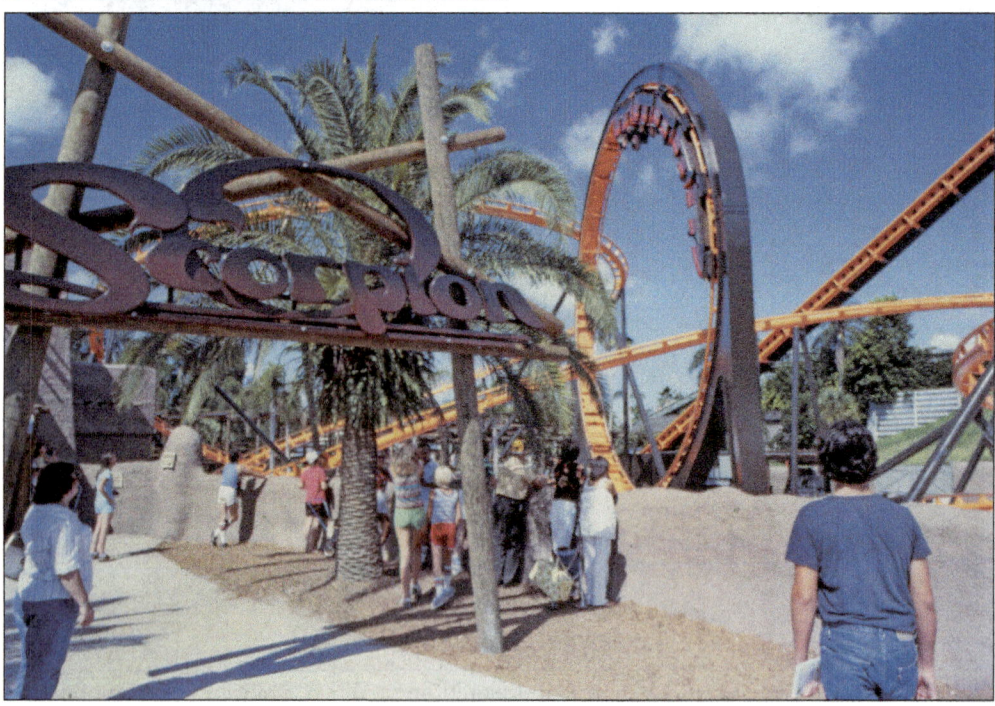

The Scorpion opened on May 16, 1980, and now ranks as the oldest roller coaster at Busch Gardens Tampa Bay. It is seen here around 1981 with its original orange-and-black color scheme. Guests continue to "feel the sting of the Scorpion" along the ride's 1,805 feet of track. The Scorpion stands 65 feet tall, features a tight 39-foot-tall vertical loop, attains speeds of nearly 50 miles per hour, and provides forces of 3.5 g's. The Scorpion was repainted in 2004, receiving red paint on its tracks and blue-colored supports. (State Archives of Florida, Florida Memory.)

Hand-rolled cigars were popular with many guests when they were sold in the Timbuktu area during the 1980s. Arturo Fuente Cigars, a long-standing cigar brand, is considered by many historians to be a Tampa tradition, dating back to the times when the city was known as the "Cigar Capital of the World." At one point in the early 20th century, more than 200 cigar manufacturers called Tampa home, most clustered in the Ybor City Latin district and employing thousands of immigrants from Italy, Spain, and Cuba. (State Archives of Florida, Florida Memory.)

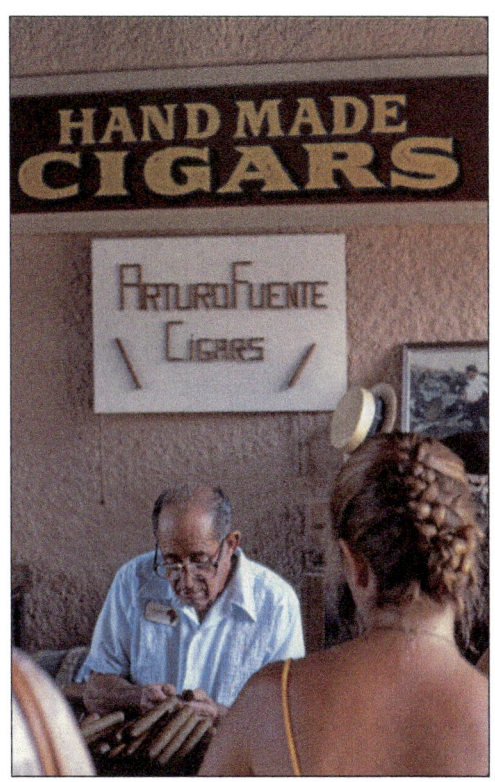

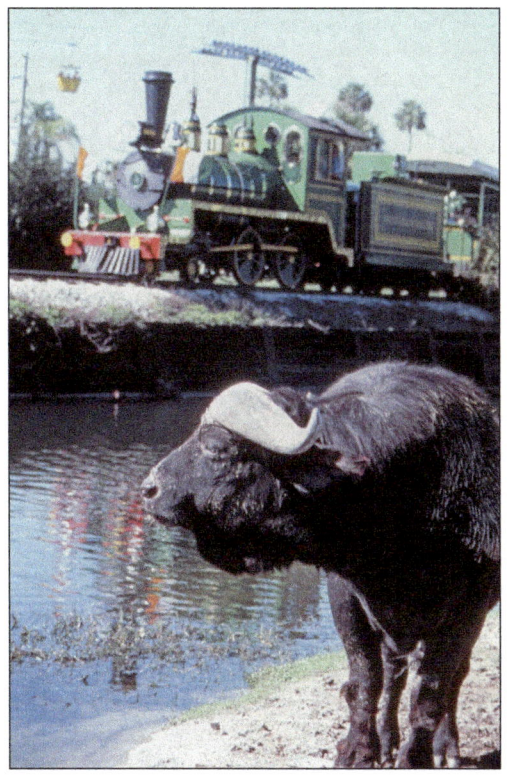

This Cape buffalo looks on as the Trans-Veldt Railway steams past along its tracks around 1980. Also known as the African buffalo, these imposing bovines measure between 6.5 feet and 11 feet long, stand 3.2 feet to 5.6 feet tall, and can weigh 660 to 1,900 pounds. While they are large animals that are up to four times stronger than a typical ox, Cape buffaloes are herbivores, feeding mainly on grass and water. (State Archives of Florida, Florida Memory.)

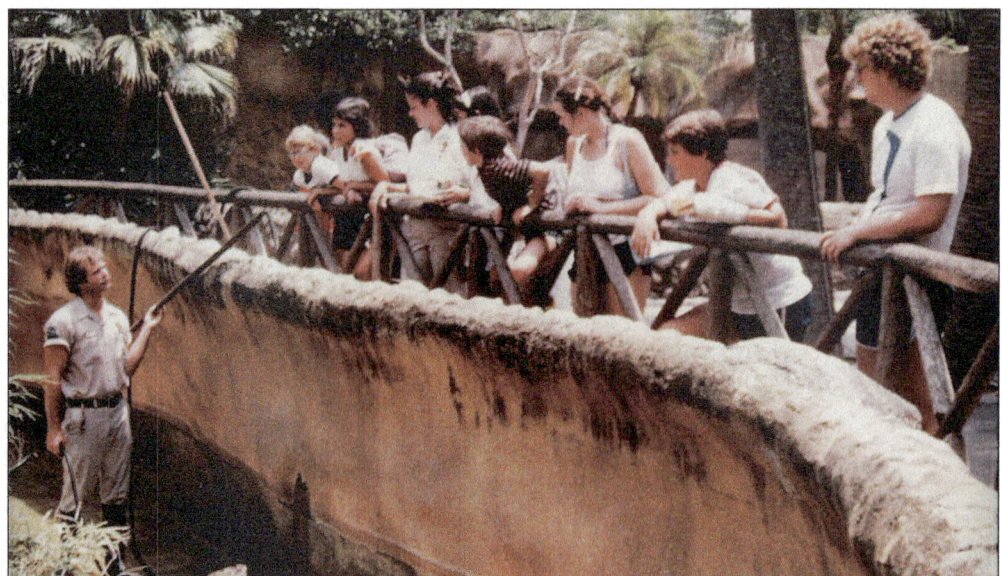

There's a lot more to being a zookeeper than just getting to play with the animals. The job is a lot of hard work. Mark Peterson interacts with guests as he cleans a habitat in the Nairobi section during the early 1980s. In addition to maintaining habitats, being a zookeeper entails having a strong knowledge of animal husbandry, the ability to understand specific dietary needs of individual animals, and educating others about conservation. (Mark Peterson.)

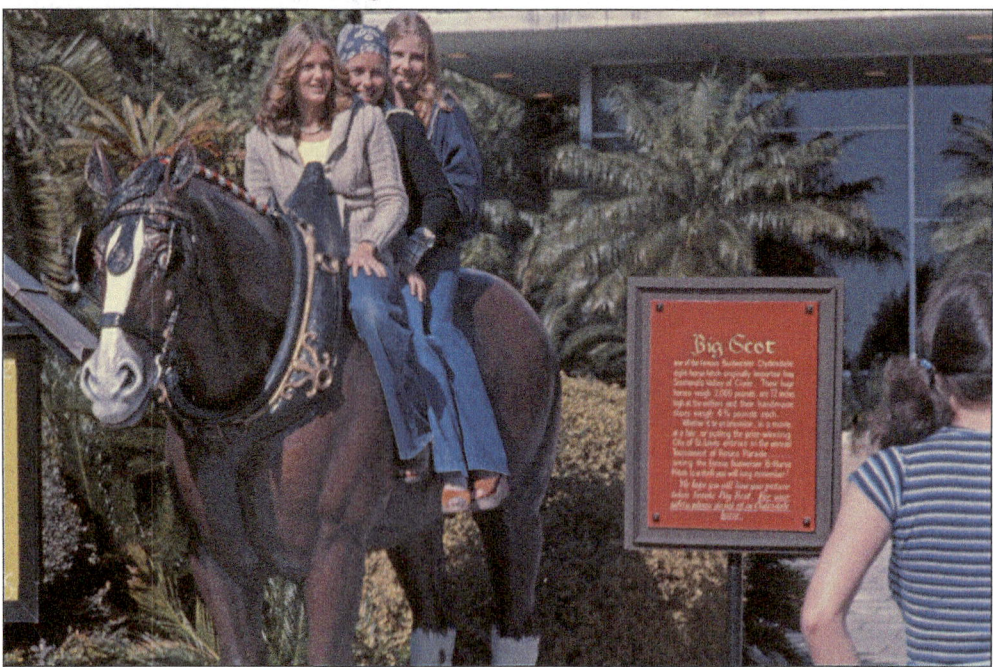

These three young women pose for a picture on Big Scot, a life-size replica of one of the famous Anheuser-Busch Clydesdales. Big Scot was one of the most frequently photographed attractions at Busch Gardens, standing sentinel for many years just outside the Anheuser-Busch brewery office building near the Busch Gardens Hospitality House, which is now known as the Garden Gate Café. (State Archives of Florida, Florida Memory.)

The Stanleyville Theater Variety Show was a crowd-pleasing program that ran from 1980 through 1994. The variety show was hosted by a master of ceremonies and offered a frequently changing array of novelty acts from around the world, including circus performers and vaudeville-style artists. The Villams, billed as "The World's Fastest Jugglers," are seen here in 1981 and performed multiple engagements throughout the span of the variety show. (Author's collection.)

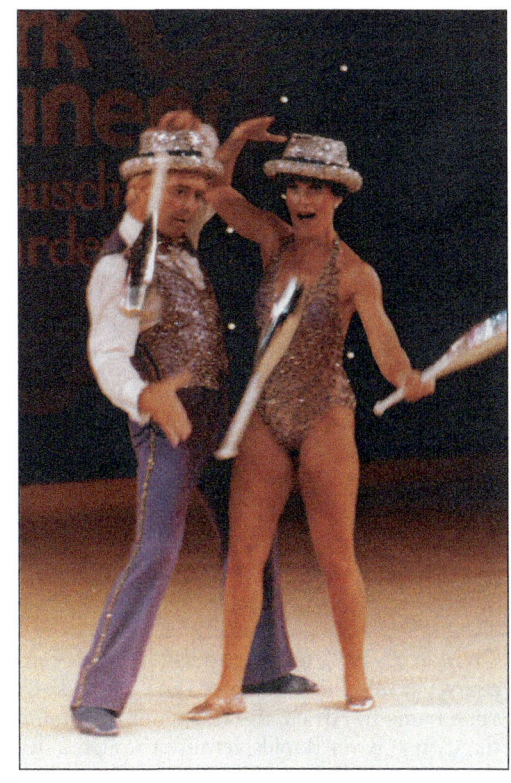

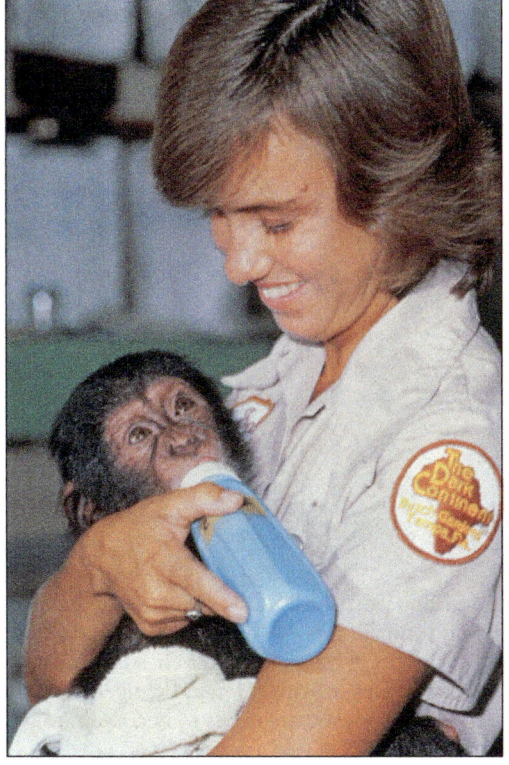

Janet Picola bottle-feeds a young chimpanzee in the early 1980s at the park's original animal training center and nursery. A common misperception among many is that chimpanzees are monkeys. The distinctions between monkeys and apes are several, but one of the most obvious differences comes down to the presence of a tail. Monkeys have tails, whereas apes, which include chimpanzees, gorillas, and orangutans, do not. Of course, as with all rules, there are some exceptions. Such is the case of the Barbary macaque, which has a nonevident tail. (State Archives of Florida, Florida Memory.)

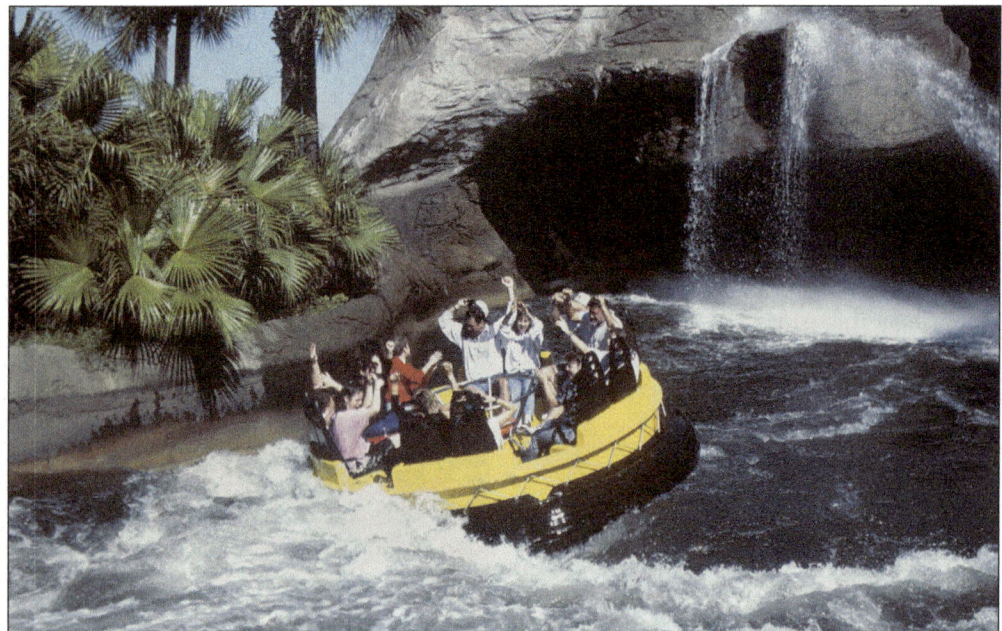

On May 26, 1982, the Congo River Rapids began soaking guests along its winding 1,380-foot-long course. While this version of the Congo is significantly shorter than the 2,920-mile river of the same name in Africa, the ride, built by Intamin, is seemingly every bit as treacherous. Riders on the Congo River Rapids venture through a dense jungle, encounter dizzying eddies, and journey through a dark cavern with a drenching waterfall. (State Archives of Florida, Florida Memory.)

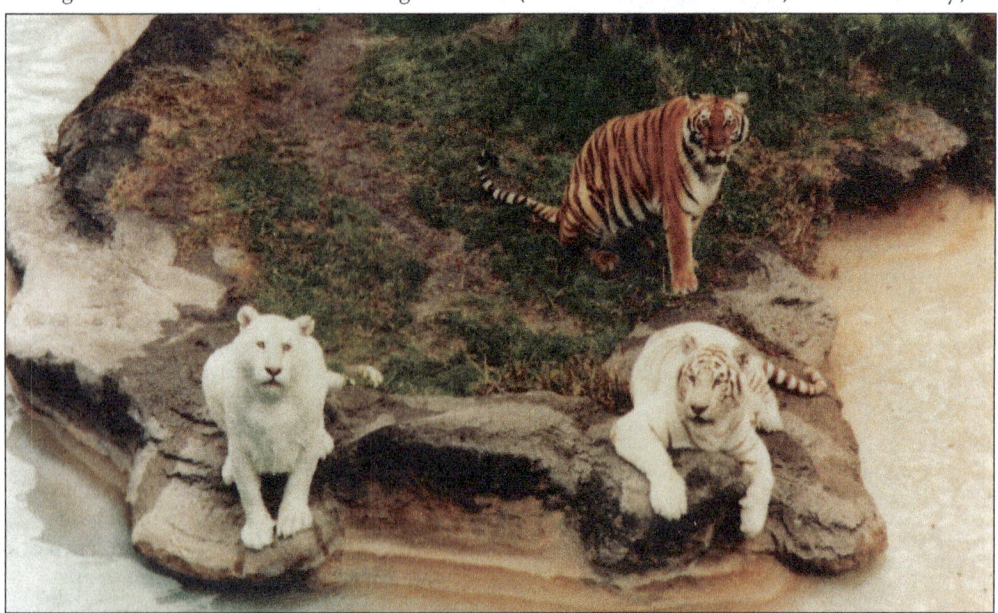

White Bengal tigers first called Claw Island home on June 29, 1982. White tigers are not albinos but rather have a gene that turns their orange hair white while keeping their stripe pattern. White tigers are adept swimmers and have keen eyesight and hearing. Generally, tigers have no known predators except for humans, who have led these majestic creatures to become rare and endangered in the wild. (Bob Kroen.)

Four
1983–1992
EXTINCTION IS FOREVER

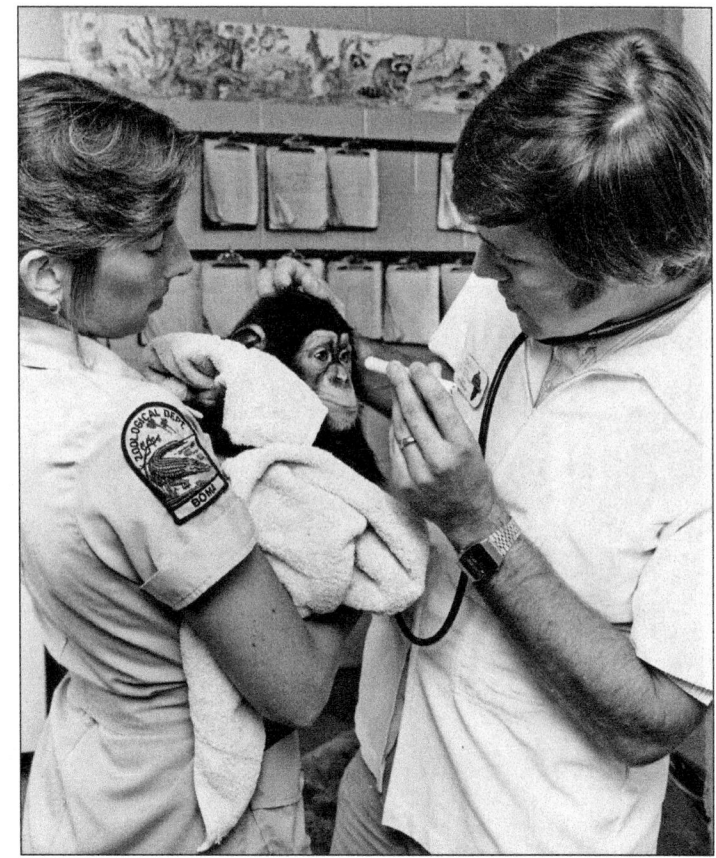

Busch Gardens Tampa Bay has provided extensive in-house zoological care for decades. This 1983 image shows Busch Gardens veterinarian Dr. John Olsen giving a checkup to baby chimpanzee Coz, who is being held by nursery attendant Pandy Sokol. The veterinarians at Busch Gardens handle both emergency and routine care and regularly attend to exotic patients as small as rodents and lizards or as large as elephants and giraffes.

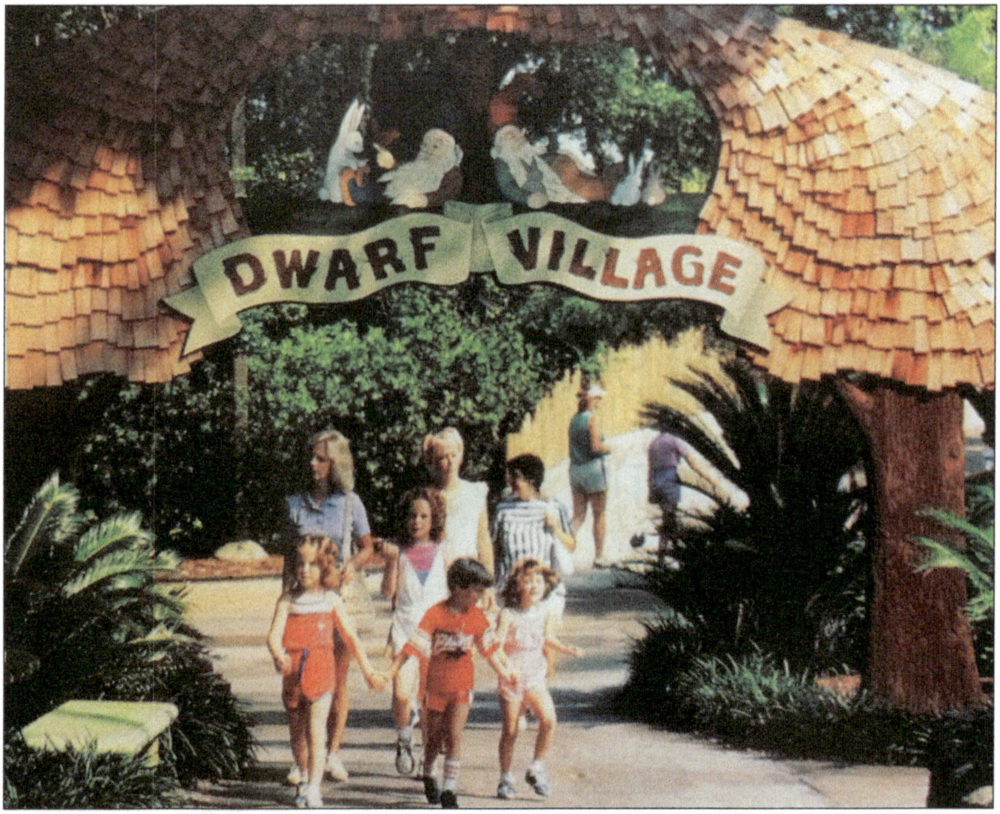

From the park's earliest days, Dwarf Village was a collection of figurines and small houses representing scenes from children's stories. In late 1983, Dwarf Village was reimagined as a whimsical children's play area aimed primarily at younger guests shorter than 56 inches tall. Dwarf Village contained many engaging play elements for young guests, including tree houses with tube slides, a sports car ride, a log ride, mazes, a cloud bounce, and a ball crawl.

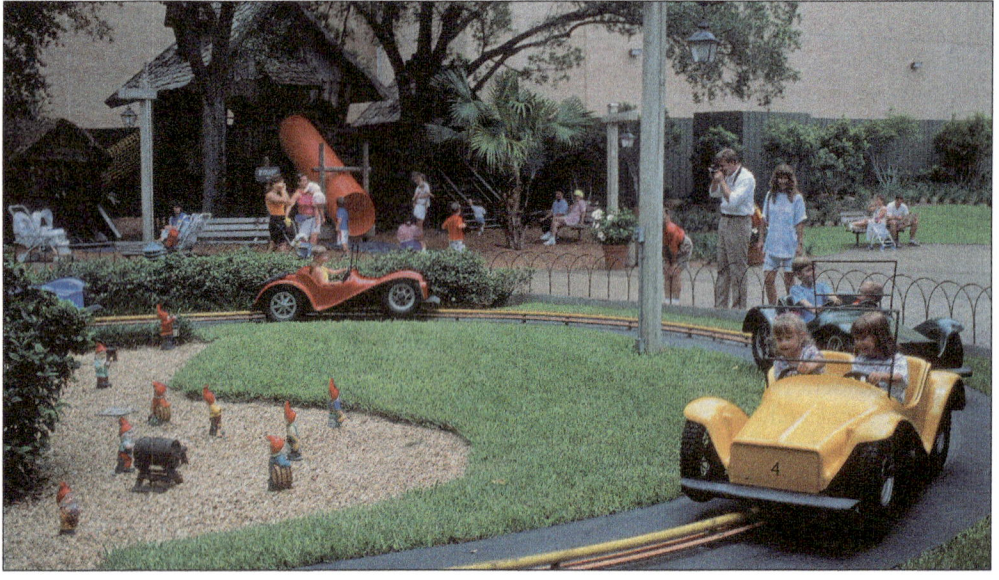

This reticulated giraffe is one of 25 that were rescued from Kenya and airlifted to the United States in early 1984. Actress and animal philanthropist Stefanie Powers was among the rescue team who brought these tall travelers to Busch Gardens Tampa Bay, where they found sanctuary on the Serengeti Plain. Giraffe populations are falling across Africa, and in more than half a dozen nations across the continent, these gentle giants are already extinct. When a species is gone, it's gone. As was the park's slogan during the 1980s and 1990s, "extinction is forever."

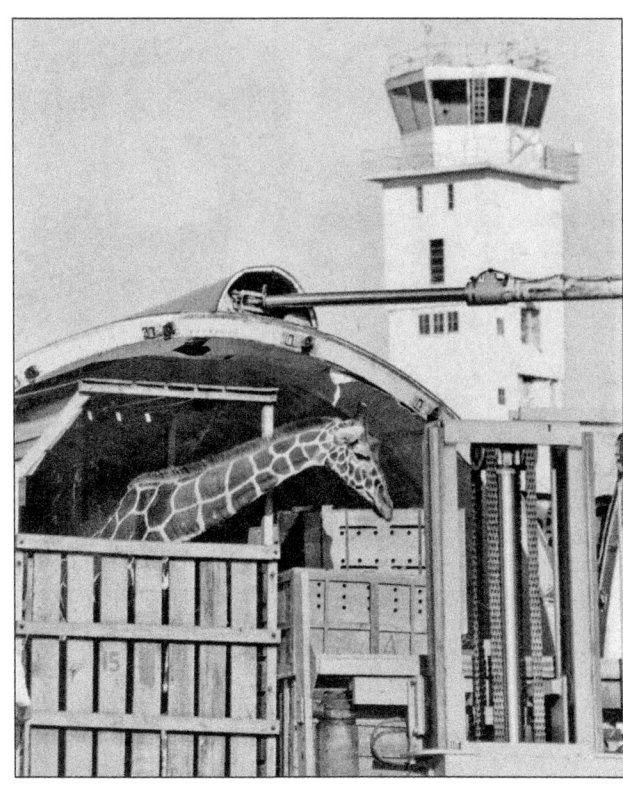

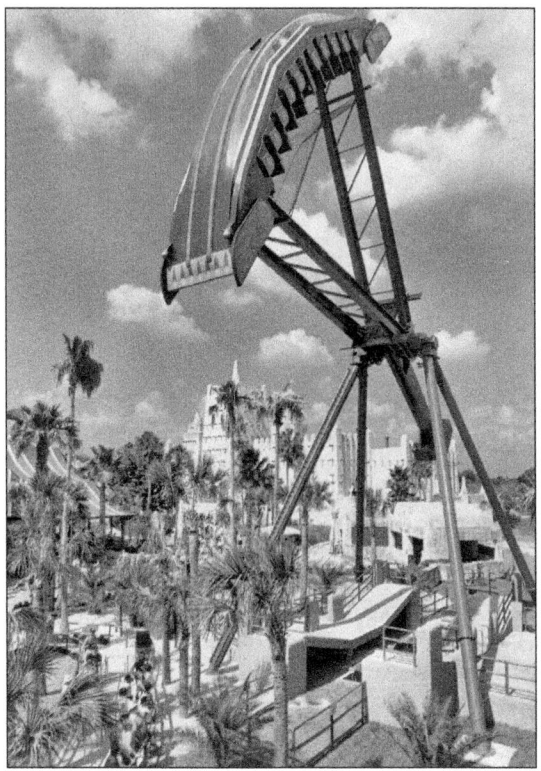

The Phoenix rose above Timbuktu for the first time on June 5, 1984. During several terrifying moments, the Intamin Looping Starship hangs it riders upside down more than 60 feet above the ground. The Phoenix is now dwarfed in size by taller rides such as its 335-foot-tall neighbor Falcon's Fury and the nearby Kumba roller coaster, but it is still very high on many guests' lists of scariest thrillers.

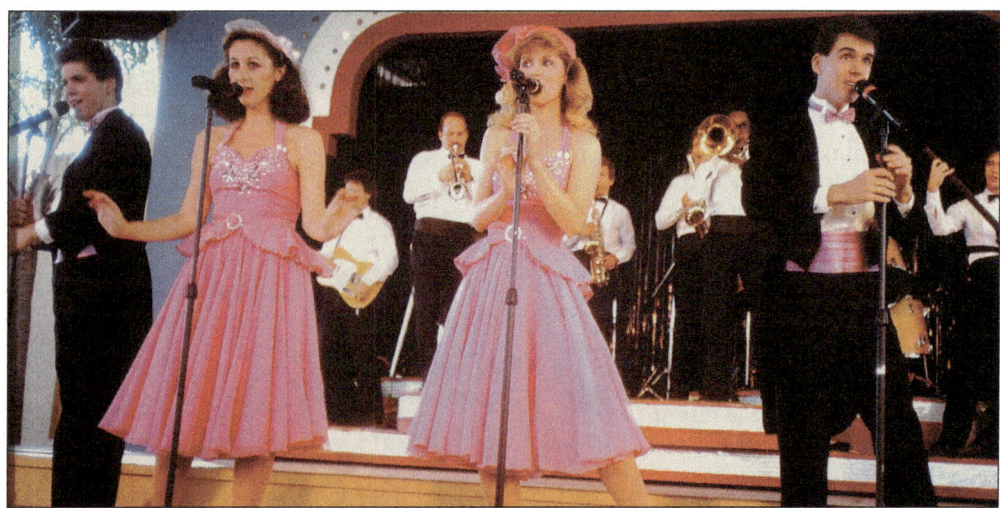

Since opening in 1983, the Marrakesh Theater in Morocco has hosted an exciting array of dazzling live shows, including musical revues such as the 1940s big band–themed *Music Express*, seen here in December 1987. In addition to choreographed musical shows, the Marrakesh Theater has also been the backdrop for animal encounters and school and church choir groups. It is also an entertainment hot spot for special events like Howl-O-Scream. (Author's collection.)

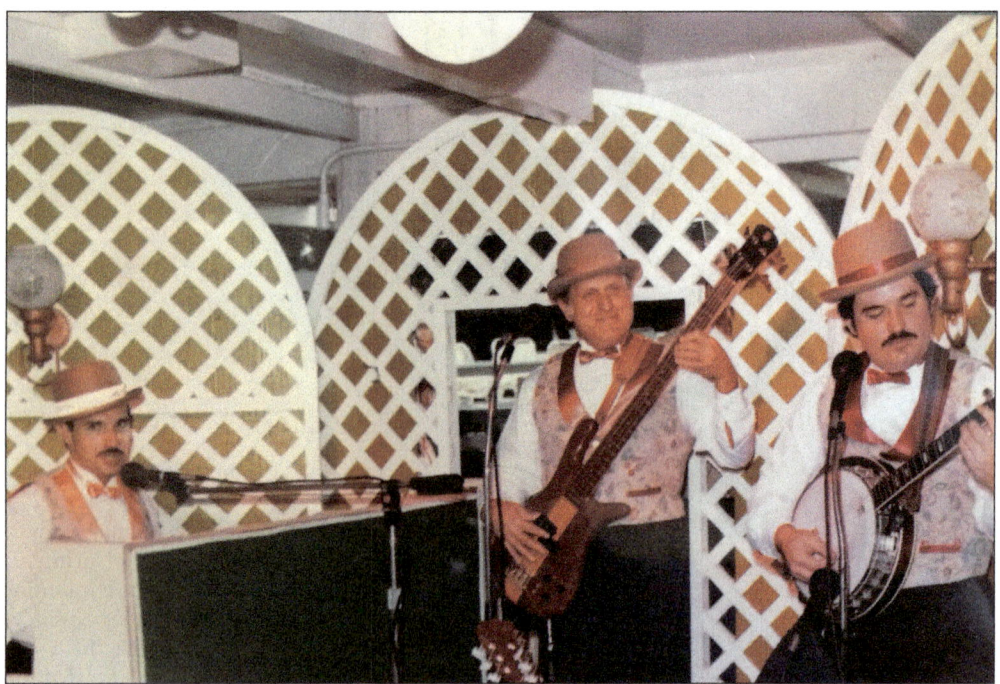

Ragtime pianist "Doctor" Dave Messick (left) leads his Doctor Dave's Good Time Trio near the Hospitality House in late 1984. In the center is bassist Andy Lalino and on the right playing banjo is Bill Norman. "Doctor" Dave's toe-tapping repertoire included old-time classics such as "Honeysuckle Rose," "Chattanooga Choo Choo," and "Hey, Good Lookin'." ("Doctor" Dave Messick.)

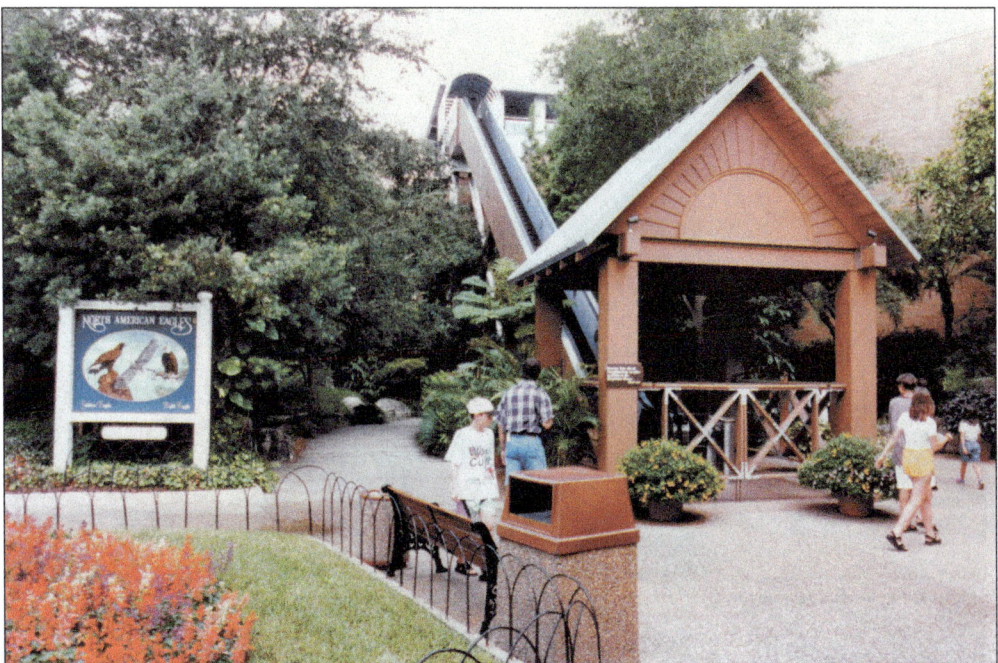

Eagle Canyon, once home to North American bald eagles and golden eagles, is seen above under the Stairway to the Stars brewery tour escalator, where it opened in January 1985 after moving from a prior location near the Bird Gardens Gift Shop (now known as Xcursions). The bald eagle, seen in the image below, is known as the national bird of the United States of America and can be readily recognized from a distance by its brown body, white head, and tail. After suffering a severe population decline, bald eagles are recovering in number thanks to conservation efforts and sanctuaries. (Below, Bob Kroen.)

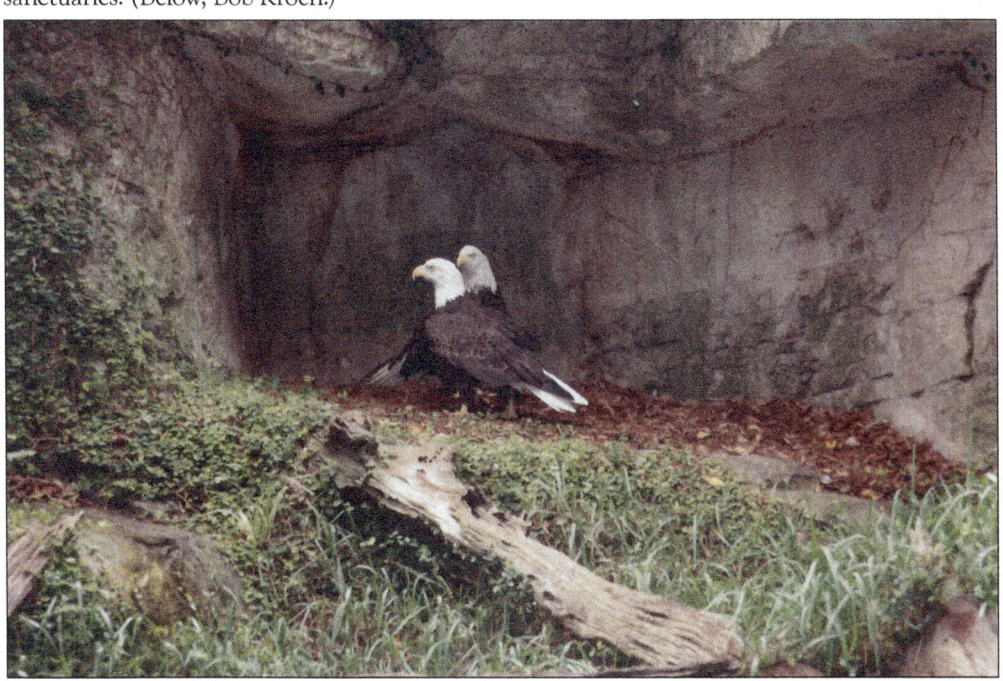

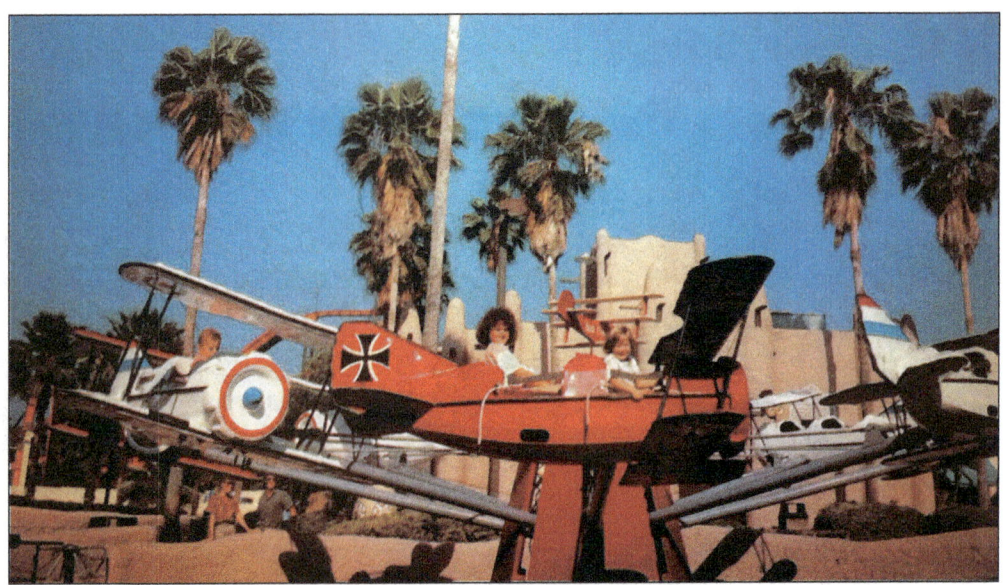

Young children enjoy the Bush Flyers plane ride in the mid-1980s. Bush Flyers, located adjacent to the Phoenix, has been a mainstay at Busch Gardens since the ride was built in Timbuktu in 1979. Today, Bush Flyers continues tempting the next generation to take flight in the skies above Pantopia.

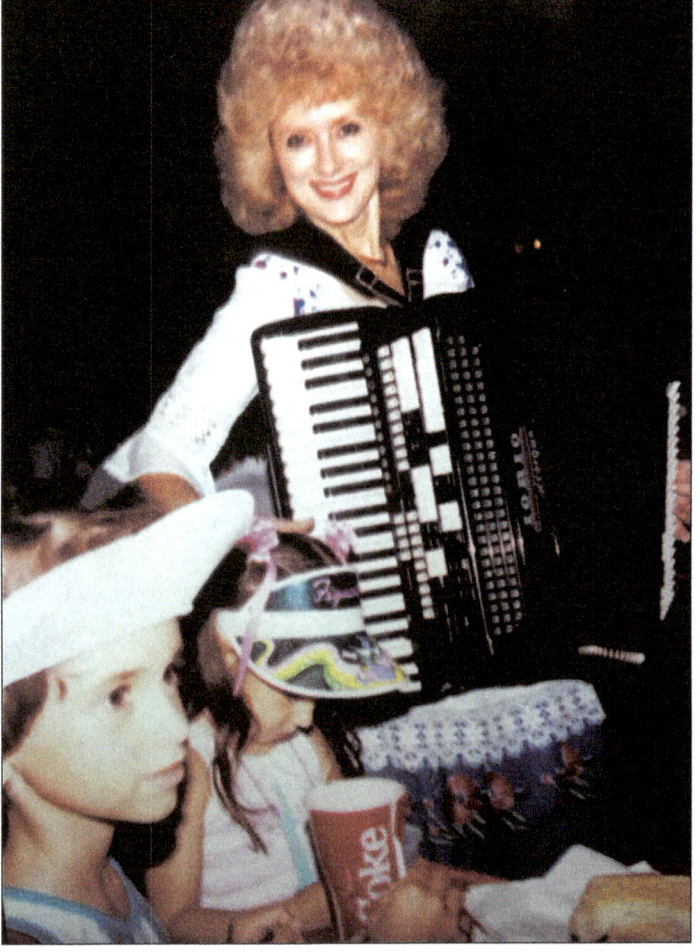

Accordionist Barbara St. Denis was a fixture at Das Festhaus in the 1980s and 1990s. St. Denis pumped out many guests' personal requests from the squeezebox and merrily entertained diners at Das Festhaus throughout the day before and after stage shows at the theater. (Author's collection.)

The Moroccan Palace Theater opened in September 1986 as the park's premier showplace. Boasting 1,100 seats, the Moroccan Palace Theater is a Broadway-style venue that has staged some of the finest performances offered at any theme park as well as numerous prime-time television specials and other premier engagements. The theater's first regularly scheduled show was a lavish musical called *Kaleidoscope*, which ran from 1986 through 1989.

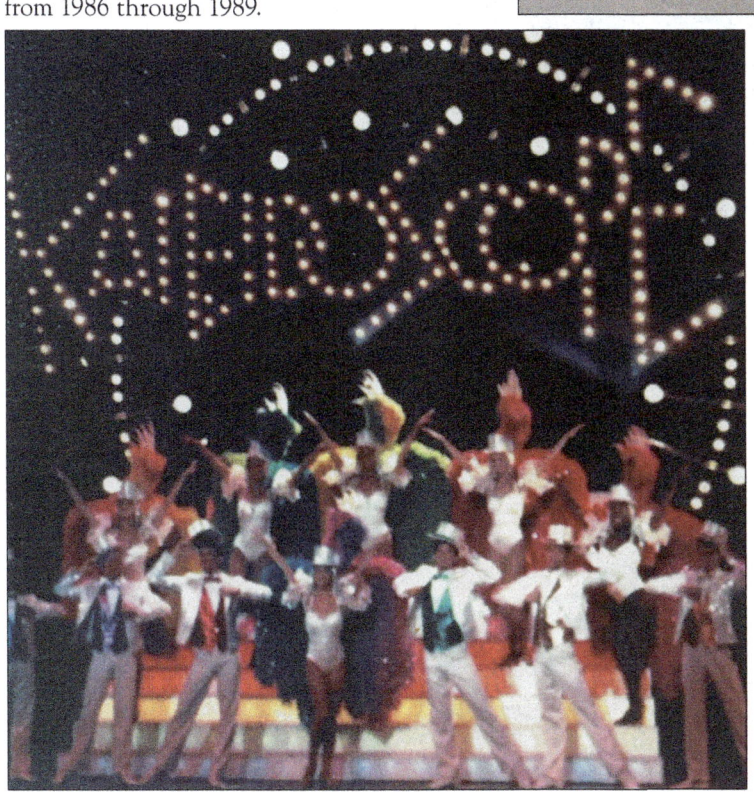

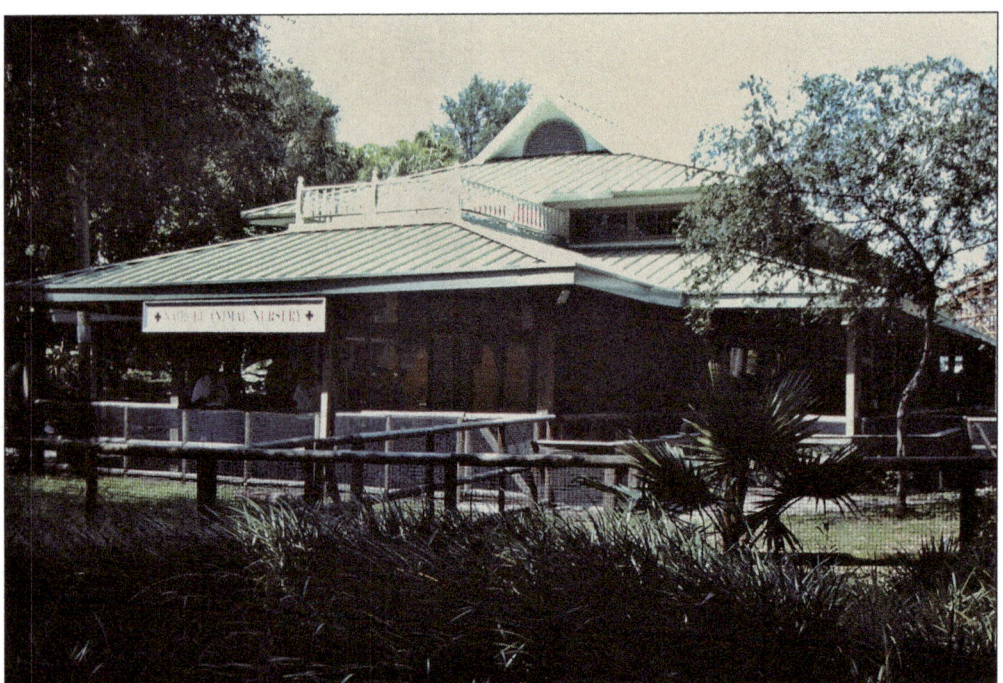

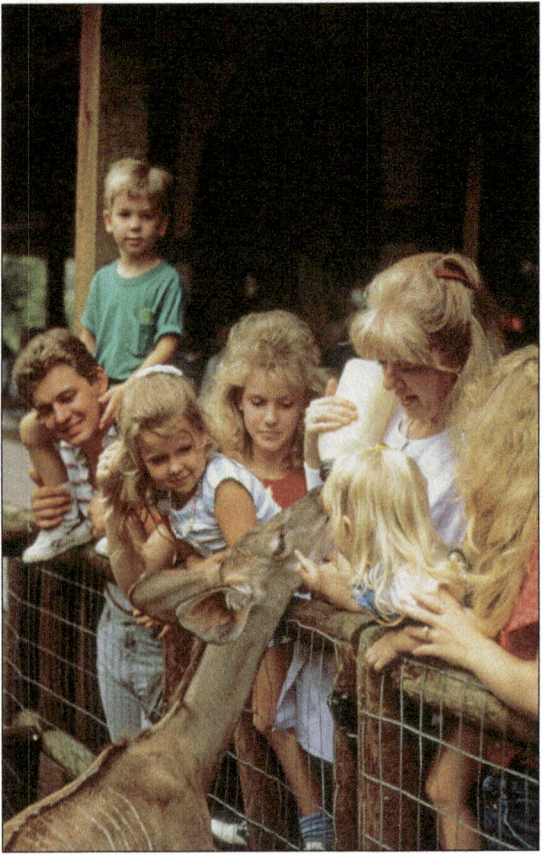

In late 1986, the Nairobi Field Station animal nursery opened in the Nairobi section. This innovative animal nursery, located near a similar facility that it replaced, had dozens of enclosures designed for creatures of all varieties and boasted an open kitchen where dietitians and other specialists prepared nourishment for the young residents of the nursery. At left, Deborah Kern Bond is seen feeding a female nyala before a group of guests at the nursery. The Nairobi Field Station was later renamed Jambo Junction, which closed in 2016. (Left, State Archives of Florida, Florida Memory.)

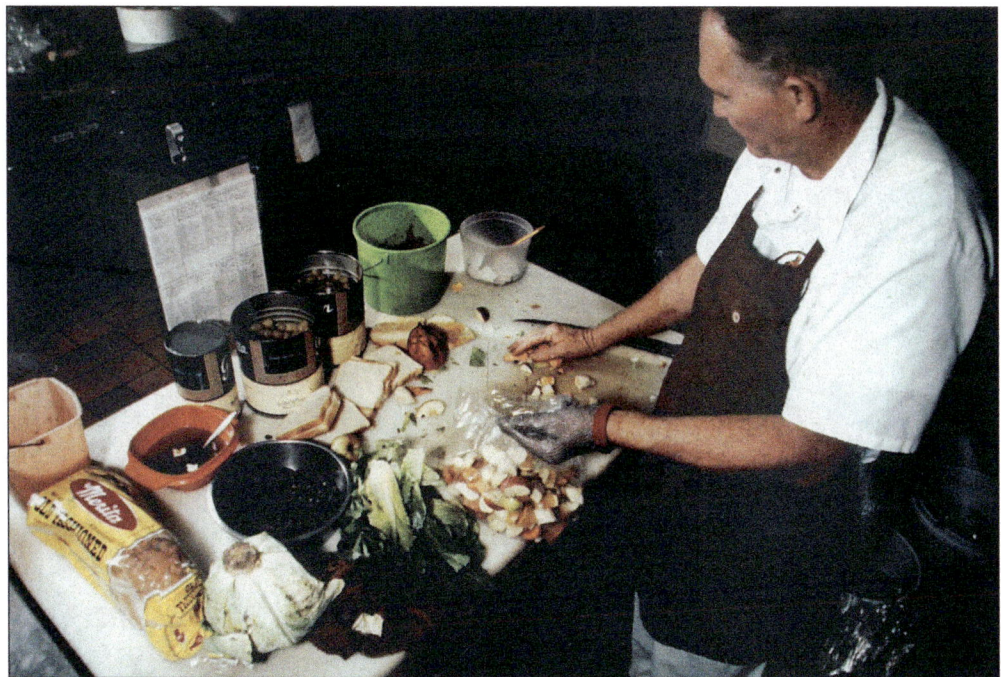

Fulfilling the dietary needs of the animals at Busch Gardens Tampa Bay is a major part of what many zoo ambassadors do at the park on a daily basis. Above, John Jernigan prepares diets for some of the residents at Busch Gardens, while at right, David Seager feeds giraffes on the Serengeti Plain. (Above, Mark Peterson; right, State Archives of Florida, Florida Memory.)

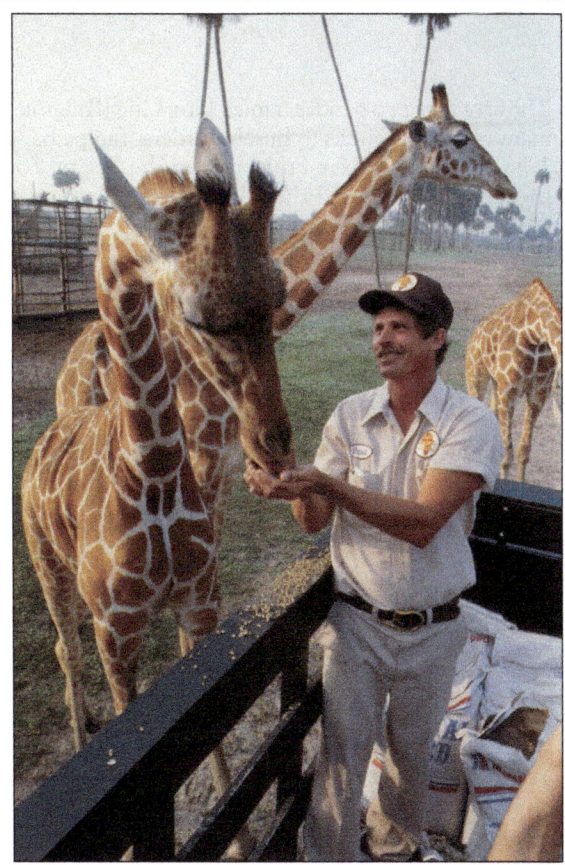

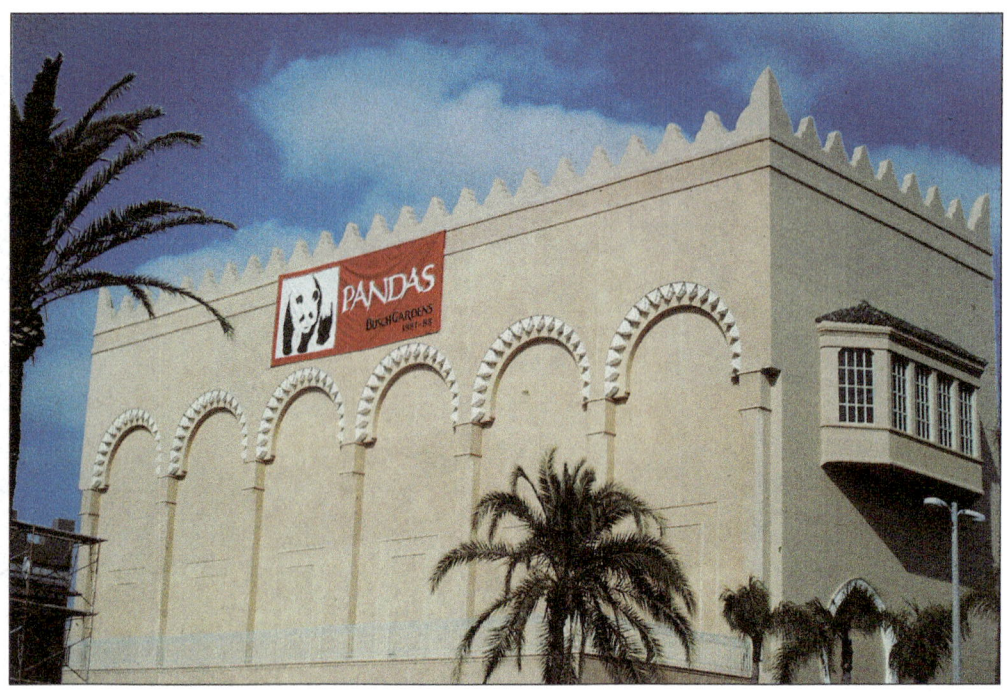

The arrival of two pandas named Ling Ling (Ringing Bell) and Yong Yong (Forever and Ever) lured many additional guests to Busch Gardens Tampa Bay during their stay from late 1987 through early 1988. The pandas were on loan from the Beijing Zoo in China and spent a few months wowing the crowds who visited them in their multimillion-dollar habitat in the southern Bird Gardens. (Above, author's collection.)

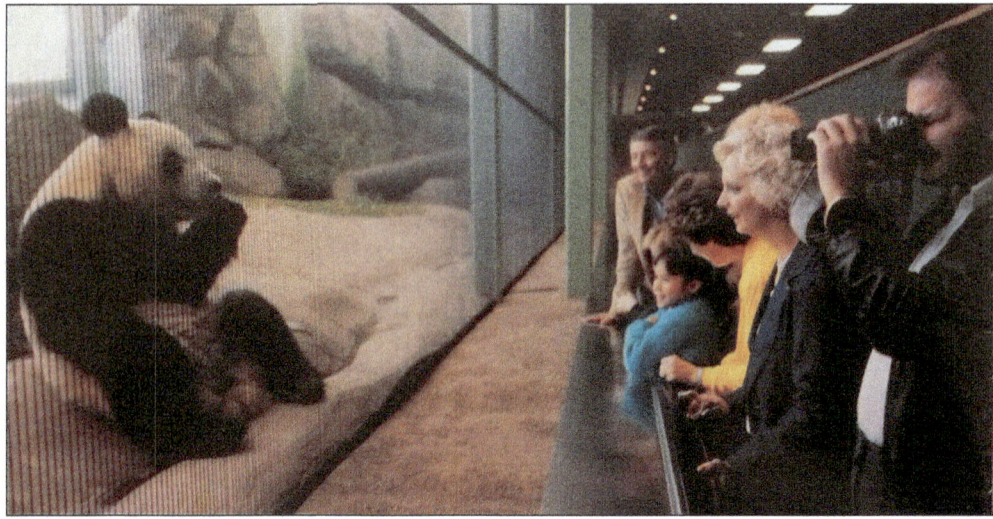

Sister park Adventure Island opened across the street from Busch Gardens Tampa Bay in April 1980 and has been drenching its guests with summery fun ever since. Some of the park's earlier attractions, such as the Tampa Typhoon (right pair of slides) and Gulfscream (left) in the image at right have given way to newer rides, such as the thrilling Colossal Curl. Meanwhile, classics like the Runaway Rapids (below) continue offering guests endless enjoyable, exciting options to beat Florida's summertime heat. (Right, State Archives of Florida, Florida Memory.)

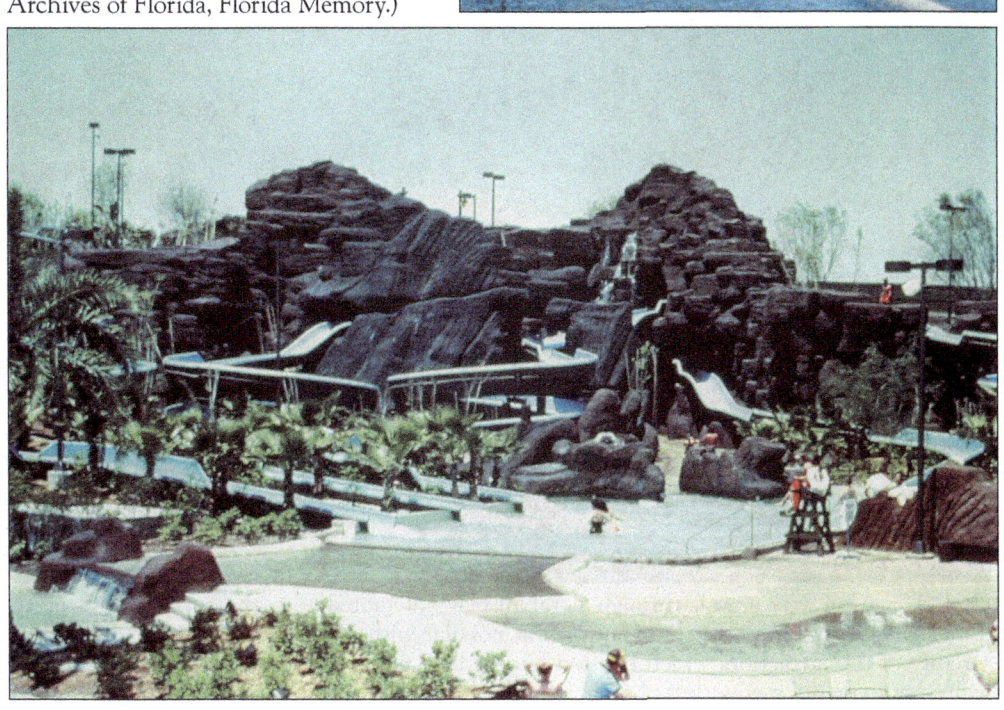

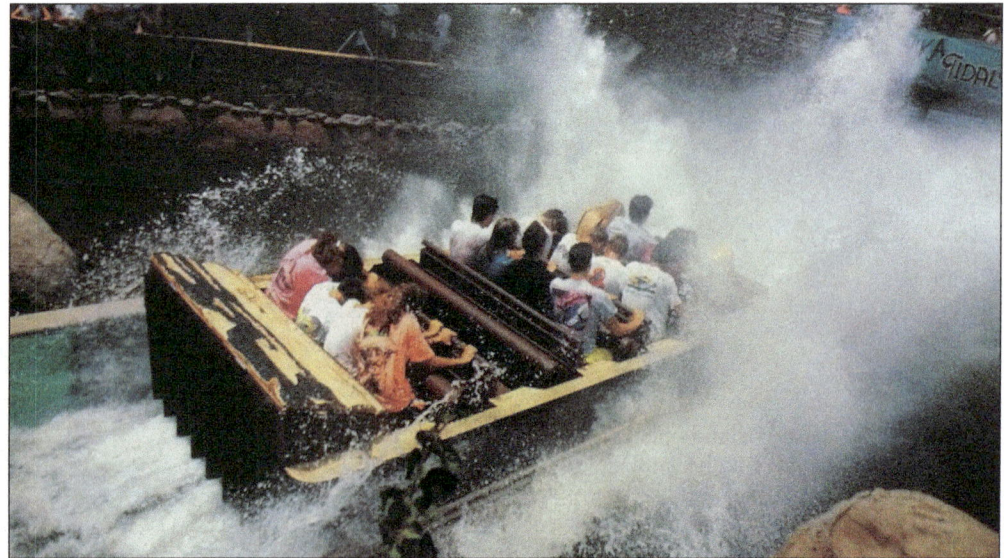

The Tanganyika Tidal Wave was an Intamin Shoot-the-Chutes boat ride that started off as a serene jungle cruise but culminated in a 55-foot drop producing a splash that soaked riders and bystanders. The Tanganyika Tidal Wave opened on July 1, 1989, and was a revamped version of the African Queen Boat Ride. Many elements of the African Queen Boat Ride, including the village scene, remained visible to guests until April 10, 2016, the day the Tanganyika Tidal Wave closed.

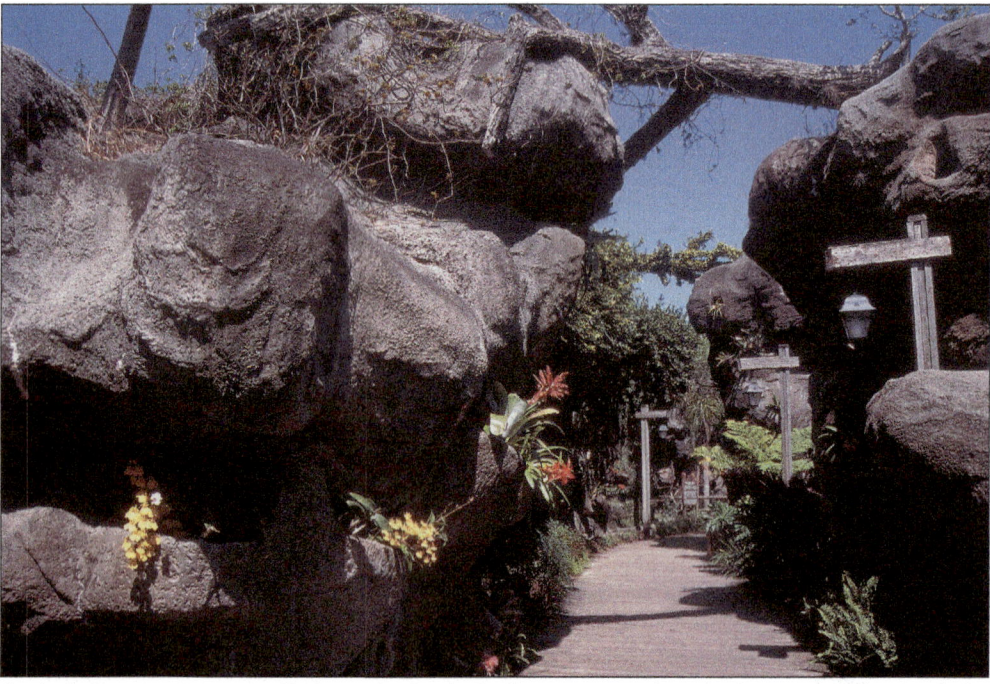

Orchid Canyon was a walk-through floral display integrated into the surroundings of the Tanganyika Tidal Wave. Orchid Canyon was popular with guests of all ages who enjoyed the serenity of the attraction, which boasted hundreds of plants growing out of naturalistic rock walls, not to mention countless photograph-taking opportunities.

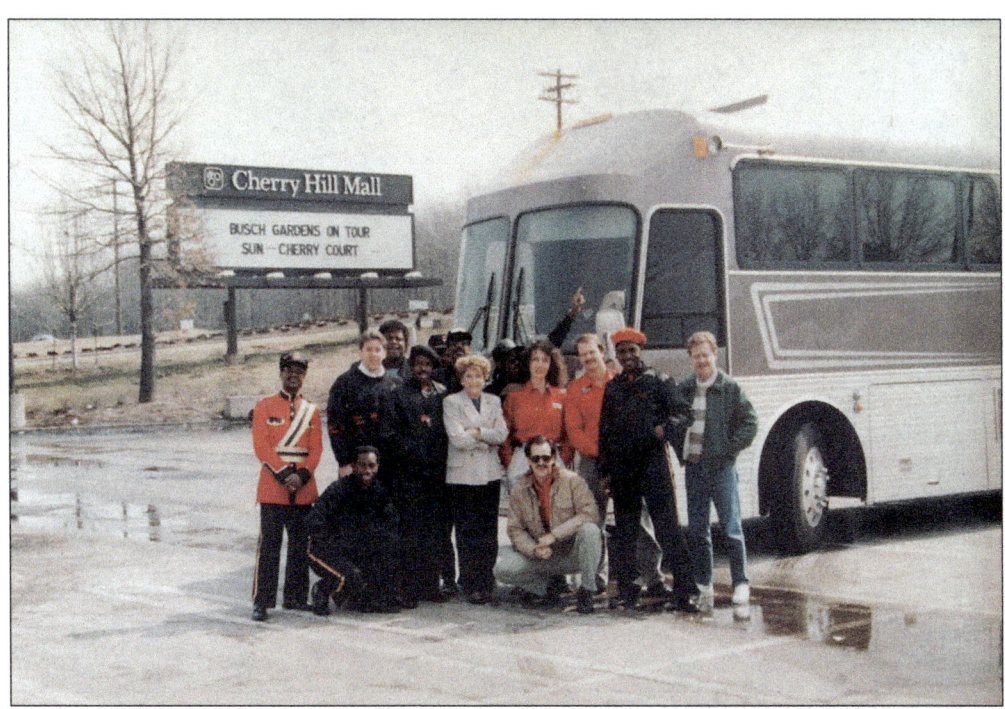

Many Busch Gardens ambassadors regularly travel outside of the park, and even outside of Tampa Bay, to educate and entertain crowds. This early 1989 photograph shows members of the Busch Gardens zoological team, the Mystic Sheiks of Morocco, and representatives from other park departments at the Cherry Hill Mall in the Greater Philadelphia community of Cherry Hill, New Jersey, where they introduced mallgoers to the exotic animals and entertainment found at Busch Gardens. During the trip, the group also made stops at local schools in the Delaware Valley. (Mark Peterson.)

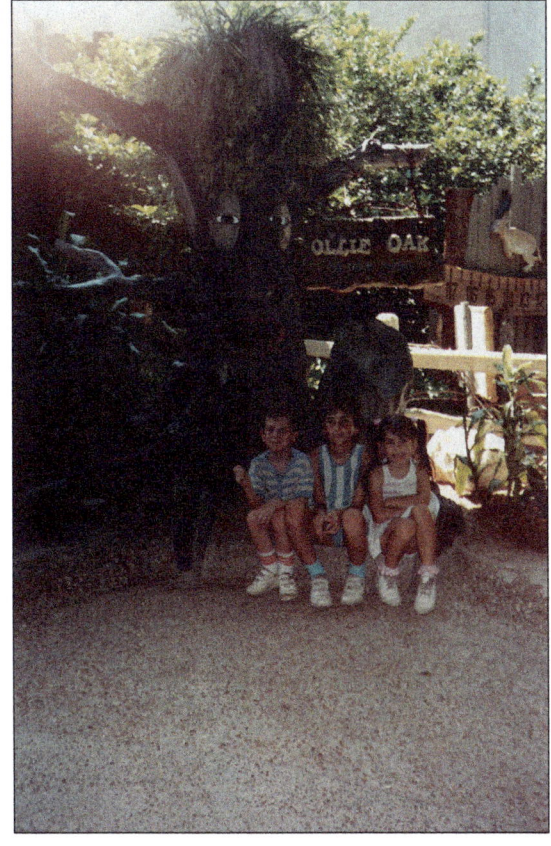

Ollie Oak was a talking tree, voiced by Frank "Rudy" Hernandez, who lived in Dwarf Village and encouraged guests to recycle their trash by tossing it into his mouth. The friendly tree had talent as a rapper, too, singing hip-hop songs about conservation. He bid all of his visitors adieu by saying "thank you very mulch." (Author's collection.)

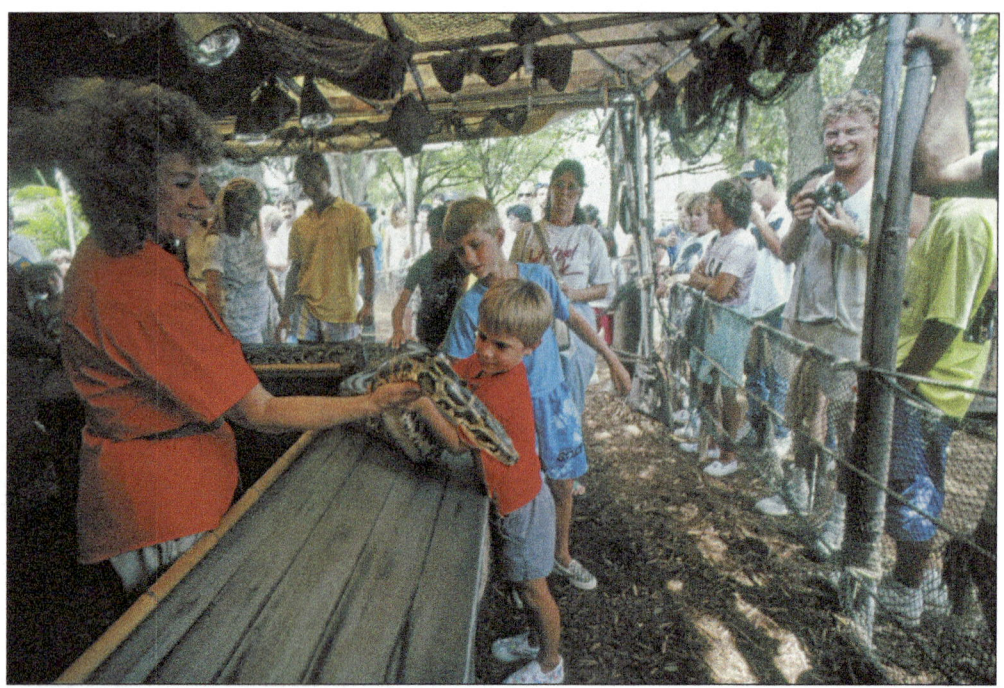

There is an opportunity to learn about the animals at Busch Gardens at just about every twist and turn in the park. One such educational encounter was the Snakes and More display in Stanleyville, seen here in the early 1990s. Educational kiosks and conservation centers are still found throughout the park today, and meet-the-keeper sessions near many of the animal habitats offer exciting opportunities for guests to find out more about the fascinating creatures at Busch Gardens Tampa Bay. (State Archives of Florida, Florida Memory.)

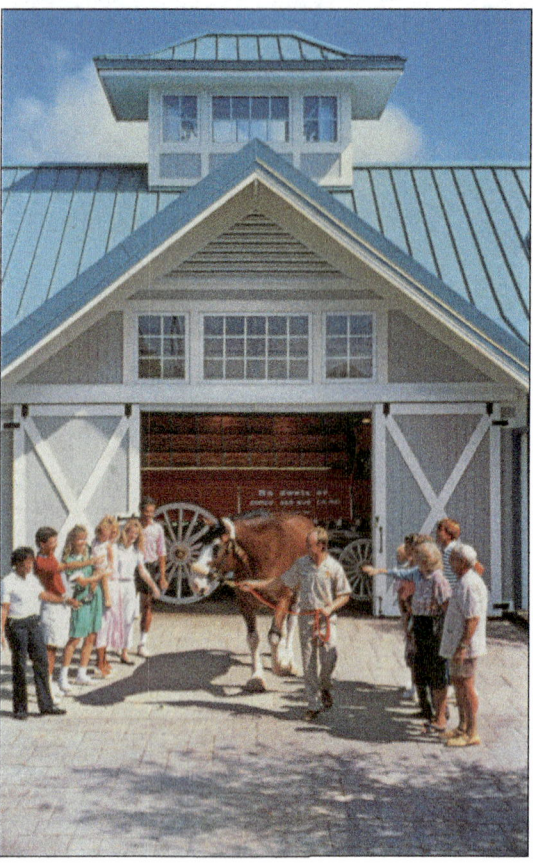

In mid-August 1989, the Clydesdale Hamlet opened just south of the monorail station. The hamlet was the quaint Tampa home of the famous Anheuser-Busch Clydesdales, and guests could get to see these majestic horses up close as they rested in their stalls or galloped around a grassy paddock adjacent to the stable. After the Clydesdales left the park in 2009, the hamlet was converted into a cheetah residence that is now incorporated into Cheetah Run. (State Archives of Florida, Florida Memory.)

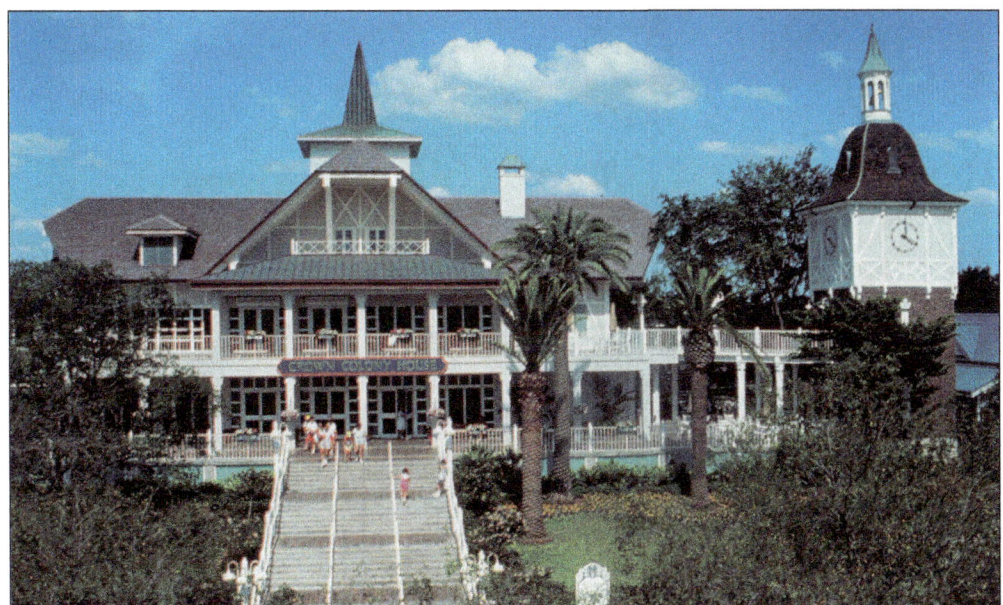

In early 1990, the restaurant formerly known as the Old Swiss House reopened as the Crown Colony House. The dining facility features two separate venues: the second floor offers a café with sandwiches and pizza, while the third floor houses a full-service upscale restaurant. Both dining areas provide outstanding views of the Serengeti Plain. The popular dining venue was renovated and renamed the Serengeti Overlook Restaurant in May 2016.

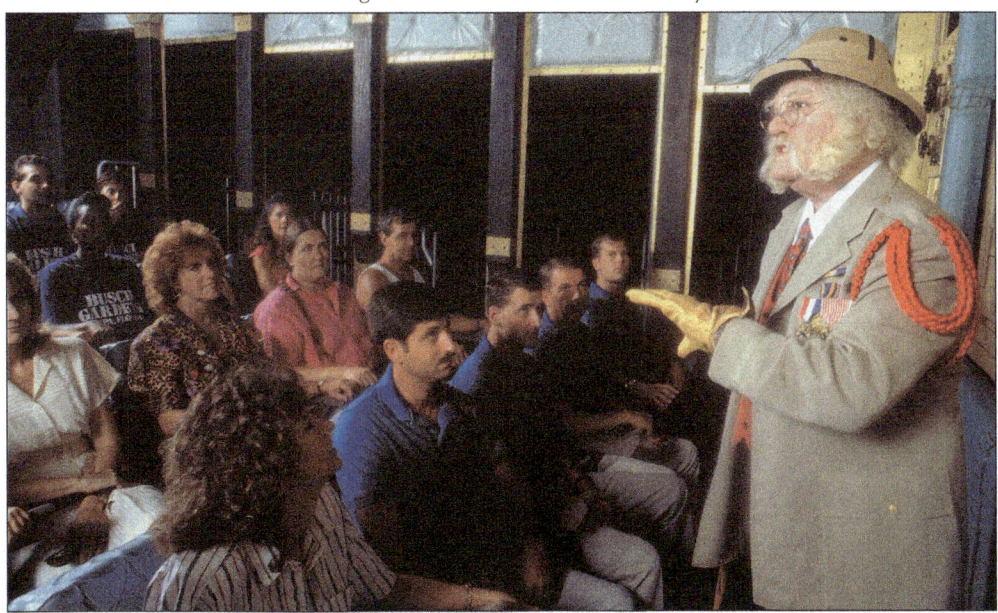

On May 23, 1991, the Questor motion-simulator ride opened near the Crown Colony House and Clydesdale Hamlet. This indoor attraction was narrated by an explorer named Sir Edison Fitzwilly, who took his guests on a wild ride through the air, under the sea, inside caves, and over a waterfall on his search for the magic Crystal of Zed. Questor was manufactured by Reflectone and closed in 1998, when it was replaced by a comedy motion-simulator experience called Akbar's Adventure Tours.

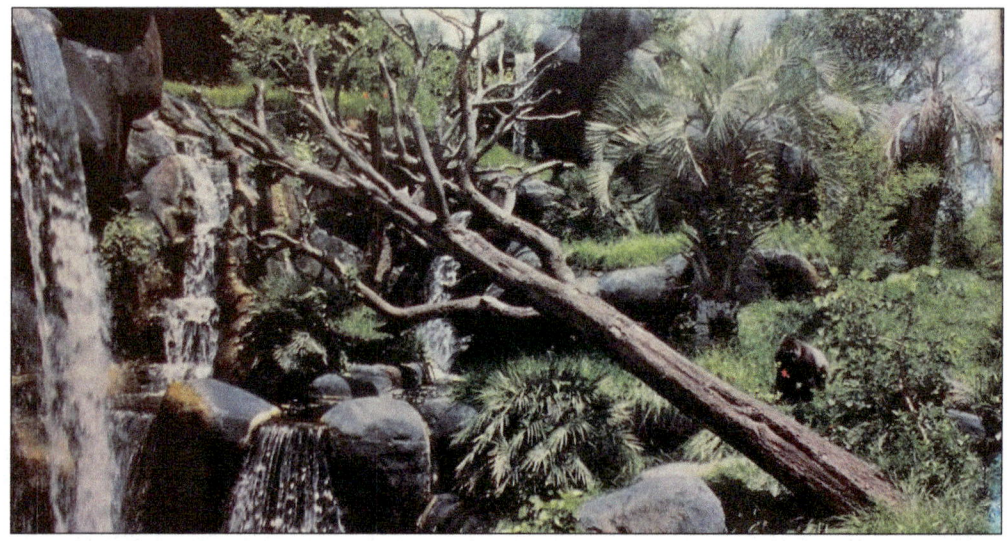

When Myombe Reserve: The Great Ape Domain opened on June 17, 1992, it introduced guests to a primate habitat unlike any other in the world. The three-acre rainforest habitat was built on the site of the original Boma area and houses chimpanzees and lowland gorillas that roam freely in lush jungle settings.

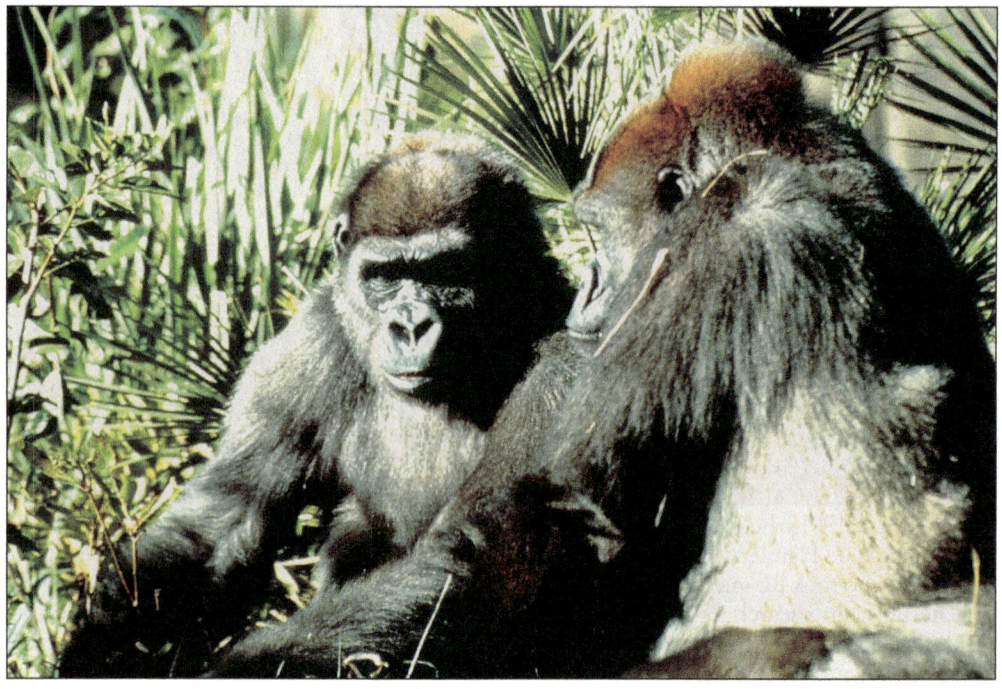

Five
1993–2008
Racing to the Top

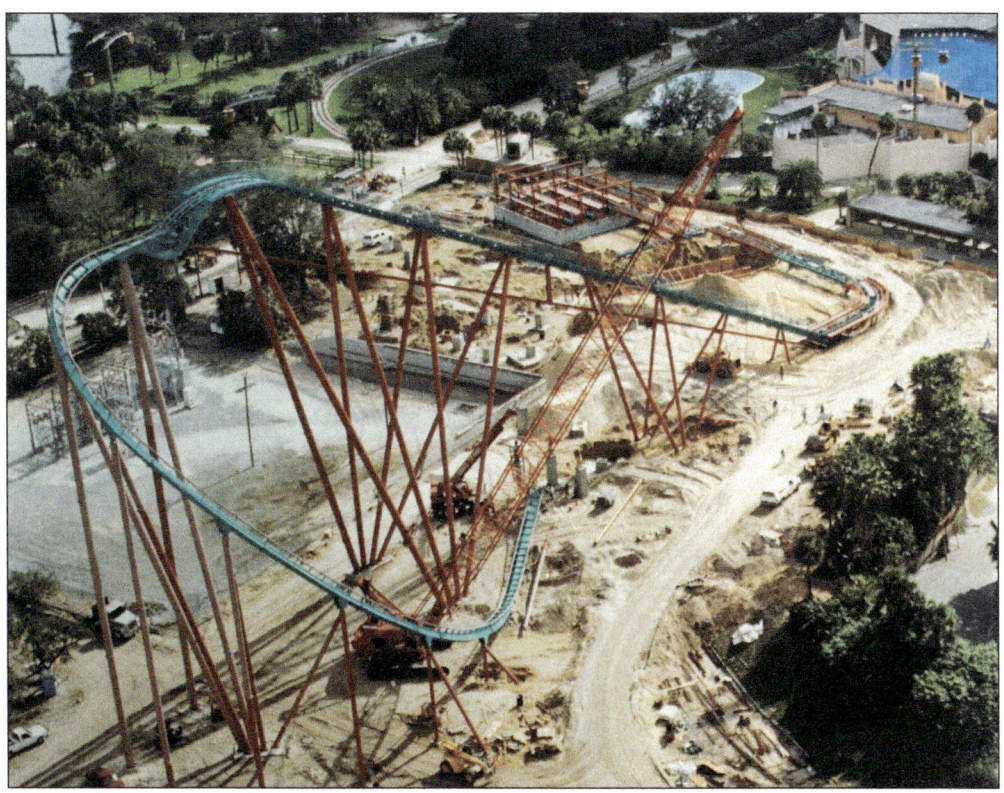

Kumba rises high above Busch Gardens Tampa Bay in January 1993. The roller coaster was manufactured by Bolliger & Mabillard of Monthey, Switzerland, and features several elements that were never before seen on any roller coaster anywhere in the world, including a vertical loop that encircles the same roller coaster's lift hill, the first dive loop, and the first zero-g roll atop a camelback hump. (Aerial Innovations.)

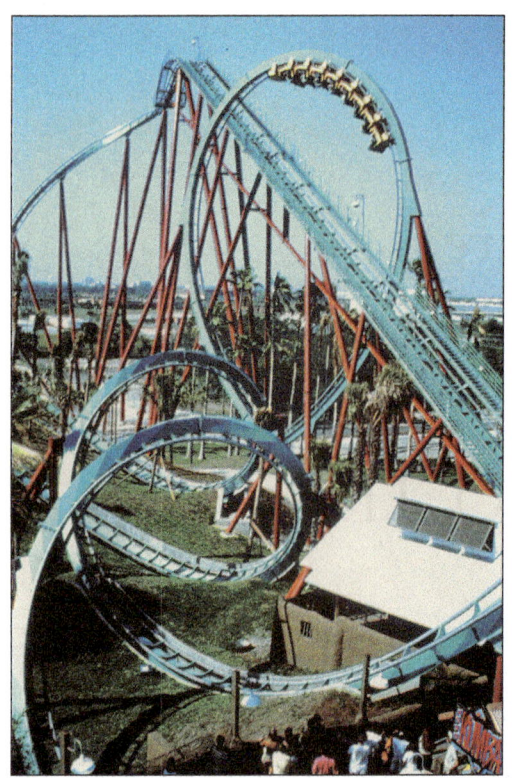

When Kumba opened on April 20, 1993, it boasted the world's tallest vertical loop and was one of the tallest, longest, fastest steel roller coasters anywhere in the United States. Kumba is 143 feet tall, 3,978 feet long, and attains speeds of 60 miles per hour. Kumba, which has seven inversions and thrills its riders with forces nearly four times greater than normal gravity, is named for the African Kikongo translation of the English word "roar."

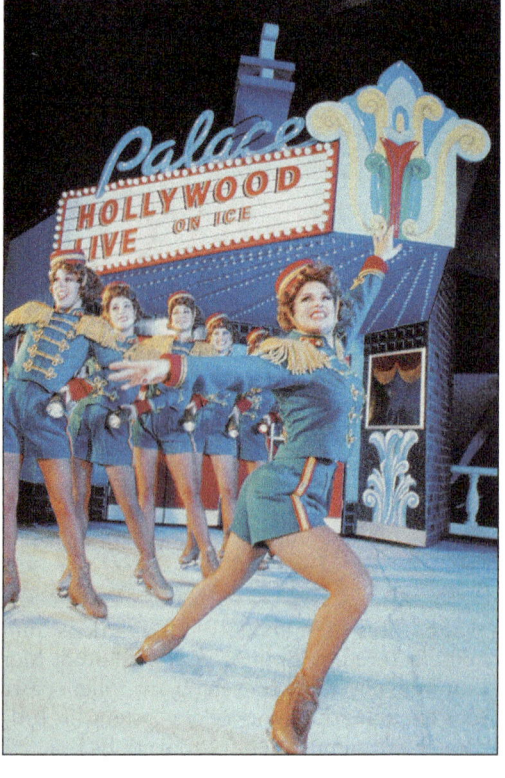

Hollywood Live On Ice was a popular ice show at the Moroccan Palace Theater that followed up the venue's previous ice extravaganza, *Around the World on Ice*. The movie-themed *Hollywood Live on Ice* featured scenes, songs, and dances inspired by some of Tinseltown's most beloved silver-screen classics.

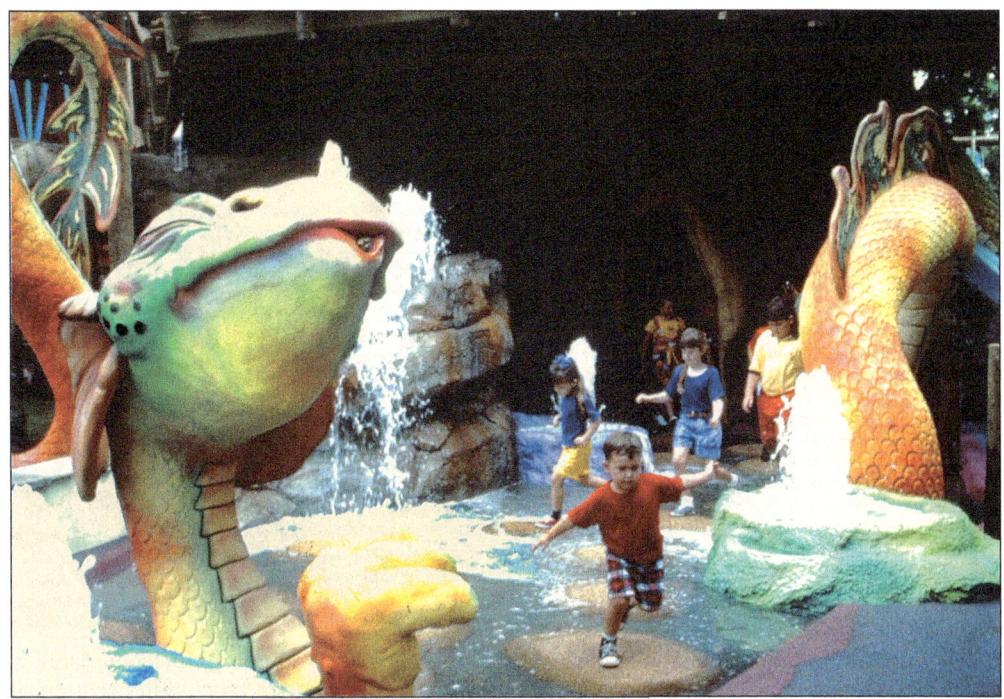

The Land of the Dragons play area debuted on May 9, 1995, in the area that was formerly the Dwarf Village children's attraction. Land of the Dragons entranced young guests with play elements, mechanical rides, and obstacle courses themed around a mystical and friendly dragon lair. The area was later re-themed and became Sesame Street Safari of Fun, which opened on March 27, 2010.

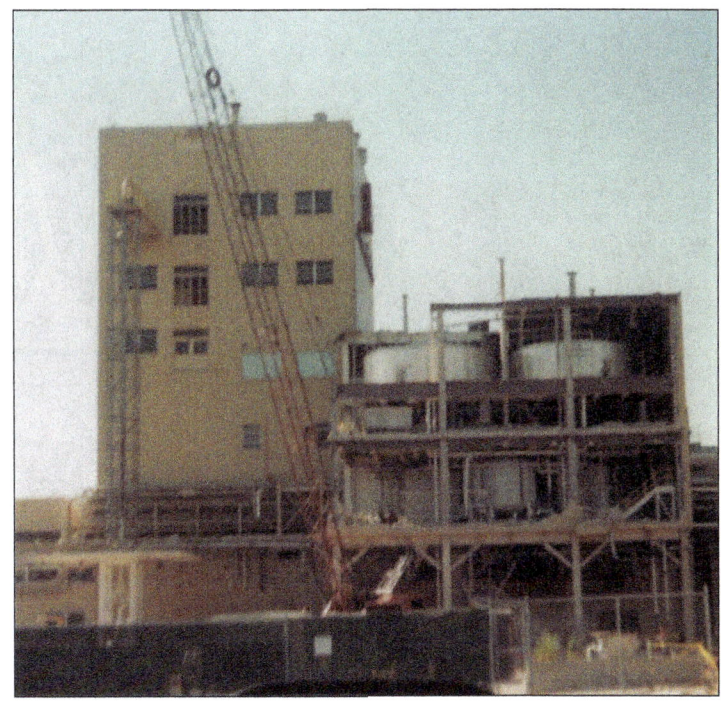

On October 25, 1995, it was announced the park's Anheuser-Busch brewery, which originally served as the anchoring feature of Busch Gardens Tampa Bay, would close. The demolition of the sprawling facility took more than one year. Several attractions would later flourish on the grounds that were once occupied by the brewery, including the Gwazi wooden roller coaster, Gwazi Park, and much of the Sesame Street Safari of Fun children's play area. (Author's collection.)

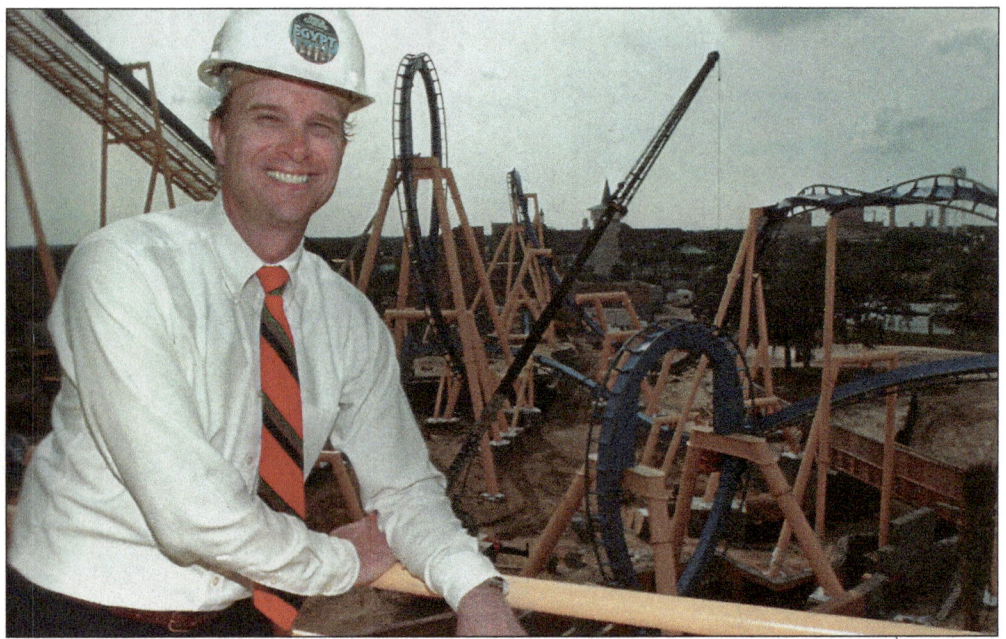

Vice president of design and engineering Mark Rose stands before Montu, a Bolliger & Mabillard roller coaster seen under construction in February 1996. Early inverted-style roller coasters, or suspended roller coasters, were designed by Arrow Development and debuted to the public in 1981. Suspended roller coaster Big Bad Wolf was a popular ride at Busch Gardens Williamsburg during its run from 1984 through 2009. Modern inverted roller coasters, such as Montu, came along in the 1990s. When it opened, Montu was the world's tallest and fastest inverted roller coaster. (*Tampa Bay Times*.)

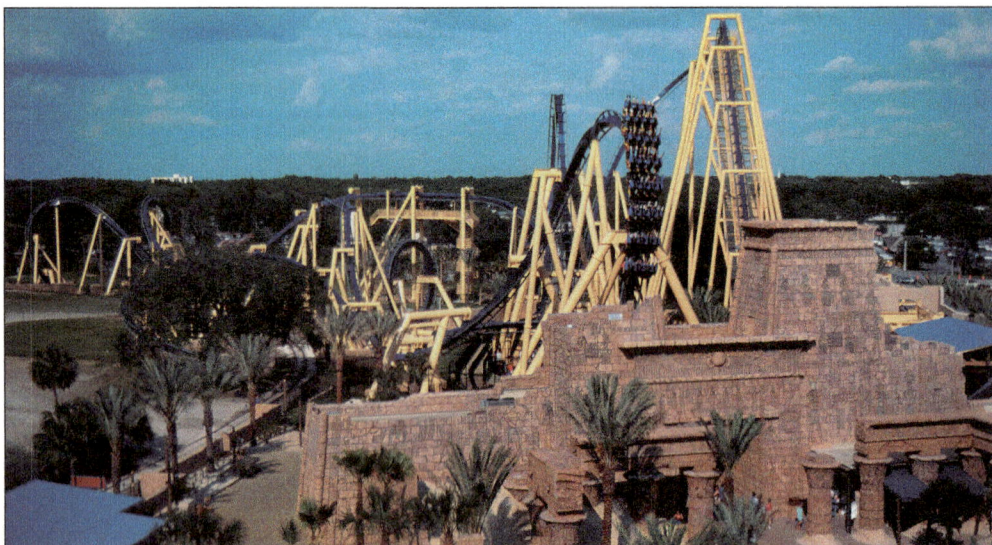

Montu, which opened on May 16, 1996, stands 150 feet tall, is 3,983 feet long, and attains speeds up to 65 miles per hour. Guests aboard Montu also experience forces nearly four times greater than that of normal gravity. The innovative and thrilling roller coaster has been featured on many television programs, has won awards in the amusement park industry, and consistently ranks well with roller coaster riding organizations many years after the ride opened.

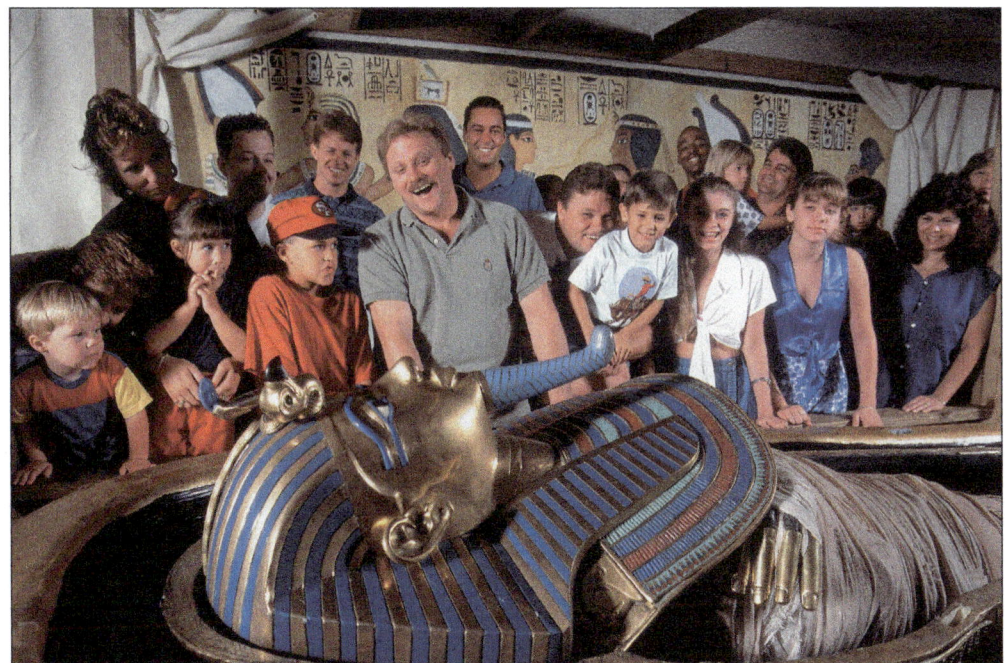

King Tut's Tomb opened in May 1996 along with Montu in the Egypt area. King Tut's Tomb is a faithful re-creation of the 1920s archeological dig that revealed the treasures and sarcophagus of Tutankhamun, the young Egyptian pharaoh who ruled sometime around 1332–1323 BC. The building that once housed King Tut's Tomb was converted into the indoor queue area for the Cobra's Curse roller coaster, which opened in June 2016.

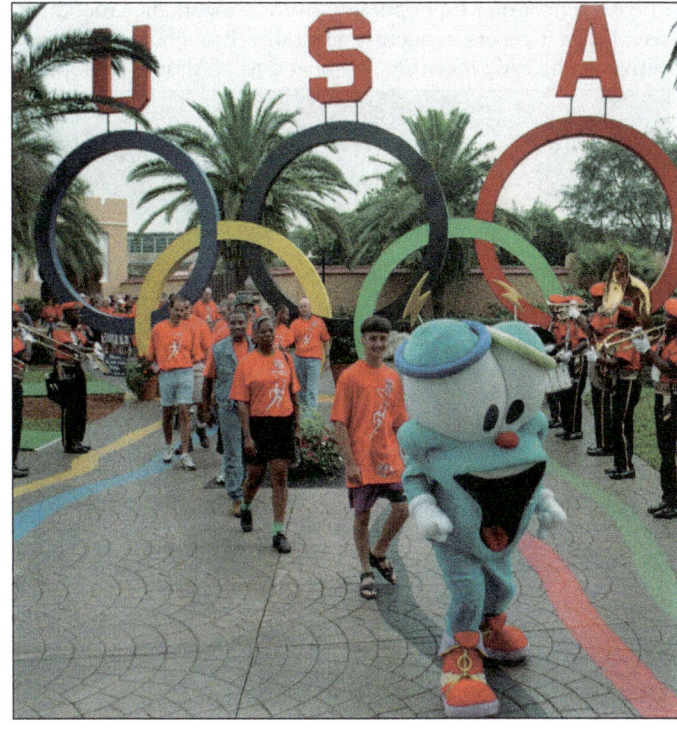

Busch Gardens was the official theme park sponsor of the 1996 Summer Olympic Games in Atlanta, Georgia. In celebration of the summer games marking the 100th anniversary of the modern Olympics, Busch Gardens opened Olympic Spirit Village in the Morocco area. The temporary attraction offered meet-and-greets with Olympic athletes, official Olympic-emblazoned merchandise, and opportunities to meet Izzy, the large-eyed mascot of the 1996 summer games, who is seen in this image leading a parade of more than 130 Olympic torchbearers in June 1996. (*Tampa Bay Times*.)

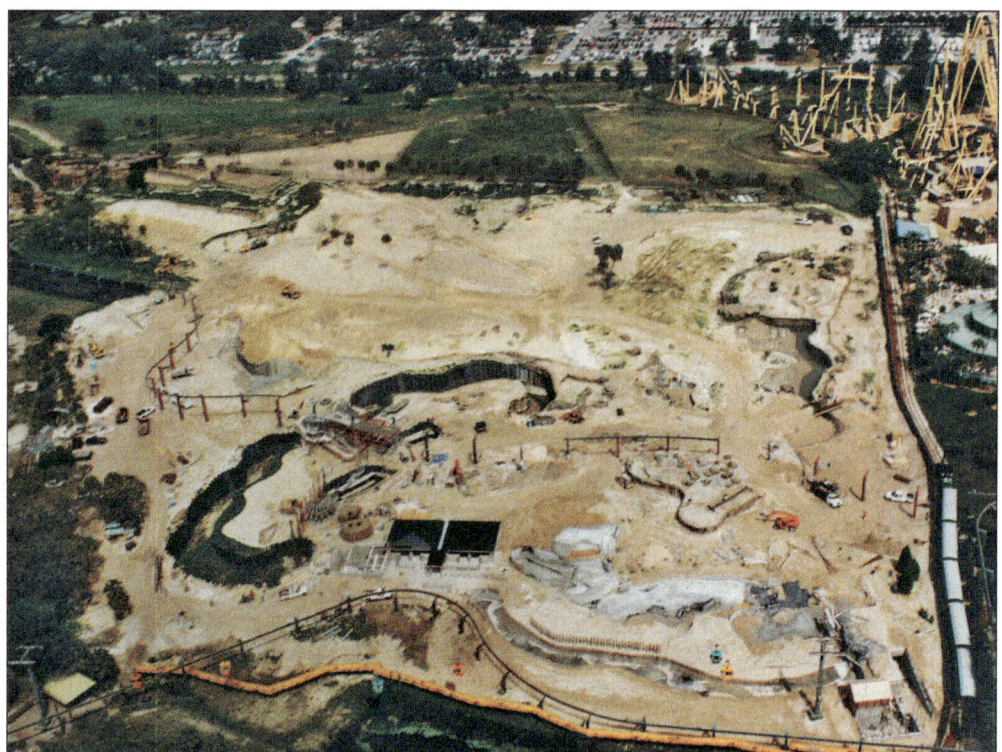

The Edge of Africa opened on July 4, 1997, and is an expansive animal habitat themed as an abandoned fishing village. At the Edge of Africa, seen above in the fall of 1996 under construction, one can encounter hippopotami, hyenas, meerkats, crocodiles, and lions, the latter of which is seen below. Keepers frequently give talks throughout the Edge of Africa, where animals are most active in the early morning and near dusk. (Above, Aerial Innovations.)

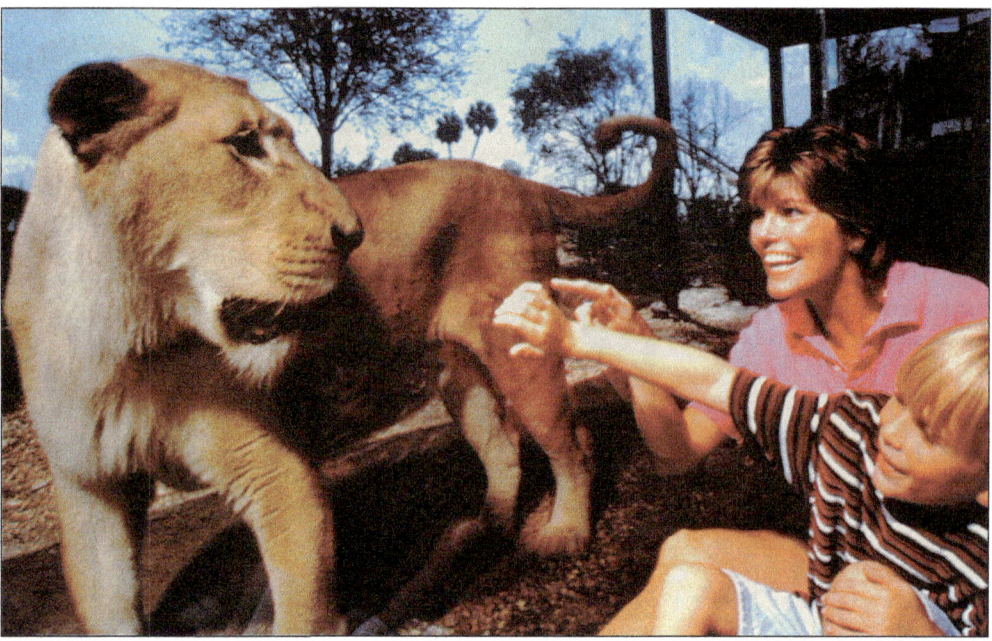

Akbar's Adventure Tours was a comedy motion-simulator ride that, like its predecessor Questor, took guests on an exciting, and often bumpy, expedition through the depths of Africa. Akbar's Adventure Tours opened on March 12, 1998, and took on the overarching theme of the adjacent Egypt section. In the film, two zany entrepreneurs (played by actors Martin Short and Eugene Levy) take their unsuspecting guests on a ragtag, dangerous tour of Egypt.

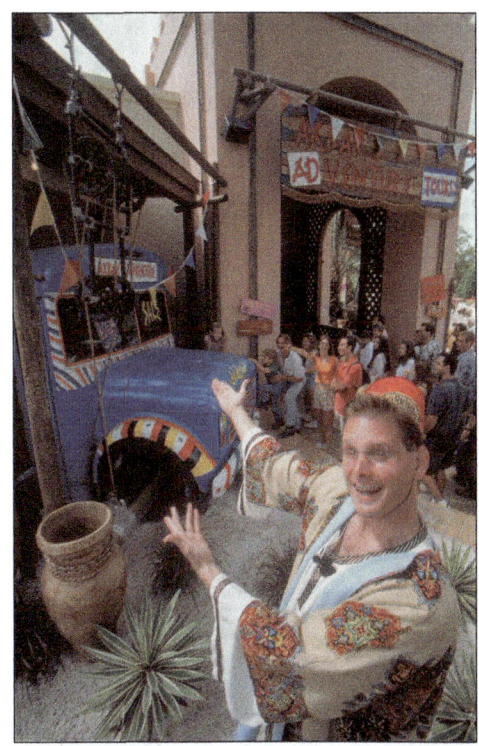

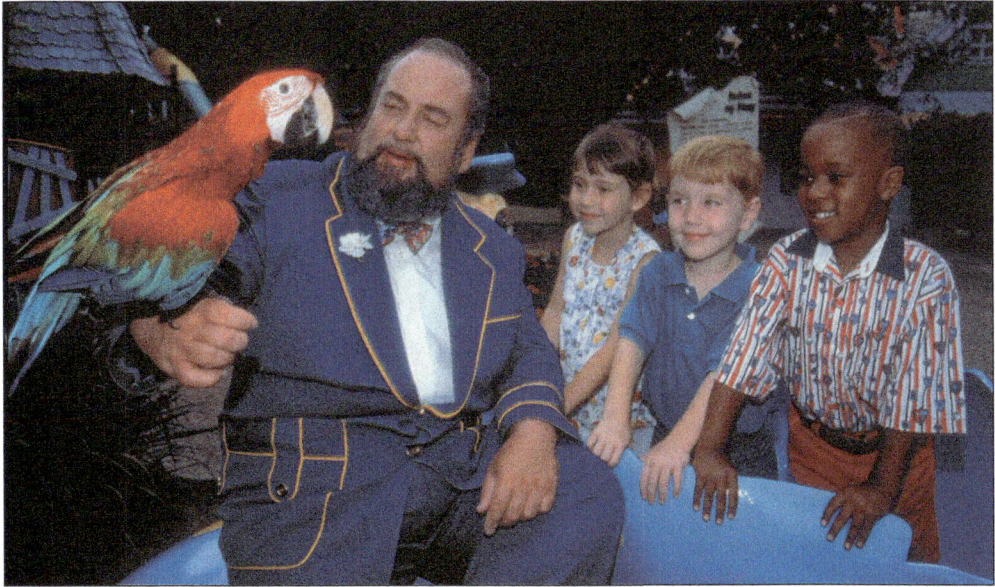

The All New Captain Kangaroo, which aired from 1997 to 1998, is one of many nationally televised programs taped at Busch Gardens Tampa Bay over the years. One of the park's first glimpses of national exposure came in the early 1960s on the original *Captain Kangaroo*, starring Bob Keeshan. Later, Dinah Shore shot her *Dinah!* variety talk show at the park twice, including an episode filmed in conjunction with the grand opening of the Timbuktu area in January 1980. *Second Noah*, a television drama about a zoo veterinarian and her family of eight adopted children, was filmed at Busch Gardens from 1996 through 1997.

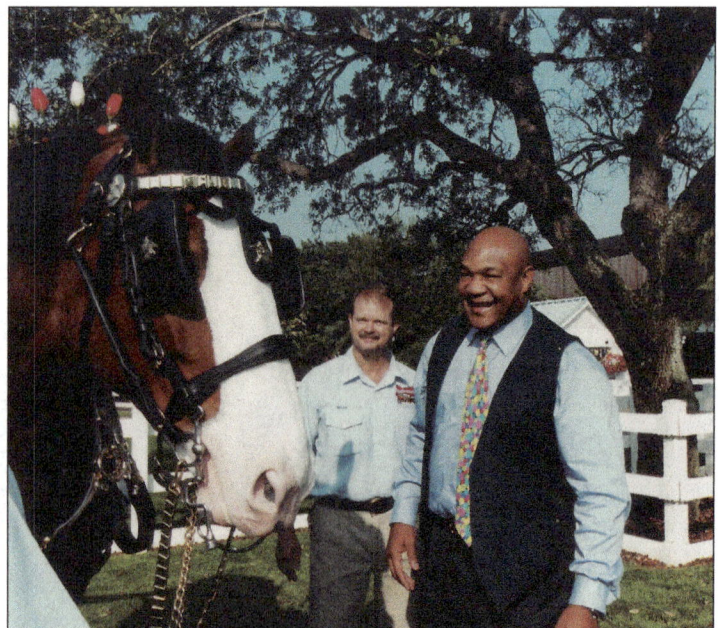

Busch Gardens Tampa Bay has lured many celebrities over the years, including world heavyweight boxing champion and inventor George Foreman. "I do remember well my visit to Busch Gardens," he said of his 2001 trip to the park, where he met Brutus the Clydesdale and trainer Mark Peterson, standing behind Foreman in the photograph. "Boy, they are giants! What a treat for a horse lover as I am." (Mark Peterson.)

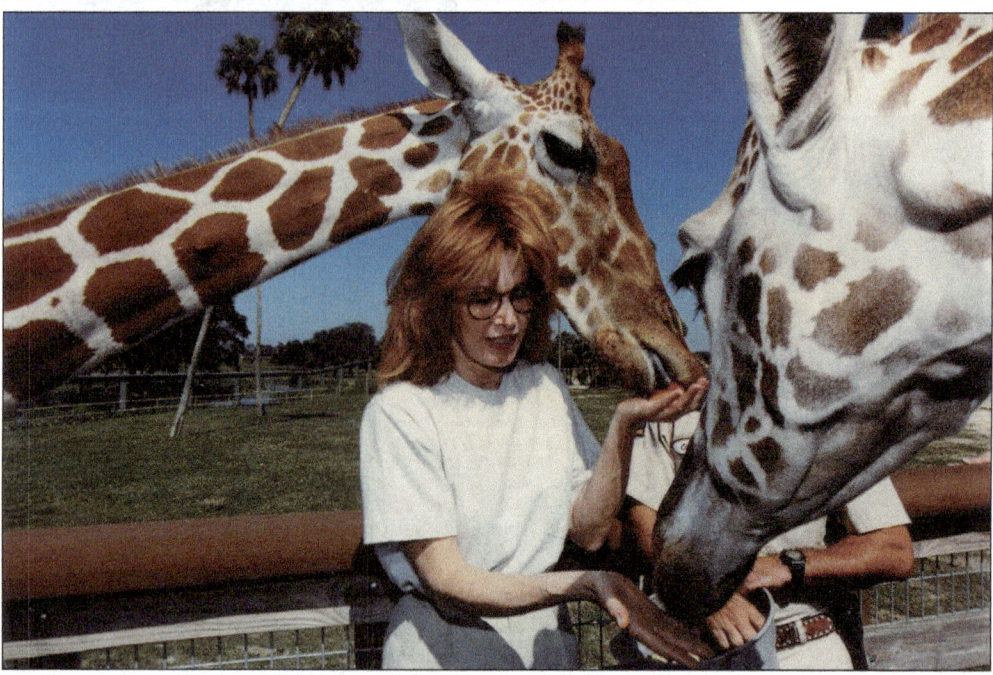

Actress and philanthropist Stefanie Powers was involved in the capture of more than two dozen reticulated giraffes during a conservation project in 1984 led by animal translocation and rehabilitation pioneer Don Hunt. Powers administered injections of vital stress vitamins and antibiotics after the giraffes were under human care. "The giraffes were transported to the United States after their quarantine period in Kenya via Pan Am cargo planes," said Powers. "They were then transported to Busch Gardens by road, and I was there in person when the giraffes arrived in Tampa." Powers has visited Busch Gardens many times, including in 2004, when she was reunited with the last remaining giraffe from the 1984 group of rescues. (Stefanie Powers.)

This young boy feeds hungry lorikeets nectar at Lory Landing. The animal encounter opened in May 1998 between the Stanleyville pedestrian bridge and Land of the Dragons, now known as Sesame Street Safari of Fun. In addition to feeding lorikeets and hundreds of other exotic tropical birds, guests who visit Lorikeet Landing can talk with keepers and take incredible photographs of pretty flora and avian fauna.

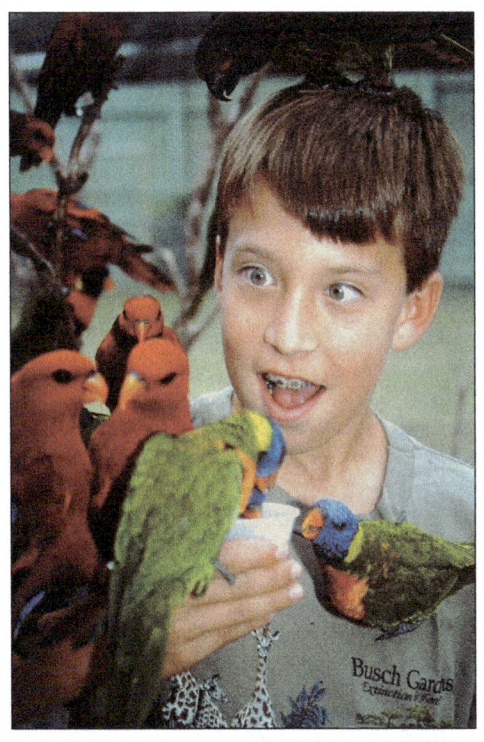

The Serengeti Safari, one of the most popular animal encounter experiences at Busch Gardens Tampa Bay today, was already a hit by the mid-1990s. The Serengeti Safari offers a unique opportunity for guests to enjoy up-close, face-to-face encounters with many of the animals on the Veldt, which may include zebras, ostriches, and gazelles. The off-road animal adventure tour even offers its guests the chance to hand-feed giraffes.

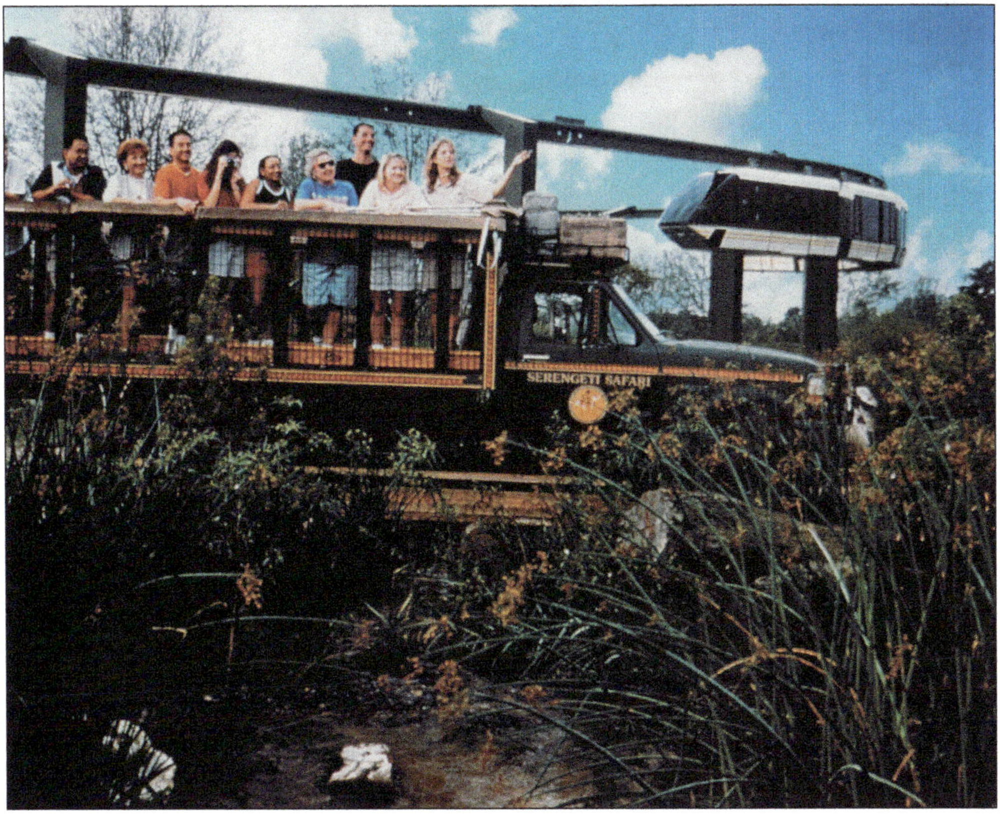

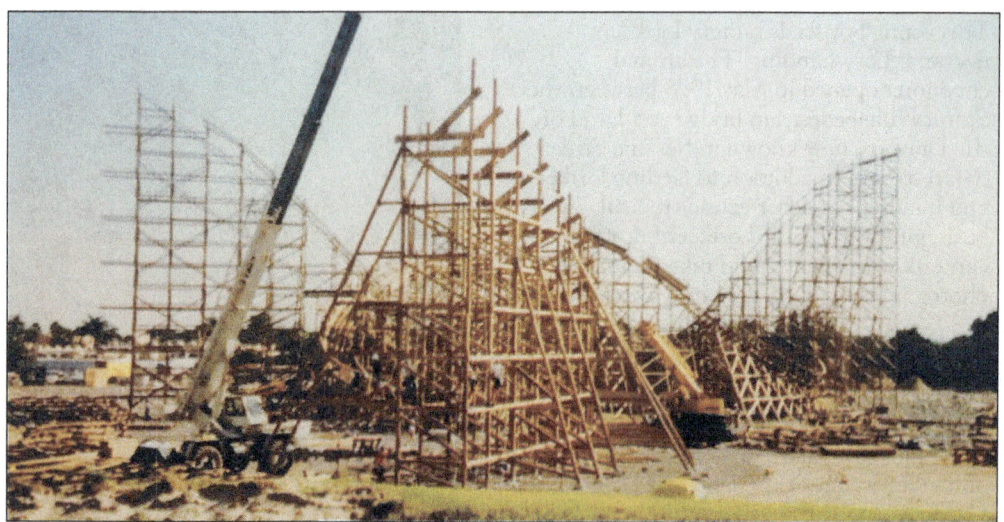

In 1998, Busch Gardens Tampa Bay broke ground on a long-awaited project: the park's first wooden roller coaster—two, to be exact. Gwazi, a mythical African creature with the head of a tiger and body of a lion, was the namesake of this dueling wooden roller coaster built by Great Coasters International. More than 1 million board feet of lumber was used in constructing the behemoth roller coaster, which rose on the site formerly occupied by the brewery. (Author's collection.)

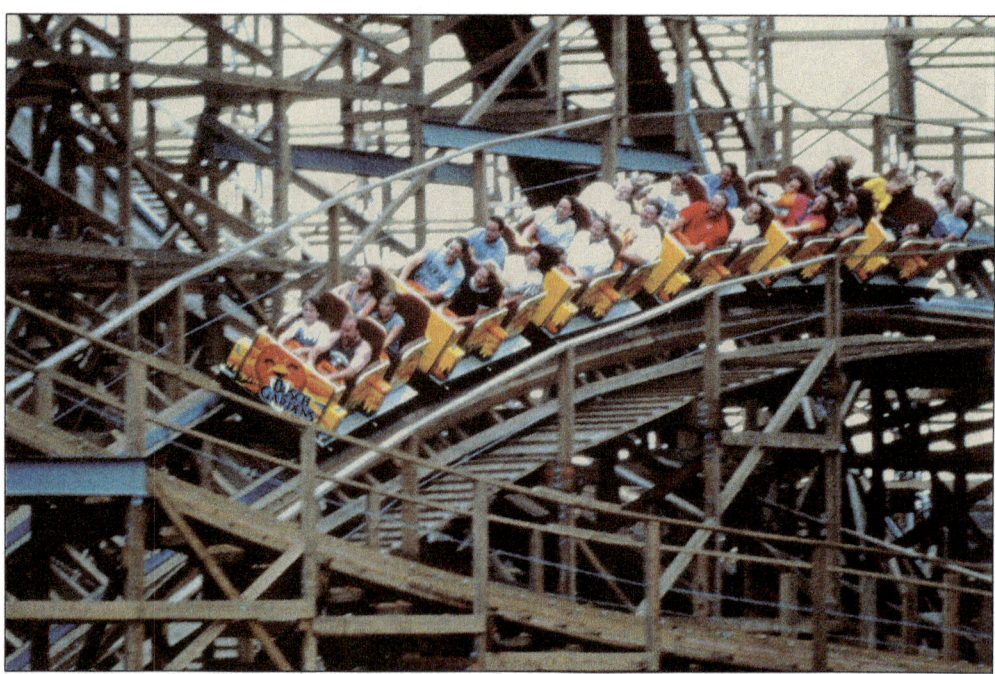

When Gwazi opened on June 18, 1999, it was Florida's first dueling wooden roller coaster. The two tracks, one lion-themed with yellow cars and the other colored blue representing the tiger, were each 3,508 feet in length. Each track boasted a 92-foot drop, top speeds of 50 miles per hour, and six fly-bys, where the two trains appeared to be on a collision course with each other. The ride's original Philadelphia Toboggan Company cars were replaced by Millennium Flyer trains in 2010. The tiger side closed in 2012, and the entire attraction closed on February 1, 2015.

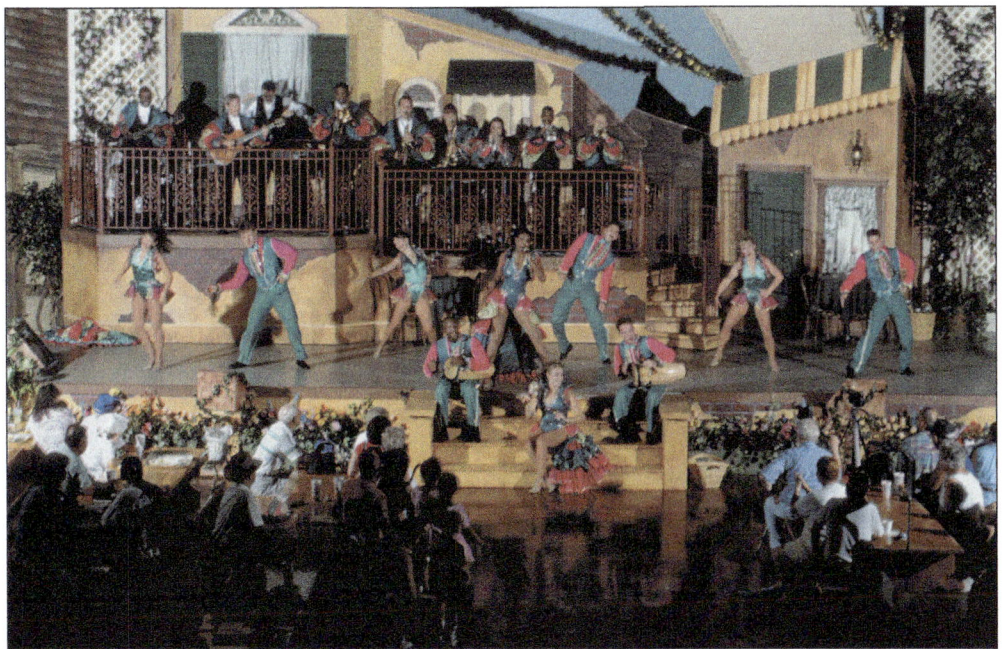

While Das Festhaus was widely known for its popular, long-running German show, there was much more than polka music and lederhosen on display there. Running concurrently for many years along with the German show was the *International Celebration* show, which paid homage to the merry music, diverse dances, and colorful costumes from countries around the world, including France, Mexico, Ireland, Germany, and Italy.

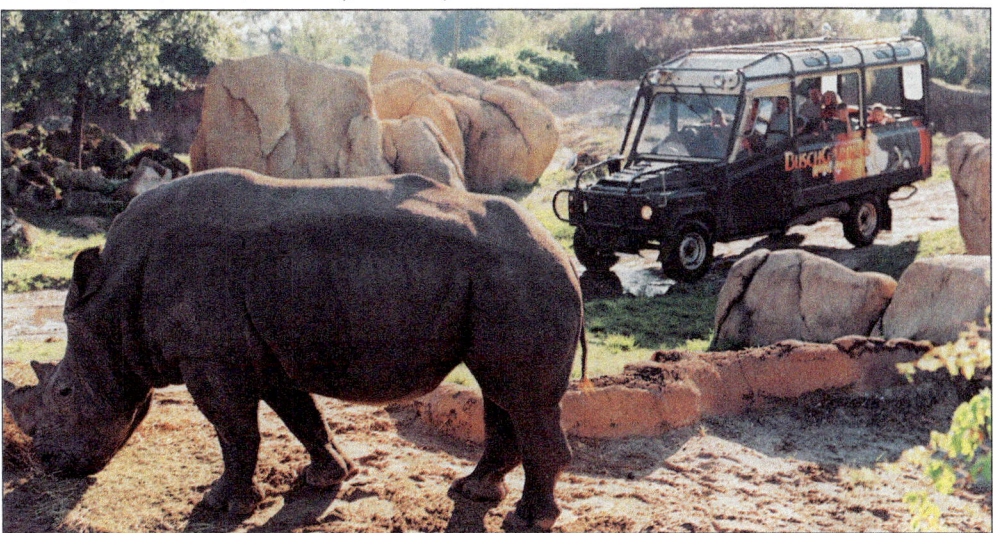

Rhino Rally, a Vekoma Safari Adventure ride, was one of the largest single attractions Busch Gardens Tampa Bay ever constructed. Opened on May 23, 2001, in the Nairobi section and encompassing a vast spread of acreage in the northern Serengeti Plain, Rhino Rally was an off-road voyage that took guests on a comical animal expedition through canyons and jungles while looking for a lost driver. The ride originally included a harrowing river segment, but that portion of Rhino Rally was incorporated into scenery for Cheetah Hunt. The exciting five-minute ride closed on September 1, 2014.

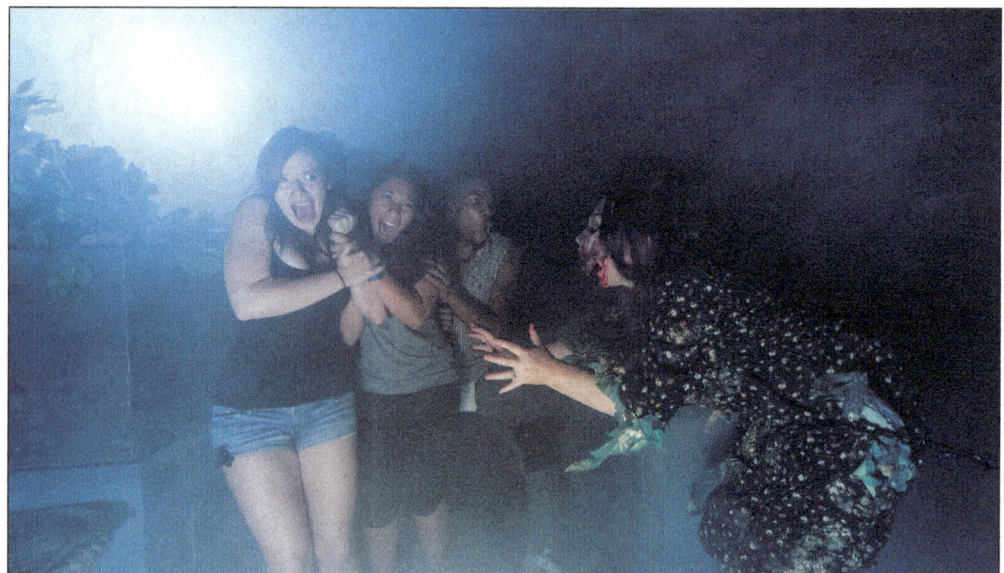

Howl-O-Scream debuted at Busch Gardens Tampa Bay in 2000 following a single-year Halloween event in 1999 called Spooky Safari. Howl-O-Scream is an annual event that takes place on select nights in September and October and features haunted houses, outdoor "scare zones," and inescapable roaming hoards.

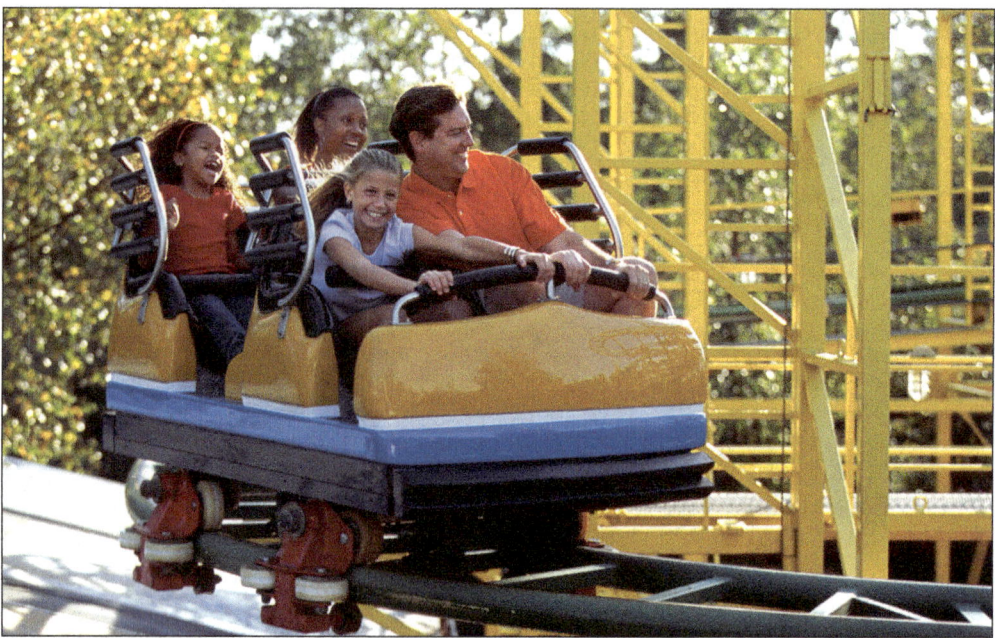

A MACK Rides Wild Mouse–style family roller coaster called Cheetah Chase opened on February 28, 2004, on a site once partly occupied by the Crazy Camel. The 1,200-foot-long, 45-foot-high roller coaster actually originated from Busch Gardens Williamsburg, where it opened in 1996 as Wild Izzy, paying homage to the mascot of the 1996 Summer Olympic Games. The ride was renamed Wilde Maus in 1997 before closing in 2003, when it was replaced by The Curse of DarKastle dark ride. Cheetah Chase was renamed Sand Serpent in 2011 to avoid confusion with another cheetah-themed Busch Gardens roller coaster, Cheetah Hunt.

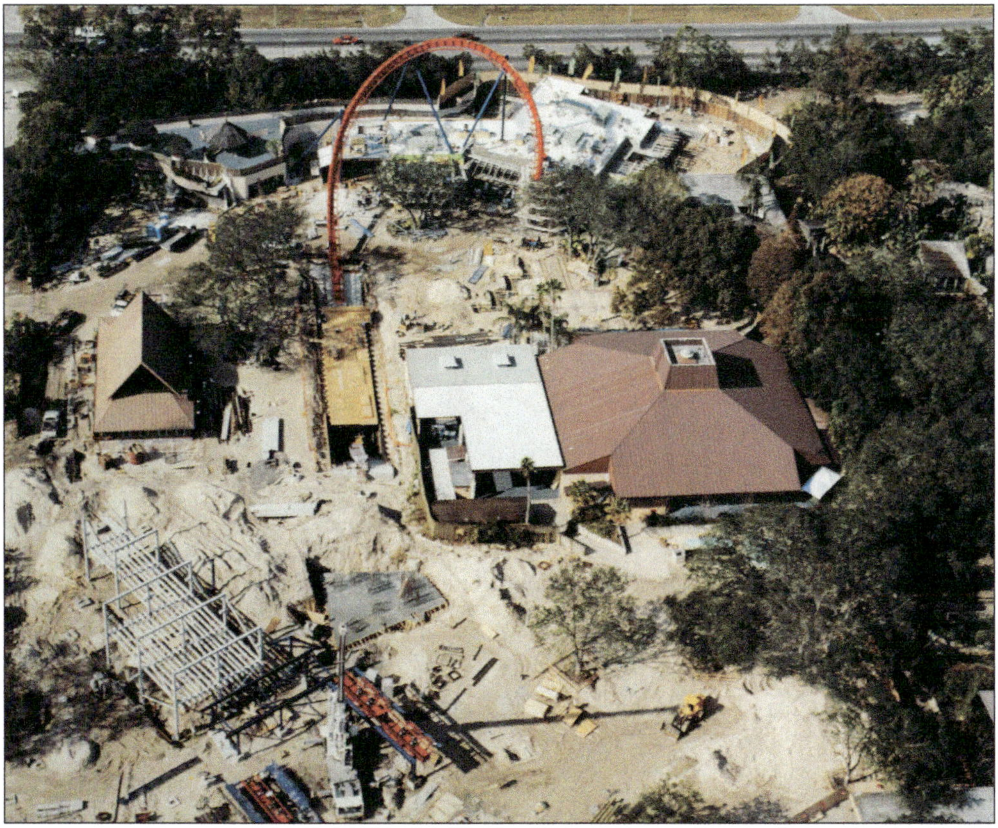

The once relatively quiet African village of Stanleyville received a thrilling makeover when construction crews broke ground on SheiKra in 2004. The roller coaster, which became the third Bolliger & Mabillard masterpiece at Busch Gardens Tampa Bay, is seen here under construction in late 2004. SheiKra originally opened on May 21, 2005, as the first dive coaster in North America and the world's longest, tallest, and fastest dive coaster—the latter two being records the red-colored Tampa Bay roller coaster lost to its blue-hued sister, Griffon, at Busch Gardens Williamsburg in 2007. (Aerial Innovations.)

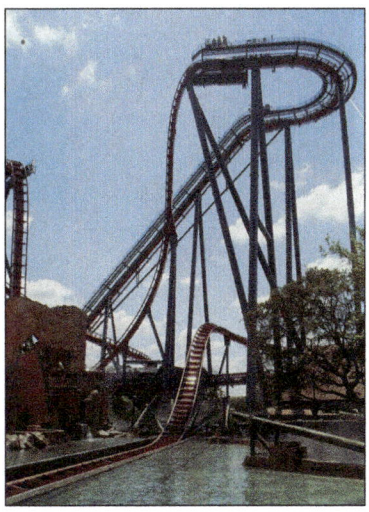

SheiKra's name derives from a hawk known as a shikra. The bird, whose name means "hunter" in Hindi, is widely found in Africa and Asia and is known to dive for its prey. Meanwhile, the SheiKra roller coaster stands 200 feet tall, features a 90-degree drop, and carries riders along 3,188 feet of track at speeds up to 70 miles per hour. SheiKra was profiled on Discovery Channel's *Build It Bigger* in 2007, the same year the ride received a significant modification when its new, floorless trains were installed that provide an experience closely mimicking the sensation of flying.

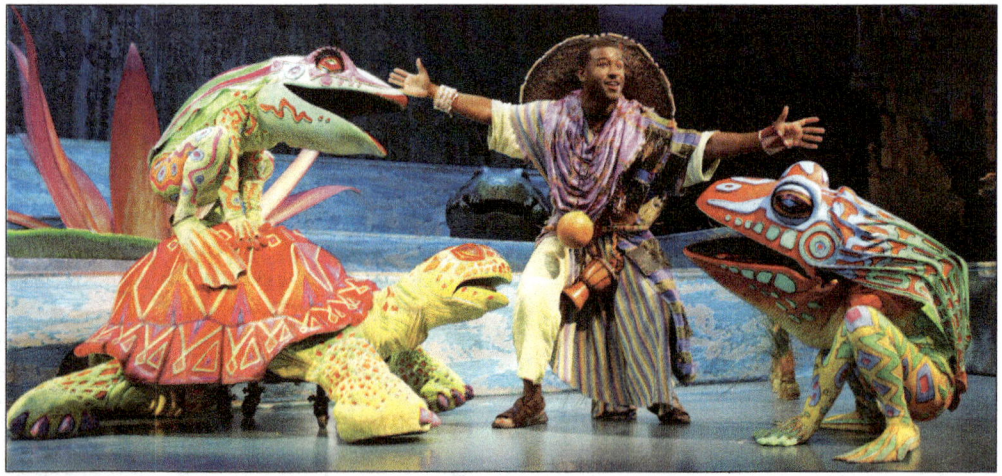

Katonga was one of the park's longest-running shows. Debuting at the Moroccan Palace Theater in 2004, *Katonga* delivered a riveting African-themed music and dance experience with vivid costumes and special effects. *Katonga* closed in 2010 as one of the park's most popular shows. With 8,842 performances, *Katonga* staged more shows than iconic Broadway hits such as *Cats*, *Les Misérables*, and *A Chorus Line*.

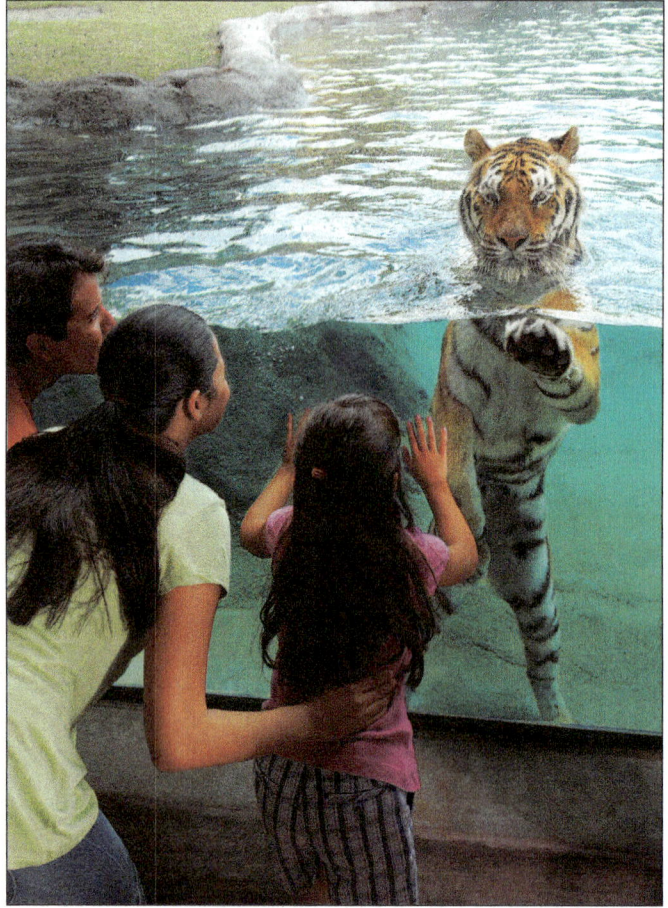

Jungala opened on April 5, 2008, in the area formerly occupied by the Python roller coaster and Claw Island. The lushly landscaped four-acre attraction features expanded habitats for the park's orangutans and Bengal tigers. Also found in Jungala is a refurbished Vivi Storehouse restaurant, renamed Bengal Bistro; a children's hang-glider ride called Jungle Flyers; Wild Surge, a family drop ride by Moser Rides; and the multilevel Treetop Trails, a play element for younger guests that includes mazes, bridges, climbing nets, and crawl tubes.

Six
2009 AND BEYOND
THE FUTURE BLOOMS

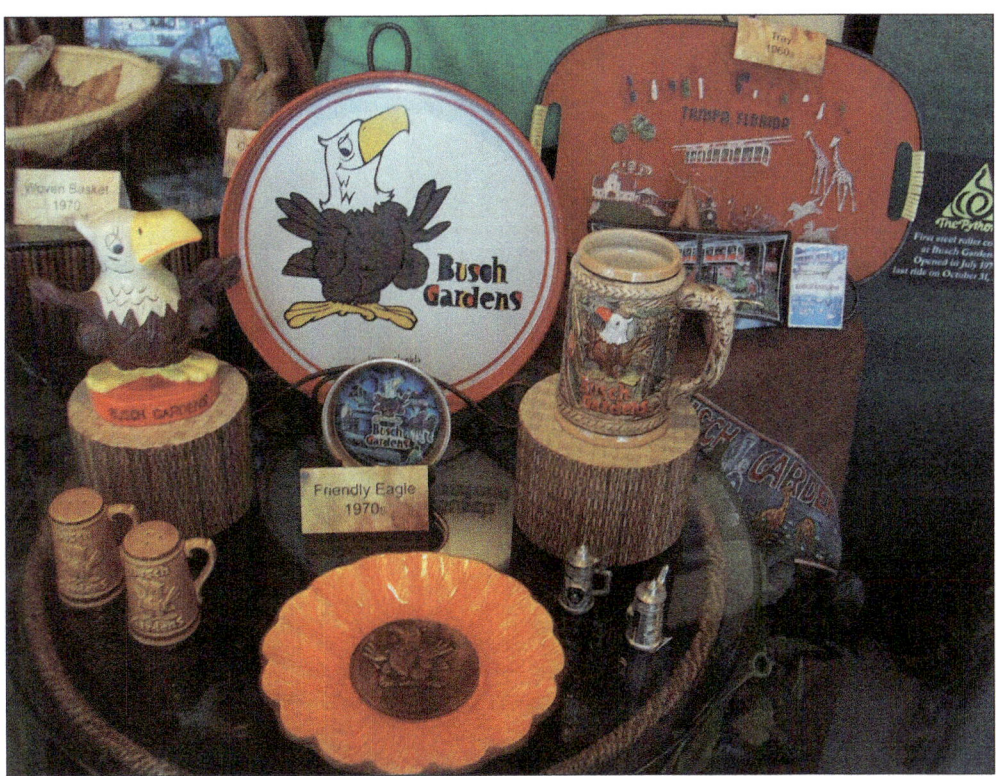

When Busch Gardens Tampa Bay celebrated its 50th anniversary in 2009, park officials converted the former Questor and Akbar's Adventure Tours building into a history museum. Dozens of photographs and displays, such as this one showcasing vintage Busch Gardens souvenirs from the 1960s and 1970s, helped guests enjoy a fun trip back in time. Incidentally, the park began its second half-century operating under a new company name, when the former Busch Entertainment Corporation became SeaWorld Parks & Entertainment on December 1, 2009. (Author's collection.)

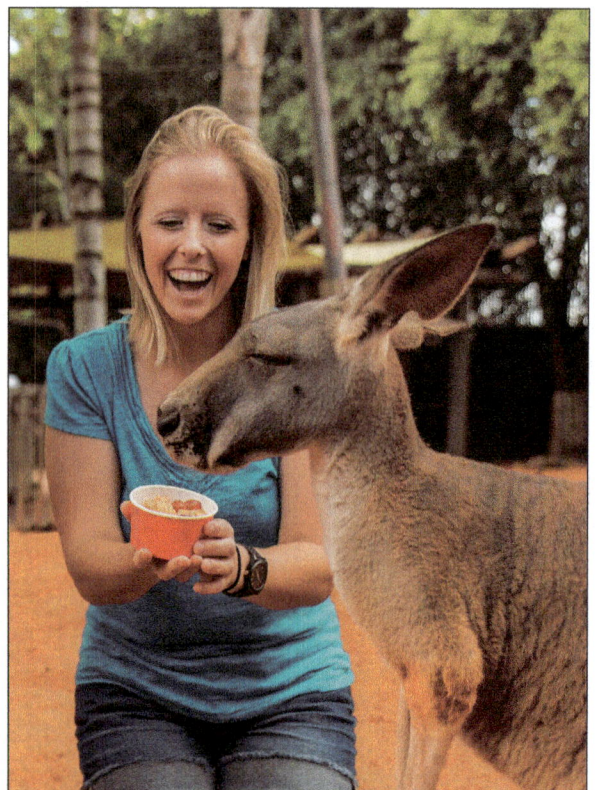

Kangaroos and their smaller, similar-looking cousins, wallabies, engage with guests in Walkabout Way. This marsupial habitat allows guests to interact with the kangaroos, wallabies, and wallaroos; ask keepers questions about these fascinating creatures; and take some "ripper" photographs of some 'roos and joeys. The word *ripper* is Australian slang for "great," while a joey is what a baby kangaroo is called when still taking up residence in its mother's pouch.

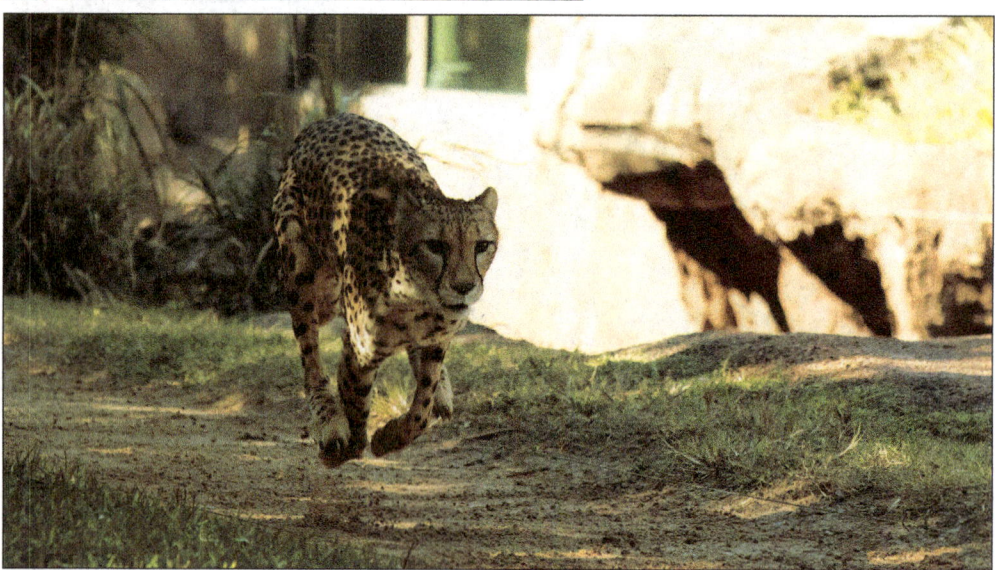

Cheetah Run is an innovative, interactive, state-of-the-art habitat between the Moroccan Palace Theater and Serengeti Overlook Restaurant where the world's fastest land mammals reside. The new habitat incorporates part of the former Clydesdale Hamlet and opened on May 27, 2011. About a dozen cheetahs call Cheetah Run home, and they take advantage of the runway in the habitat where they can run up to their full capability if they choose. Cheetahs can spring at speeds of up to 70 miles per hour.

Cheetah Hunt is a steel triple-launch roller coaster that opened on May 27, 2011, along with its neighboring attraction, Cheetah Run. Built by Intamin, the same company that manufactured the Phoenix and Congo River Rapids, Cheetah Hunt whisks riders along 4,429 feet of track at speeds up to 60 miles per hour. The queue house for Cheetah Hunt is located in the former monorail station, which was decommissioned in 1999 along with the closure of the monorail.

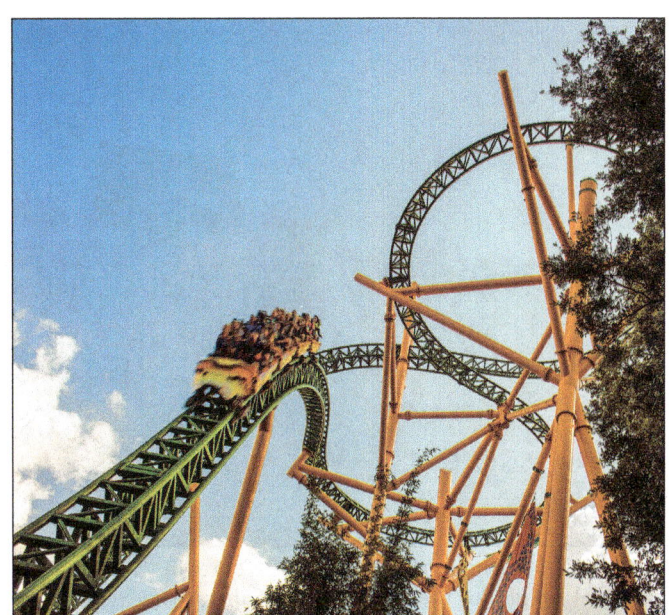

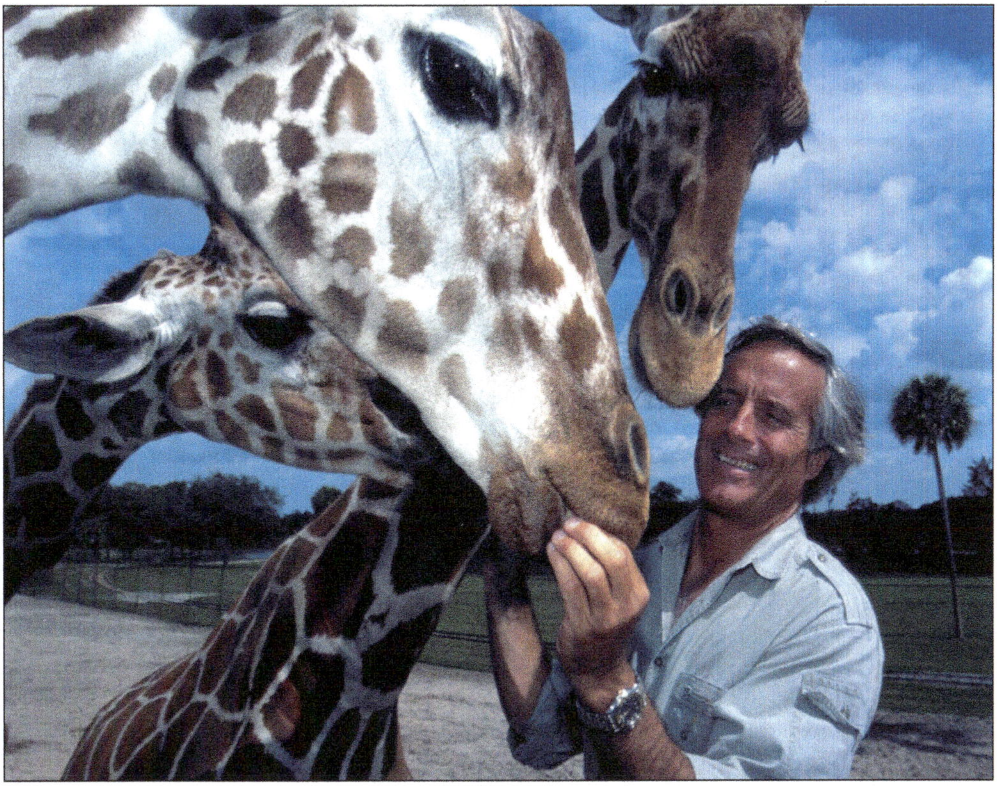

Director emeritus of the Columbus Zoo "Jungle" Jack Hanna feeds giraffes on the Serengeti Plain. The longtime zookeeper has been on numerous television shows talking about animals and conservation, and he taped various programs from his base camp studio at Busch Gardens. Hanna regularly draws huge crowds with his educational and entertaining presentations when he visits Busch Gardens Tampa Bay.

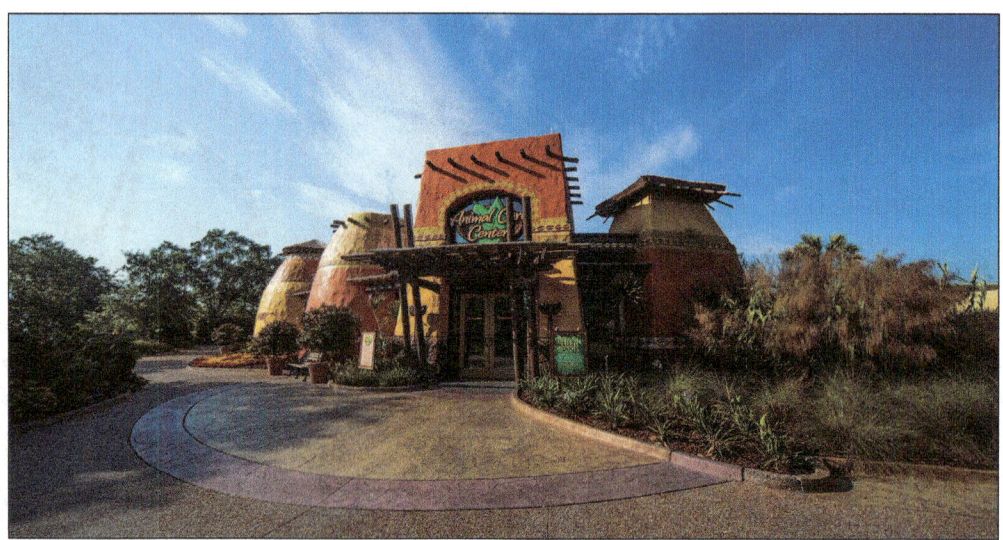

The 16,000-square-foot Animal Care Center in the Nairobi area of the park is the main in-park medical facility for the thousands of animals that reside at Busch Gardens Tampa Bay. Guests can watch through glass as veterinarians and technicians perform various procedures throughout the day at the facility. In addition to medical suites, the Animal Care Center also has a large kitchen where dietitians and other ambassadors prepare food, present educational talks, and answer guests' questions. "The Animal Care Center at Busch Gardens is one of the finest at any zoo in the world," said popular animal expert Jack Hanna in 2012.

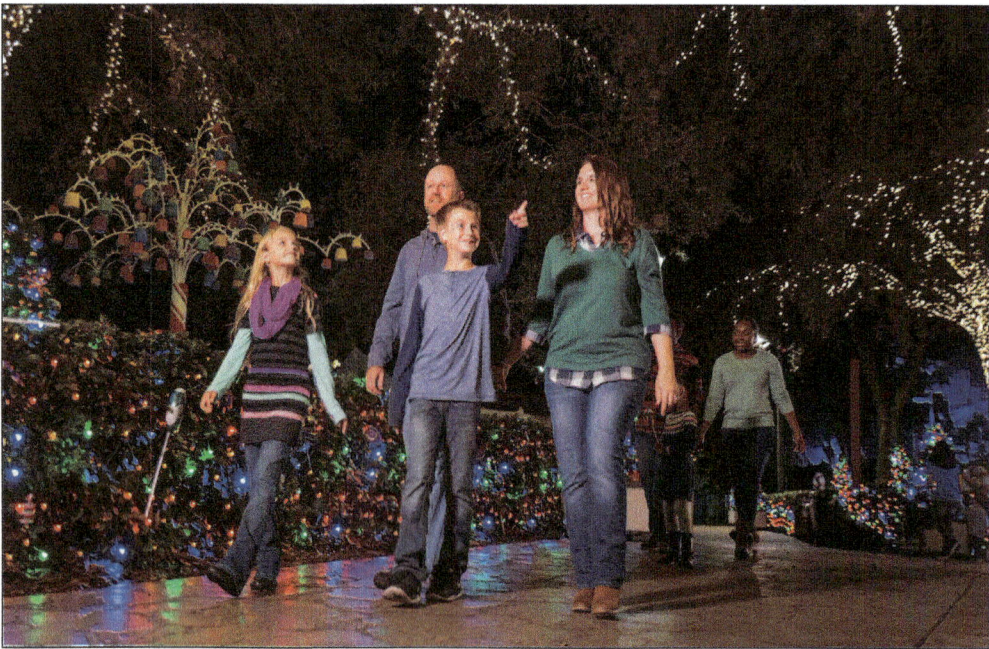

In 2012, Busch Gardens Tampa Bay began decking its halls for a new annual event called Christmas Town. Featuring holiday-themed shows, attractions, and more than 2 million lights, Christmas Town is held on select nights during November and December. Guests can shop for unique gifts, catch a jolly show filled with holiday cheer, sip hot chocolate, and get their photographs with Santa Claus.

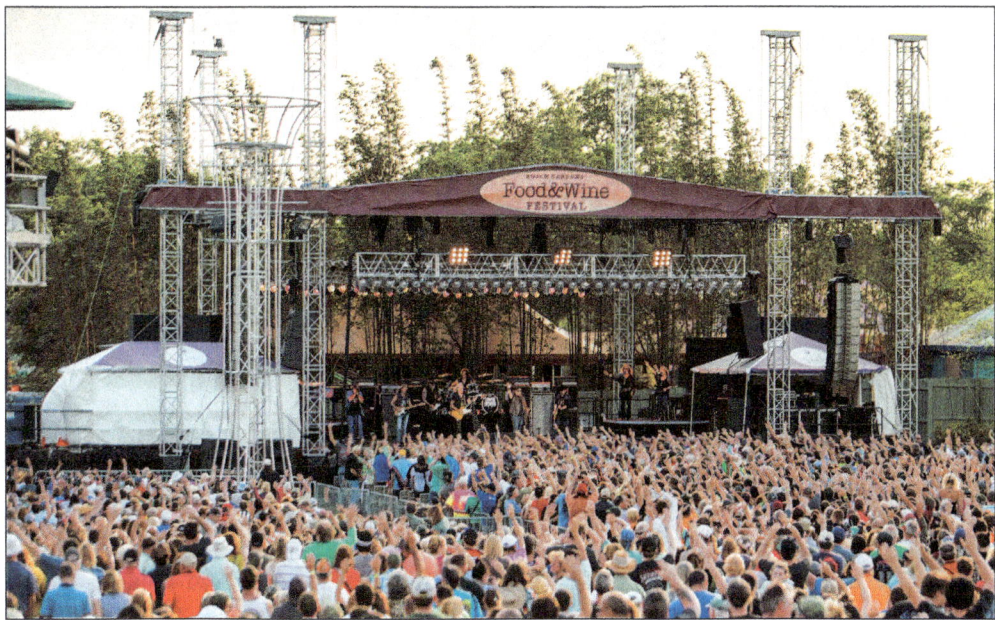

The Busch Gardens Tampa Bay Food and Wine Festival debuted in 2015 to huge crowds. Dozens of epicurean vendors serve up their finest fare in the spring, luring swarms of hungry foodies from all over to taste tempting treats representing the savory flavors of multiregional United States cooking as well as appetizing international foods.

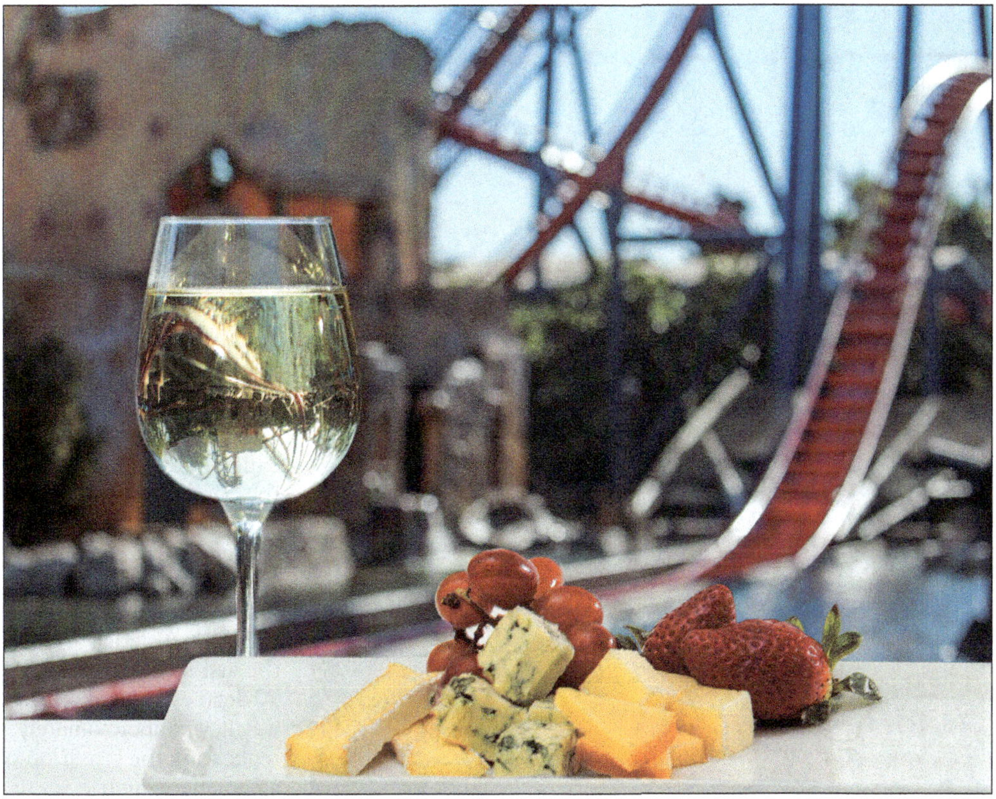

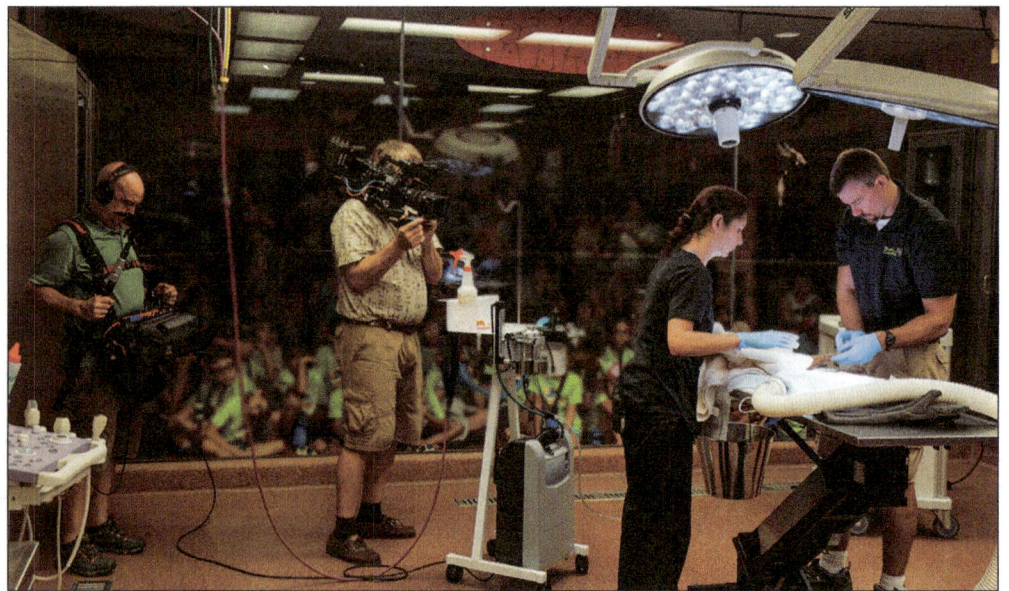

The Wildlife Docs is an educational television series profiling the daily lives of veterinary staff that work at Busch Gardens Tampa Bay. The show, which premiered on October 5, 2013, is hosted by actress and conversationalist Rachel Reenstra and is produced in partnership by SeaWorld Entertainment and Litton Entertainment.

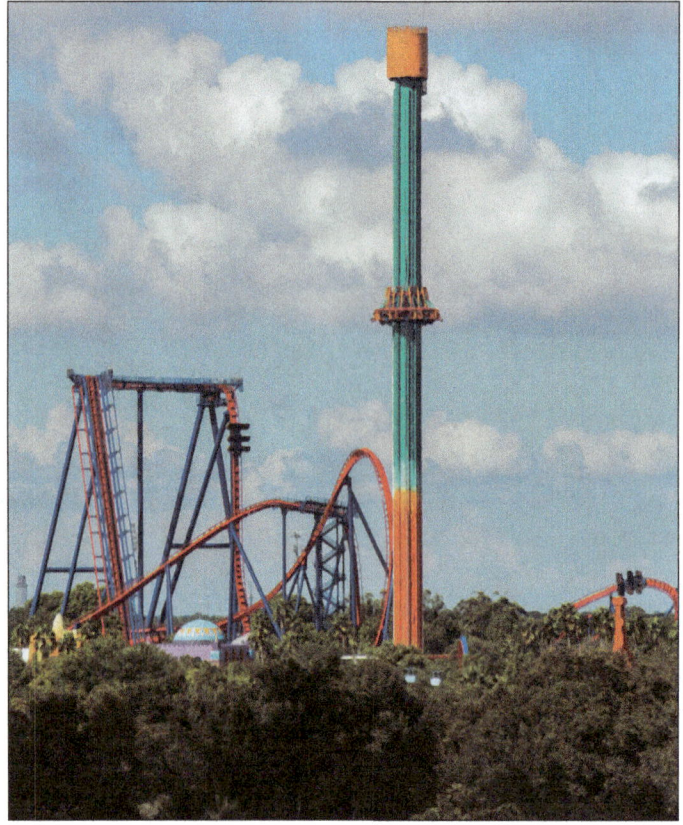

Falcon's Fury is a 335-foot-tall drop tower that rises high above Pantopia. The Sky Jump drop tower, built by a subsidiary of Intamin called IntaRide, replaced the Sandstorm orbiter ride and officially opened on September 2, 2014. Falcon's Fury became the tallest freestanding drop tower in North America and the first to tilt its riders 90 degrees forward on the way down, approximately replicating the sensation of a parachute jump.

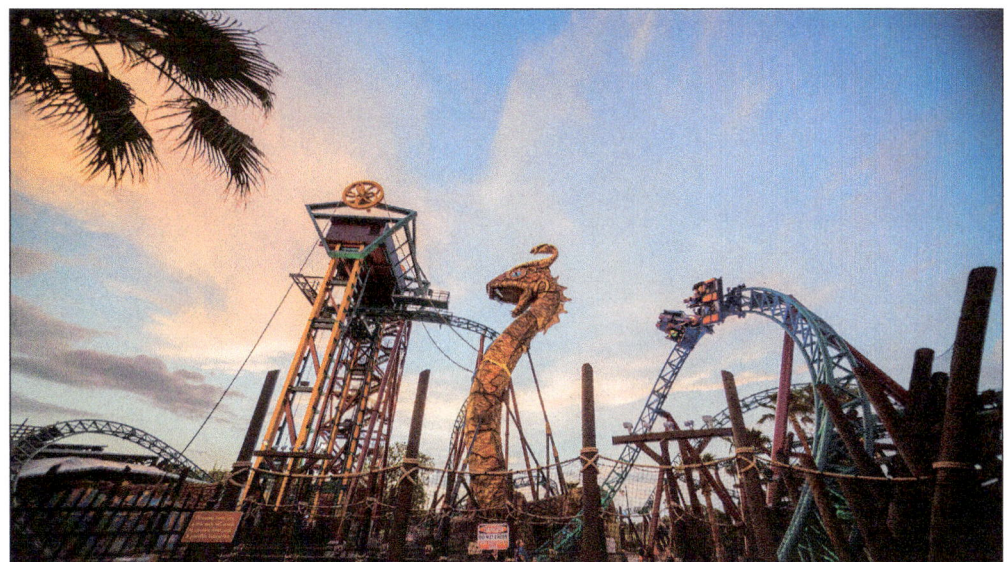

Cobra's Curse is a unique ride that puts a whole new twist in family roller coasters. The MACK Rides roller coaster opened on June 17, 2016, and features spinning cars that ascend to the top of the 70-foot-high ride by an unusual vertical elevator lift. Coming face-to-fang with the 80-foot snake king, the individually spinning cars turn about along overbanked curves based on the weight distribution of the passengers within the train. The roller coaster is located just northwest of Montu, and the ride queue is located in the former King Tut's Tomb building.

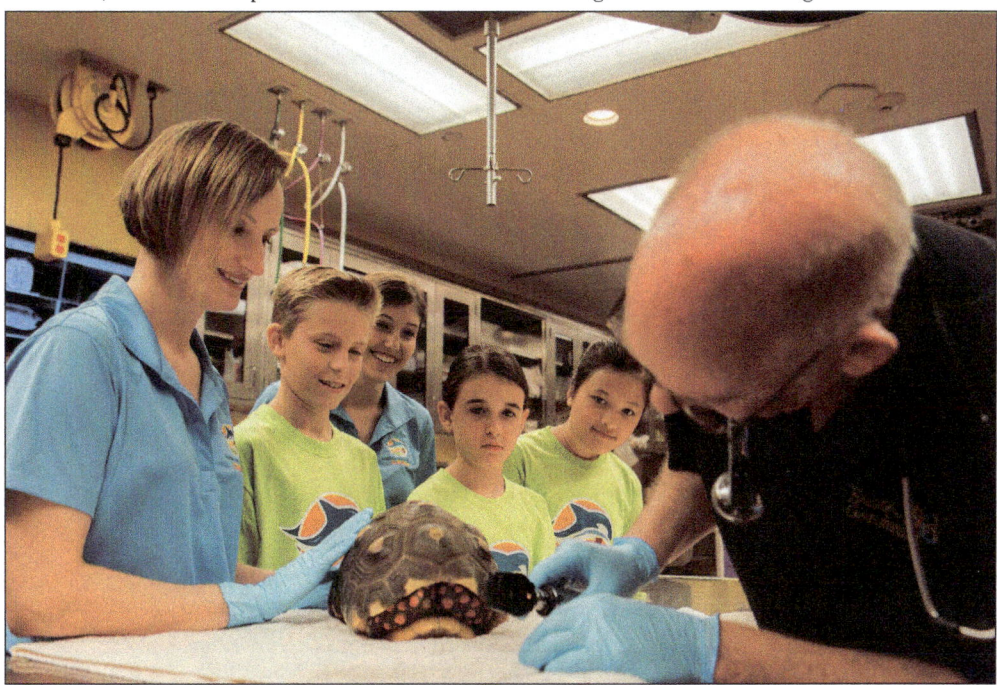

The next generation of Busch Gardens Tampa Bay ambassadors has already been born. Aspiring zookeepers should study the sciences, volunteer with local animal shelters and farms, and take college courses in zoology and the behavioral sciences. Who knows? Perhaps the children in this image will someday work as animal ambassadors at Busch Gardens.

Visit us at
arcadiapublishing.com

CPSIA information can be obtained
at www.ICGtesting.com
Printed in the USA
LVOW05*1015040318